From Registration to Recounts:

The Election Ecosystems of Five Midwestern States

A Project of *ELECTION LAW @ MORITZ* AT
THE OHIO STATE UNIVERSITY
MORITZ COLLEGE OF LAW

By Steven F. Huefner, Daniel P. Tokaji, & Edward B. Foley

with Nathan A. Cemenska

Published by The Ohio State University Michael E. Moritz
College of Law. The authors alone are responsible for all
statements of fact, opinions, recommendations, and conclusions
expressed. Publication in no way implies approval or endorsement
by The Ohio State University, or any of its faculties, including The
Ohio State University Michael E. Moritz College of Law.

Cover and design by Andrea Reinaker. Select photos taken by
Jo McCulty. Photographs made possible courtesy of the Franklin
County Board of Elections.

ISBN 978-0-9801400-0-2

CONTENTS

	PAGE
List of Tables	ii
Acknowledgements	iii
Executive Summary	v
Introduction	1

PART I: OVERVIEW

| Chapter 1: Background and Methodology | 5 |
| Chapter 2: Primary Components of an Election Ecosystem | 11 |

PART II: ELECTIONS IN THE FIVE STATES

Chapter 3: Ohio's Election Ecosystem A Poster Child For Reform	21
Chapter 4: Illinois' Election Ecosystem From Illegalities to Inconsistencies	59
Chapter 5: Michigan's Election Ecosystem Statewide Stability, But Local Vulnerabilities	85
Chapter 6: Wisconsin's Election Ecosystem Progressive Reform And Decentralized Administration	111
Chapter 7: Minnesota's Election Ecosystem A Model Today, But Will It Last?	137

PART III: LESSONS LEARNED

Chapter 8: General Observations	163
Chapter 9: Recommendations for Nine Areas of Election Administration	173
Chapter 10: Specific Reforms for the Five States	187

| Appendix A: Individuals Consulted | 199 |
| Appendix B: Bibliography of Works Consulted | 201 |

| About the Authors | 206 |

LIST OF TABLES

	PAGE
Table 1: State Provisional Voting Data	32
Table 2: Ohio Rejected Provisional Ballots, November 2006	49
Table 3: Ohio Rejected Provisional Ballots, November 2006: Large Counties	52-53
Table 4: Voter Turnout Percentages by Election Year	87
Table 5: Election Administration Systems	142
Table 6: Provisional Voting in Large Jurisdictions	182-183

ACKNOWLEDGEMENTS

This study was made possible by a generous grant from the Joyce Foundation, whose Midwest-focused Money and Politics Program is dedicated to preserving and strengthening those values and qualities that are the foundation of a healthy democratic political system. We also appreciate the personal assistance of Lawrence Hansen, Joyce Foundation Vice President.

Separately acknowledged in Appendix A are the many dedicated election administrators, public officials, leaders of public interest organizations, and others with special knowledge of or expertise in election administration who generously spent time talking with us, including members of the Midwest Democracy Network, an emerging alliance of state-based civic organizations whose reform agendas include improved election administration.

In addition, a number of other organizations and individuals contributed to this study. First, we are grateful to the Moritz College of Law and its administration for supporting our research and providing us a collegial professional home. In turn, we appreciate the encouragement and assistance of our colleagues at the Moritz College of Law, especially Terri Enns and Donald Tobin, Senior Fellows of *Election Law @ Moritz*. Terri in particular provided an extra measure of assistance on multiple occasions. Laura Williams, the *EL@M* Program Administrator, has worked tirelessly on an almost endless number of logistical details throughout the study. We also appreciate the help of Irene Mynatt, Mandy Fowler, and Kim Egger, our office staff over the life of the study.

Among other members of the Moritz community for whose contributions we are grateful, Andrea Reinaker, Moritz Graphic Designer, deserves special praise for working above and beyond the call to help us to prepare the manuscript for publication. Barbara Peck, Moritz Chief Communications Officer, helped to keep us on deadline, and she and Rob Phillips, Moritz Communications Coordinator, proofread the manuscript. J.D. Barlow, Tim Meager, and Merida Weinstein each supplied logistical support.

We also are grateful for Moritz Associate Dean and Law Librarian Bruce Johnson and the Moritz Law Library, whose dedicated staff provided prompt and efficient research assistance on many occasions. In this regard we especially appreciate the help of law librarians Matt Steinke and Paul Venard.

Over the course of the study many Moritz College of Law students also have helped with research. These include Sarah Cherry, Melissa Eakin, Kelle Hinderer, Katie Jory, Nick Kamphaus, Damien Kitte, Larry Lanham, Ryan Meadows, Debra Milberg, Veronica Norman, Benjamin Shepler, Chris Tamms, Anthony Tedesco, and Elliot Thomes. We have welcomed the opportunity to work with each of these capable individuals.

Finally, we are grateful to our families, not only for their encouragement and support, but also for their patience and longsuffering.

SFH   DPT   EBF   NAC

EXECUTIVE SUMMARY

THE SUBJECT OF ELECTION REFORM has garnered enormous public attention since the dramatic 2000 presidential election. From voting machines to provisional ballots to voter identification requirements, the "nuts and bolts" of the country's election systems have generated concern across the political spectrum. Yet in the face of considerable disagreement over what changes should be made, the debate has too often proceeded without an adequate understanding of existing rules and practices. Particularly in need of scrutiny is how the changes required by the Help America Vote Act of 2002 ("HAVA"), passed by Congress in response to the 2000 presidential election, as well as many recent state-initiated changes, have altered the election environments at the state and local level.

This report seeks to help fill that gap by describing the results of a yearlong study of election administration in five key Midwestern states: Illinois, Michigan, Minnesota, Ohio, and Wisconsin. Not only have these five states historically played a pivotal role in national politics, but they also provide examples of a variety of approaches to election administration. The views and experience of these five states – some five years after HAVA's passage and one year before the 2008 general election – are therefore of significance not only regionally but also nationally.

THE ECOSYSTEM MODEL

We have divided the election administration topics addressed in this report into nine areas: (1) institutional arrangements; (2) voter registration; (3) challenges to voter eligibility; (4) voting technology; (5) early and absentee voting; (6) polling place operations; (7) ballot security; (8) provisional voting; and (9) vote counting, recounting, and contests. We approach this study with the conviction that, within each state, these nine areas should be understood as constituting an election "ecosystem." By that, we mean that changes in any one part of the system are likely to affect other areas, sometimes profoundly.

Part I of the report (Chapters 1 and 2) sets forth the goals and methodology of our report. A healthy election ecosystem should promote three core values: access, integrity, and finality. The value of access seeks to ensure that all citizens in our representative democracy can readily and equally participate in the selection of those who represent them (and in decisions regarding ballot issues). The value of integrity seeks to ensure that the election process occurs in a fair, accurate, and transparent manner that protects voter privacy and minimizes the potential for fraud. The value of finality recognizes that the outcomes of elections need to be determined expeditiously and conclusively. These values are sometimes in tension with one another, but a sound election ecosystem must serve them all. As part of our analysis of the election laws and practices of the five states, in each state we conducted a series of interviews with state and local election officials, as well as with others knowledgeable about a particular state's election system. Though focused on these five states, the study provides insights on election administration that are of national importance.

FINDINGS IN THE FIVE STATES

Part II of the report (Chapters 3 through 7) draws upon the nine areas of analysis to describe the distinctive features of each state's system for administering elections, including the manner in which the state has endeavored to comply with HAVA's requirements and significant issues that have emerged in each state in recent years. Each state chapter is followed by a summary description of that state's law and practice in each of the nine areas of election administration. We discuss the states in an order roughly reflecting the health of their election ecosystems, beginning with the states having the most pressing problems.

OHIO FINDINGS

No state's election system has received greater attention in recent years than Ohio's, and for good reason. The state's recent history exhibits serious issues in a variety of areas, including voter registration, provisional ballots, voter identification, and voting technology. In the 2004 election, voters in some parts of the state reportedly experienced lines of up to ten hours. Cuyahoga County, where Cleveland is located, has had some especially troubling problems in recent elections, including difficulties in transitioning to new voting technology and polling places opening late. Key features of Ohio's election ecosystem are:

■ *The prominent role of the secretary of state*, including former Secretary of State Kenneth Blackwell and his successor, Jennifer Brunner;

■ *Deficiencies in the state registration database* required by HAVA, which falls short of the goals set by Congress and the needs of local election officials;

■ *Variations in the administration of elections across counties*, especially in provi-

sional balloting, the training of poll workers, and election technology;

■ *Troubles in Cuyahoga County*, Ohio's most populous county, which includes Cleveland; and

■ *Persistent election litigation*, including over twenty active suits pending against the state as of January 2007, relating to every aspect of Ohio's election ecosystem.

ILLINOIS FINDINGS

Illinois has a long reputation for political corruption, and not without some justification. Its history of election fraud and abuse, although diminishing, has contributed to a culture of suspicion and lack of cooperation between election officials that disserves the state's highly decentralized ecosystem. The various counties and cities with responsibility over elections conduct their business in many different ways. The state's biggest challenge is to put the past aside and work together to create a reasonably consistent experience for every voter and a reasonably consistent treatment of every ballot. The distinctive features of Illinois' election ecosystem include:

■ *Decentralized administration* with a relatively weak central elections authority that does not effectively ensure consistency across counties and cities;

■ *A history of fraud* that, while diminishing, continues to pose risks and to foster distrust and lack of cooperation among the highly decentralized local election officials;

- *Chicago and Cook County*, two huge, separate election jurisdictions that face a level of complexity in administering elections that is unsurpassed in the Midwest;

- *Inconsistencies across jurisdictions* within the state, on everything from provisional voting to post-election procedures, a phenomenon largely attributable to the lack of a strong central authority; and

- *The risk of litigation*, especially Equal Protection claims similar to those brought in Ohio, should there be a close election.

MICHIGAN FINDINGS

Michigan has experienced fewer election administration problems than Ohio or Illinois in recent years, although Detroit's mishandling of absentee ballots in that city's 2005 municipal election was the culmination of years of concern about the city's election administration. Michigan is now implementing a voter identification requirement that had been on hold for a decade until the state supreme court, divided on party lines, approved it earlier this year. The partisan split in the state judiciary over this issue highlights a concern over whether state courts generally are well-suited to handle potential election litigation in a manner that will inspire public confidence. Key features of Michigan's election ecosystem are:

- *The predominant role of municipal officials*, including over 1,500 city and township clerks who have primary responsibility for running elections.

- *A healthy working relationship between state and local election officials*, marked by the responsiveness of the state's bu-

reau of elections to municipal clerks, which contributes greatly to consistency in the administration of elections;

- *Michigan's "Qualified Voter File,"* now almost a decade old, which serves as Michigan's HAVA-compliant statewide voter database and has been a model for other states;

- *A uniform system of optical-scan voting*, now in use throughout the state; and

- *Concern about the state supreme court*, now bitterly divided along party lines on voter identification and other issues, should potentially determinative election litigation come before it.

WISCONSIN FINDINGS

Wisconsin's current election system retains features of the political culture associated with the LaFollette era of progressive reform. Since 1976, the state has permitted voters to register at the polls on Election Day, a reform that has spurred exceptionally strong turnout. Wisconsin has mostly been free of the accusations that have dogged some election officials in other states, particularly those elected on a partisan basis. At the same time, Wisconsin's decentralized system of running elections – in which responsibility rests among 1,851 municipal clerks – has a downside. Foremost among the challenges is the difficulty of achieving uniformity in the administration of elections across the state. Key features of Wisconsin's election ecosystem are:

- *A culture of nonpartisanship and professionalism* in the administration of elections, which helps ensure consistency among Wisconsin's municipalities;

- *An Election Day registration system,* which has successfully increased turnout without increasing fraud, and has the added benefit of reducing reliance on provisional ballots;

- *Problems in the state voter registration database,* including slowness in the system, the inability to check voter records against other records, and problems in generating absentee ballots;

- A *system for resolving post-election disputes* that likely would be seriously tested in the event of a close statewide race, especially if Wisconsin were the critical state in a presidential election.

MINNESOTA FINDINGS

Minnesota, another Election Day registration state, has the highest percentage of voter participation in the nation, with virtually no evidence of unlawful voting. Elections in both 2004 and 2006 were widely regarded as having gone smoothly throughout the state, with minimal problems. Yet in the recent past the state also has weathered some serious criticism that its election officials, particularly its former elected secretary of state, have behaved in an excessively partisan fashion. And its underlying culture of cooperative decisionmaking shows some signs of waning, thus increasing the chances that the state's election processes may become a casualty of partisanship. Key features of the state's election ecosystem are:

- A *healthy political culture* that emphasizes both civic engagement and electoral integrity;

- *The central role of the secretary of state* in

Minnesota election administration, though sometimes one that has been played controversially;

- *The importance of Election Day registration,* which is largely responsible for the state's exemplary turnout and has been a model for other states; and

- *Uniform technology and sound procedures,* which help promote consistent and fair treatment of voters across the state.

GENERAL OBSERVATIONS AND RECOMMENDATIONS

Our examination of Ohio, Illinois, Michigan, Wisconsin, and Minnesota yields valuable insights for election administration across the United States. The specific background and traditions of each state substantially influence its election ecosystem. Nevertheless, we think it possible to draw some general lessons, which are set forth in Part III (Chapters 8 through 10). Our key observations and recommendations include:

- *Statewide equality should generally trump local autonomy.* It is critical for states to accord equal treatment to all their citizens, especially with respect to the casting and counting of ballots. Therefore, although each state ought to do more to foster local experimentation, this should occur only within a framework that guarantees the essential equality of the right to vote.

- *A strong state elections authority is critical.* The health of a state's election ecosystem depends on having an effective state elections authority, which can promote statewide consistency, avoid any appearance of bias, and provide helpful guidance to local election officials. State legislatures must give their election officials the tools to enforce consistency in the application of state law across counties and municipalities.

■ *States should work to improve both access and accuracy by relaxing barriers to registration and complying with existing federal laws governing registration.* One way of doing this is Election Day Registration ("EDR"), a reform that has achieved great success in increasing participation in Minnesota, Wisconsin, and the other states in which it has been implemented. EDR also has the side-benefit of virtually eliminating the need for provisional ballots, although for a state fearful of EDR, an alternative would be "provisional EDR," in which new registrants at polling places would cast provisional ballots that would count upon verification of their registration information.

■ *States should provide clear guidance on provisional ballots.* States that rely on provisional ballots must set clear rules for both who should receive a provisional ballot and the circumstances under which provisional ballots will be counted. It is also critical that the process for verifying and counting provisional ballots be transparent.

■ *States should consider in-person early voting instead of expanded absentee voting.* In-person early voting promotes convenience, without the same risks of fraud and error that exist with liberalizing absentee voting by mail.

■ *Election integrity efforts should focus on "insider" fraud.* Problems of election fraud today almost always involve absentee voting or insider corruption. States should avoid instituting practices that might constitute barriers to voter participation in the name of preventing fraud and focus on refining the checks against insider fraud.

■ *State and local officials must continue to enhance poll worker recruitment and training.* Among the greatest challenges facing our democratic system is the difficulty in staffing polling places with an adequate number of sufficiently trained workers. Larger, economically depressed urban areas are especially likely to have problems. Local entities should be encouraged – and funded – to experiment with new ways of attracting and preparing poll workers.

■ *States should reexamine their post-election procedures, to ensure the evenhanded and prompt resolution of disputes.* It is of the utmost importance that vote counting and recounting be conducted in an evenhanded manner, either by nonpartisan officials or bipartisan teams. None of these five states has in place a final arbiter of a post-election dispute with the institutional credibility that both sides would perceive as fair. In that sense, all of these states – and probably most states in the country – have failed adequately to prepare for the next election.

■ *Congress should revisit the statute governing presidential election disputes.* The timetable for resolving presidential elections needs to be revised to give states more time to resolve post-election disputes before the "safe harbor" date under federal law (now thirty-five days after the election).

SPECIFIC REFORMS FOR THE FIVE STATES

Chapter 10 recommends priority reforms tailored to the existing election ecosystems of each of the five states in this study. We have kept our list to the three most important priorities, both to maximize the ability of policymakers to focus on a few critical goals and to reduce the prospects of destabilizing change.

OHIO REFORMS

■ Develop bipartisan leadership over election administration.

■ Replace the elected chief elections officer with a nonpartisan statewide elections director.

■ Create nonpartisan tribunals to resolve election disputes.

ILLINOIS REFORMS

■ Replace the state board of elections with a nonpartisan statewide elections director.

■ Increase trust in the integrity of state elections by making local election officials more accountable.

■ Create nonpartisan tribunals to resolve election disputes.

MICHIGAN REFORMS

■ Update the Qualified Voter File.

■ Enhance the chief election officer's ability to ensure consistency among municipalities.

■ Improve poll worker recruitment and training.

WISCONSIN REFORMS

■ Create a strong election division of the new Government Accountability Board.

■ Improve the Statewide Voter Registration System.

■ Reform the post-election dispute resolution processes.

MINNESOTA REFORMS

■ Improve poll worker recruitment and training.

■ Experiment with in-person early voting, instead of expanding mail-in absentee voting.

■ Develop nonpartisan institutions for administering elections and resolving disputes.

We close with one final, overarching theme that has repeatedly arisen throughout our study: Improvement of each state's election ecosystem depends upon nonpartisan and professional administration at every level, something that will require *structural* and not just attitudinal changes. We are optimistic about the prospects for reaching this goal, but recognize that it will take dedicated and concerted efforts on the part of elected officials, administrators, and citizens alike to get us there.

INTRODUCTION
ELECTION REFORM

THE SUBJECT OF ELECTION REFORM has garnered enormous public attention since the dramatic 2000 presidential election. From voting machines to provisional ballots to voter identification requirements, the "nuts and bolts" of the country's election systems have generated concern across the political spectrum. Yet in the face of considerable disagreement over what changes should be made, the debate has too often proceeded without an adequate understanding of existing rules and practices. Politicians and advocates often have put forward their own preferred solutions, without taking the time to gather evidence drawn from the actual experience of the state and local entities that run American elections.

Particularly in need of scrutiny is how the changes required by the Help America Vote Act of 2002 ("HAVA"), passed by Congress in response to the 2000 presidential election, as well as many recent state-initiated changes, have altered the ecology of the election systems of each state. Such information is a necessary predicate to recommending what can be done prospectively to improve the administration of elections.

This book seeks to help fill that gap by describing the results of a yearlong study of the statutory, regulatory, and judicial frameworks shaping the election administration procedures of five key Midwestern states: Illinois, Michigan, Minnesota, Ohio, and Wisconsin. Not only have these five states historically played a pivotal role in national politics, but they also are broadly representative today of the political

character of the country as a whole. In these states, perhaps more than in other regions of the nation, reside the proverbial "median voters," whom both major political parties endeavor to persuade. As a result, statewide races in these states tend to be particularly competitive and close, making the need for a well-working electoral system especially pressing.

Since the 2000 election, each of these bellwether states has undertaken the challenge of revamping its election system. In the fall of 2006, gubernatorial contests in all five of these states provided an opportunity to test the current conditions of their revamped electoral systems. Anticipating this event, in the summer of 2006 we set out to monitor and study how the election systems in these states would function, first analyzing in detail each state's legal landscape governing the conduct of elections, and then paying careful attention to the difficulties that unfolded in these states during the 2006 "midterm" election season. Thereafter, in each state we conducted a series of interviews and meetings with local and state election administrators and officials, seeking to understand how the underlying statutory and judicial standards governing election processes in these states are actually applied on the ground.

We believe that the views and experience of these five states' election administrators and other officials, and more generally the manner in which these states now conduct their processes of democracy – some five years after

HAVA's passage and one year before the 2008 presidential election – are of significance not only regionally but also nationally. Accordingly, in the pages to follow, we report the results of our study, in the form of both a state-by-state analysis and a cross-state comparison of fundamental matters of election administration, accompanied by some general observations and recommendations on these matters.

Part I contains two chapters. Chapter 1 provides background concerning the need for our study and outlines our research methodology. Chapter 2 then describes in more detail the particular matters of election administration that we have included in this study, grouped into the following nine areas: (1) institutional arrangements; (2) voter registration; (3) challenges to voter eligibility; (4) voting technology; (5) early and absentee voting; (6) polling place operations; (7) ballot security; (8) provisional voting; and (9) vote counting, recounting, and contests. As Chapter 2 explains, these related topics should be studied not in isolation but instead as an election "ecosystem," in which each area affects, sometimes profoundly, several other areas.

In Part II, Chapters 3 through 7 describe what is occurring in these nine areas within the five states, including the manner in which each state has endeavored to comply with HAVA's requirements. These state-specific chapters identify the most significant aspects of the state's statutory, regulatory, and judicial frameworks that govern election processes. They also assess how well each state's election ecosystem in fact is working.

In Part III, the three concluding chapters then contain some general conclusions and observations, as well as specific proposals for im-provement and reform. We both compare these states, and consider how each state can achieve more fair, efficient, and effective election administration. We believe that these proposals in particular, and this study generally, will be of interest to key state public officials, legislators, election administrators, election scholars, and opinion makers. We hope that the study will help to elevate the accuracy of the debate concerning election processes and to guide policymakers as they work to shape election ecosystems that are efficient, effective, fair, and accessible to all citizens.

PART I: OVERVIEW

Chapter 1: Background and Methodology

Chapter 2: Primary Components of an Election Ecosystem

CHAPTER 1
BACKGROUND AND METHODOLOGY

IT IS AN OBVIOUS but frequently unexamined truth that democracy – the exercise of government power at the direction of its citizens – depends on a sound method for measuring citizen preferences. Accordingly, the United States repeatedly sends election observers to other countries to monitor how successfully they are promoting core democratic values in the conduct of their elections. This study is an effort to monitor and report on how well we are promoting core democratic values in the conduct of our elections here at home.

We have approached this study with the conviction that a healthy election ecosystem should promote three core values: access, integrity, and finality.[1] The value of access seeks to ensure that all citizens in our representative democracy can readily and equally participate in elections. The value of integrity seeks to ensure that this voting process occurs in a fair, accurate, and transparent manner that protects voter privacy and minimizes the potential for fraud. The value of finality recognizes that elections, and any resulting disputes over their outcome, must be concluded expeditiously, so that political representatives can serve with their electorate's full confidence at the time appointed for the start of their terms. These three values inform this study of election administration in Illinois, Michigan, Minnesota, Ohio, and Wisconsin.

The history of voting in the United States is one of increasing *access* to the electoral process. From removal of property qualifications, to the adoption of the Fifteenth Amend-

ment, to the granting of women's suffrage, to passage of the Voting Rights Act, to the reduction of voting age to 18, the proportion of the general public eligible to vote has increased. To be sure, progress has not always come easily. It has in fact been sporadic, marked by short periods of rapid change, often followed by long periods of stasis or even backsliding.

Practical barriers to participation remain. Examples include polling places that are inaccessible to certain voters, such as those with disabilities or limited English proficiency; polling places that are overcrowded or open only during inconvenient hours; potential voters intimidated from going to the polls; and registration requirements that impede some eligible voters from qualifying to vote.

The history of voting in the United States is also one of remarkable improvements in the *integrity* of the electoral process. The anonymous ballot was one early reform that reduced the potential for corruption, by making it much more difficult for voters to sell their votes or be coerced into voting a particular way. Partly to reduce the risk of ballot box stuffing, paper ballot voting gave way to machine voting, which although also manipulable was seen as rendering outright vote fraud more difficult. The focus of attention now has shifted to the security of electronic voting mechanisms, which are also potentially manipulable but otherwise may provide the most accurate form of voting yet. Today, the largest potential for vote fraud likely lies in the processes for voting by absentee ballot. The processes for both Election Day and absentee voting therefore merit continuing refinement to enhance the integrity of our election systems. In addition, the relationship between the mechanisms of voting and the individuals responsible for administering these mechanisms also merits continuing attention, in order to promote the proper training and neutrality of election boards and judges.

While the values of access and integrity figure prominently in the history of electoral reform and are widely accepted as touchstones of a strong election system, the value of *finality* has received comparatively little attention. Indeed, some aspects of our contemporary election ecosystems may actually be working to undermine the prospects for finality, as our election processes become increasingly complicated (and the number of matters on each ballot grows), and as these processes are increasingly litigated.

The 2000 presidential election brought home the importance of the value of finality, as the entire country witnessed how awkward and unsettling it is to have election outcomes ultimately resolved in court after a bitter and protracted legal battle – and ultimately terminated only because the clock had run out.[2] Occasional resort to the courts to resolve close elections, with the lingering uncertainty about who will be the victor, may be inevitable, but frequent lawsuits are not a desirable feature of a sound election system. Rather, the processes should be designed to maximize the likelihood that the outcome will be determined quickly and conclusively, with minimum court involvement after Election Day.

All three of these values – access, integrity, and finality – should successfully coexist in a sound

election ecosystem. However, the excessive promotion of any one of these values can sometimes create tension with the others. For instance, enhanced judicial review of election procedures and irregularities may help to enhance access or to identify and resolve some types of electoral fraud, but could come at the cost of prolonged uncertainty about electoral outcomes. The debate over voter identification provides another example of this tension. To some observers, requiring all voters to prove their identity at the time that they vote is an important step in protecting the integrity of the voting process. Others, however, see some voter identification requirements as doing little to prevent fraud while significantly reducing access to the polls for certain classes of voters. Voter identification rules may also disserve the goal of finality, to the extent that they result in more provisional ballots being cast, which may be fought over after an election.

In addition to giving rise to questions about such matters as the appropriate form of judicial supervision over electoral processes, or the proper structure of a voter identification requirement, state election systems also give rise to a number of other questions about how to reconcile the values of access, integrity, and finality. Chief among these questions today is how to implement the provisional ballot requirements mandated by the Help America Vote Act ("HAVA"), which Congress enacted in 2002.[3] Although provisional balloting received a fair amount of attention in the 2004 election, particularly in Ohio, a number of issues deserve further attention. At stake is determining how best to minimize the number of eligible voters who are forced to vote a provisional ballot while maximizing the number of provisional ballots that are actually counted (among those cast by eligible voters), all while streamlining the process for speed and transparency.

The creation and use of the statewide electronic voter databases mandated by HAVA has also posed new questions for our election ecosystems. These databases have the potential to resolve some provisional balloting problems, and to reduce the prospects of electoral fraud, but if not implemented carefully they may also result indirectly in denying some citizens the right to vote. Moreover, potential problems with the registration databases may be every bit as serious as, yet much harder to identify than, glitches in the operation of a voting machine technology.

Indeed, today the most pressing issues surrounding the mechanics of voting involve not just what machines to use but how to implement those technologies. These questions include how to ensure that election boards and poll workers are adequately trained in the set up and operation of the equipment, know how to assist voters properly, can troubleshoot problems effectively, and will safeguard the integrity of the selected equipment throughout the process. Allegations of misconduct in the handling of ballots, electronic data packs, and memory cards in the 2005 Detroit mayoral race and the 2006 primary election in Ohio's Cuyahoga County (home to Cleveland) are but two examples of the need for clear and sensible procedures in this area. Related issues also include how to allocate the voting systems to ensure that each precinct has enough equipment, and how to keep the equipment maintained properly.

Separate and apart from questions about how readily courts ought to intervene in adjudicating claims of election fraud are questions about

when courts should supervise the recounting of close races. For instance, a large number of provisional ballots could prevent a prompt determination of an election's outcome, and provide fuel for contentious litigation. Under what circumstances, and with what evidentiary showings, should courts intervene to resolve close races?

These are some of the aspects of contemporary election processes in the United States that we discuss in the pages to follow. By analyzing election administration in the five key states of Illinois, Michigan, Minnesota, Ohio, and Wisconsin, this study identifies ways in which specific election procedures may fall short. By considering each state's election ecosystem as a whole, the study illuminates the extent to which these states are currently fostering the values of access, integrity, and finality overall. After describing what is and is not working in each state, the study offers some reflections on what makes a healthy election system and recommends some systematic approaches to these problems and challenges. We hope these recommendations will enable a state to enhance these values throughout the entirety of its election ecosystem.

In conducting this study, we proceeded as follows. After breaking the topic of election administration into the nine subtopics presented briefly in the Introduction (and discussed in more detail in Chapter 2), we used these nine areas to identify and research the answers to more than fifty core questions relevant to understanding the legal framework within which each state's existing election ecosystem operates. This research began in the summer of 2006, when we commenced working under a Joyce Foundation grant, and proceeded throughout the 2006 election season. We conducted this research with the substantial assistance of a number of law student research assistants, and *Election Law @ Moritz* web editor Nathan Cemenska, who has continued to collaborate in numerous aspects of the preparation of this report. We then posted a full set of answers for "50 Questions for 5 States" on the *Election Law @ Moritz* website, where it remains available (at http://moritzlaw. osu.edu/electionlaw/election06/50-5_index.php). We invited the election administration communities in each state to review the answers and to alert us to any errors or omissions. In addition, shortly after the November 2006, election, we prepared and also published to the *Election Law @ Moritz* website a report on the election administration experiences of each state in the 2006 election (at http://moritzlaw.osu.edu/electionlaw/election06/November2006Votingin5KeyStates.php).

After the 2006 election, we focused our attention on collecting input from local election administrators in each state by arranging and conducting a series of meetings where we encouraged local officials to speak freely and frankly about their experiences. We also sought and collected input from many other knowledgeable individuals in each state, including state (in addition to local) election officials, election attorneys, government prosecutors, and various advocacy and interest groups. In each of the five states we held at least two such meetings, and in some cases several more, in addition to gathering additional information by telephone and e-mail. Appendix A contains a list of those individuals with whom we met or from whom we received information helpful to our study.

Meanwhile, throughout the study we have collected and analyzed relevant social science research and legal scholarship, including works by various political scientists, other election law research organizations, and a number of recent government reports. Appendix B contains a bibliography of the works that we have consulted. We also have reviewed the "State Plans" that each state prepared pursuant to the Help America Vote Act. Additionally, as a core component of our research, we have reviewed court decisions addressing election controversies in each state. These cases shed light on the practical, political, and psychological factors that influence how courts intervene in the processes of election administration, and in turn help to complete the understanding of each state's ecosystem. As part of this component of the study, we developed a typology of election contests, described in greater detail in Chapter 2, which we used to examine how each state would handle several types of prototypical election problems.

Throughout the study, we have benefited enormously from our interactions with, as well as the previous work of, the many knowledgeable election law scholars, political scientists, reform advocates, and election officials with whom we share an interest in these issues. Yet our study has confirmed that, notwithstanding all the attention given to matters of election administration since 2000, the field remains underdeveloped in confronting the foundational issues of democratic government that it involves. Indeed, nothing approaching this type of comprehensive analysis of individual states' systems of election administration has previously been done. For instance, in its 2005 report the Carter-Baker Commission did not comprehensively assess the experience of states in implementing existing election laws (at a time when key provisions of HAVA had not yet become effective).[4] Similarly, the Century Foundation's working group report, while making some recommendations for state-level reforms, did not undertake the detailed analysis of specific states' election systems that follows.[5] Likewise, the Government Accountability Office's report on the 2004 election did not approach its analysis from a systemic perspective.[6] We certainly are indebted to, and have built upon, these and other previous contributions to the field of election administration, but we nevertheless believe that the analysis herein makes an important new contribution.

REFERENCES

1. Different sets of values of course are also possible. *See, e.g.,* Tova A. Wang, *Competing Values or False Choices: Coming to Consensus on the Election Reform Debate in Washington State and the Country*, 29 SEATTLE U. L. REV. 353, 354 (2006) (identifying such possible values as access, participation, efficiency, integrity, accuracy, and finality).

2. For a sampling of the voluminous literature about the 2000 election, see Richard A. Posner, BREAKING THE DEADLOCK: THE 2000 ELECTION, THE CONSTITUTION, AND THE COURTS (2001); THE VOTE: BUSH, GORE, AND THE SUPREME COURT (Cass R. Sunstein & Richard A. Epstein eds., 2001); Symposium, *Recounting Election 2000*, 13 STAN. L. & POL'Y REV. 1 (2002); Gillian Peele, *The Legacy of Bush v. Gore*, 1 ELECTION L.J. 263 (2002).

3. Pub. L. No. 107-252, 116 Stat. 1666 (codified at 42 U.S.C. §§ 15301-15523).

4. *See* Commission on Federal Election Reform (Carter-Baker Commission), *Building Confidence in U.S. Elections*, Sept. 2005. Two of this report's co-authors, Professors Foley and Tokaji, served on that working group.

5. *See* The Century Foundation, *Balancing Access and Integrity: The Report of The Century Foundation Working Group on State Implementation of Election Reform*, July 2005.

6. *See* Government Accountability Office, *The Nation's Evolving Election System as Reflected in the November 2004 General Election*, June 2006.

CHAPTER 2
PRIMARY COMPONENTS OF AN ELECTION ECOSYTEM

ELECTION ADMINISTRATION involves a multitude of processes and events, supervised and implemented by a variety of state and local officials and offices. Although no one rubric for analyzing these activities and individuals is necessarily preferable, in this study we have chosen to organize election administration sequentially into eight topical areas "from registration to recounts." But first, critical to understanding this entire sequence is an understanding of the particular administrative structures that a state has chosen for overseeing its elections. Accordingly, as the first of nine areas of focus, we examine each state's institutional arrangements for conducting elections. We then turn our attention to the eight sequential categories of the election administration process, beginning with the steps by which a citizen qualifies to vote, and ending with the way in which a contested election is finally resolved.

As a preliminary to the state-by-state chapters that follow, this chapter introduces in more detail the matters that we have reviewed in each of these nine areas, as well as the principal ways in which we believe that these matters ought to be understood as an election ecosystem. The nine areas are: (1) institutional arrangements, including the role of partisan, nonpartisan, or bipartisan bodies in exercising authority over election administration matters; (2) voter registration, including both how registration occurs and how the state manages its database of electors; (3) challenges to voter eligibility; (4) voting technology and equipment;

(5) early and absentee voting; (6) polling place operations, including poll worker training; (7) ballot security, including voter identification requirements; (8) provisional voting; and (9) vote counting, recounting, and post-election contests. We have deliberately chosen not to include in our study any of the processes by which candidates or issues qualify to be on the ballot, or any of the regulations that govern the way in which campaigns occur, including the complex and shifting mix of state and federal laws regulating campaign finance contributions and expenditures. Instead, we have limited this study to the administration of the voting processes themselves.

1. Institutional arrangements. In 2004, Ohio attracted a great deal of negative publicity because its elected secretary of state, Kenneth Blackwell, was actively and publicly involved in supporting individual candidates and ballot issues (and generally positioning himself to run for governor in 2006) at the same time that he was responsible for administering the state's elections. While some were critical of Secretary Blackwell for his political activities, others were critical of an administrative structure that placed responsibility for election administration in the hands of an official elected on a partisan basis and subject to the political realities of the day. In this respect, however, Ohio is far from unique. In fact, throughout the country the predominant form of institutional arrangement is to assign an elected secretary of state the responsibility of serving as the state's chief election officer.

Three of the five states in this study, including also Michigan and Minnesota, follow this same approach.

By contrast, Illinois and Wisconsin use a state board of elections to oversee their election administration systems. In Illinois, the state board consists of eight members, appointed on a bipartisan basis by the governor with the consent of the state senate. In Wisconsin, the state board has historically consisted of eight or more appointees, one designated by each of the following individuals: the governor, the chief justice of the state supreme court, the majority and minority leaders of both houses of the state legislature, and the head of each political party in the state that received at least ten percent of the vote in the preceding gubernatorial election. But while the Wisconsin board has final responsibility over election administration, in practice it has delegated most day-to-day matters to its nonpartisan executive director. However, as of September 2007, Wisconsin has completely restructured its board, creating a new Government Accountability Board to handle both election administration as well as campaign finance regulation, as discussed in Chapter 6.

The five states differ not only in what individual or body has state-level responsibility over elections, but also in how much authority resides at the local level, and in how reliant local election administrators are on their state level counterparts. In addition, the five states also differ in whether local level responsibility for operating the polls and administering elections resides primarily with the counties, as in Ohio and Illinois, with the municipalities, as in Michigan and Wisconsin, or involves more of a hybrid, as in Minnesota. The states also differ in whether local administration is the responsibility of a county or municipal clerk, either elected or appointed, or instead occurs under the direction of a bipartisan elections board.

2. Voter registration. Turning to the sequence of processes involved in conducting elections, the first step in most states is to create a roster of voters by requiring eligible individuals to register to vote. One alternative, now employed only in North Dakota[1] but more common in the days when America was heavily agrarian, is to forgo registration entirely and permit eligible voters simply to appear at their polling place and declare their eligibility on Election Day. Several other states, including Minnesota and Wisconsin, in some fashion permit voters to register at the polls on Election Day. But the overwhelming majority of American states, including Ohio, Illinois, and Michigan, require voters to register to vote in advance of the election.

Advance registration provides states a period of time in which both government officials and private individuals can confirm the eligibility of those seeking the authorization to vote. However, it may entirely foreclose from voting some citizens who are otherwise eligible to vote but who have failed to take the required steps ahead of time. Meanwhile, although Election Day registration may make it easier for citizens to vote, it may also complicate states' ability to check their eligibility. With multiple examples of both approaches among the five states in our study, we have examined the particular requirements that each state uses to conduct its voter registration process, and the ways in which these registration requirements serve to promote both access to the polls and the integrity of an election.

Closely related to each state's voter registration requirements is the way in which the state manages its database of registered electors. The Help America Vote Act ("HAVA") required all states by 2006 to develop and implement a statewide electronic database of registered voters, as a means of promoting greater accuracy in the registration lists and of reducing the chances of vote fraud through multiple voting.[2] Because Michigan already had a statewide electronic system in place, it has had the easiest time complying with this HAVA requirement. However, as discussed in the chapters to follow, to a greater or lesser degree the remaining states in our study have struggled to implement and use their statewide voter database effectively.

3. Challenges to voter eligibility.
Also closely related to the mechanics by which eligible voters are included on the roster of voters are the processes by which election officials check voter eligibility. These processes include reviewing registration applications for *prima facie* compliance with a state's eligibility requirements, correcting duplicate names that result when voters submit multiple applications, and purging from the registration list voters who were once eligible but are no longer. Electronic databases are making it increasingly easy to eliminate duplicate names, as well as to conduct systematic purges of voters who have been convicted of a felony, which in all five states renders a citizen ineligible to vote at least during the individual's period of incarceration. Purges also can occur in response to mass mailings to identify voters who have moved, or in response to specific challenges to individual voters. Finally, in some states the eligibility of individual voters may be challenged at the polls, either by other voters or by the political parties' designated "challengers." Each state has its own set of processes by which its registration lists are purged and updated.

4. Voting technology.
In all five states, registration requirements are one type of voting preliminary, used to determine which individuals will be allowed to cast a ballot. Also preliminary to the actual voting itself is choosing a type of voting equipment and preparing the ballots. In the 2000 presidential election, Florida showed the nation that problems can occur both as a result of the type of voting equipment used, as exemplified in the difficulties in determining how to conduct a recount of punch card ballots, and as a result of poor ballot design, as exemplified not only in the infamous butterfly ballot of Palm Beach County but also in the multiple page optical scan ballot used in Duval County.[3]

Accordingly, since 2000 the most common election "reform" around the country has been to change voting equipment, although this change has not happened overnight. By some accounts, the 2006 election saw the largest one-time swap of equipment, with almost one-third of the country's voters using a type of equipment different from what they had used in the previous election, and more than two-thirds using something different from what they had used in 2000.[4] These changes also are partially a result of the Help America Vote Act, which created heavy financial incentives for states to abandon punch card voting systems.[5]

Furthermore, in some states these changes have occurred uniformly throughout the state, while in other states individual counties or municipalities have been free to make their own choice of equipment. But from among a wide range of new equipment options, states and localities have sometimes struggled to decide what to use. In large part this is because the newer equipment has not eliminated the prospect of serious election administration problems. Sophisticated electronic voting machines bring concerns about computer viruses, including the possibility of deliberate or accidental distortion or loss of the actual votes cast. In response to some of these concerns, an increasing number of states are requiring that electronic voting machines also generate a paper audit trail that voters can peruse as they vote to confirm the accuracy of their ballot. The choice of election technology also implicates the way in which disabled voters will be able to participate in the voting process, as some types of equipment are clearly better than others for individuals with certain disabilities.[6]

5. Early and absentee voting. Once states have established who can vote and using what equipment, it is time for voting to begin. Because not all voters may be able to vote in person on Election Day, all states make some provision for voting at an alternative time or place. Traditional absentee voting rules allowed voters who could not get to the polls, either because of a physical impediment or because they would be absent from their voting precinct, to request a paper ballot that they could mark at home and return prior to Election Day. In recent years, many jurisdictions have expanded their absentee voting processes to allow any voter to cast an absentee ballot for any reason. Meanwhile, other jurisdictions have begun to permit voters to appear at select locations prior to Election Day to cast an early vote.[7]

Increased use of absentee and early voting has the promise of increasing access to the polls,

but brings with it greater risks to the integrity of the election. This is especially true for absentee ballots cast at remote locations, such as homes or businesses, where voters may be subject to intimidation or bribery, rather than in polling locations, where the voters can vote in secret. But to a lesser extent it may be true of early voting as well, if the period of early voting itself distorts the underlying election campaigns. In turn, some forms of absentee and early voting may increase the costs of election administration, and they inevitably alter the type of work that poll workers and election judges are needed to perform, as next discussed.

6. Polling place operations. Traditionally, the heart of the democratic process has been the casting of votes at the polls. Notwithstanding the substantial increase in the amount of early or absentee voting occurring in many states, most of the voting in the five states in this study, at least for the near future, is likely to continue to occur at the polls on Election Day. A critical component of a state's election administration process therefore is how polling place operations are conducted during this daylong event.

In no small part, how polls operate is a function of how poll workers are recruited and trained. In most states, the vast majority of election officials are volunteers who receive a modest stipend for staffing the polling places from the time the polls open until the time they close. They are expected to attend a training program, typically a couple of hours long, in the days prior to the election. In practice, however, local boards of election or their elections directors often have difficulty even recruiting the necessary number of poll workers, let alone getting them all to attend the training programs. The state-specific chapters to follow include individual states' experiences in this regard.

Polling place operations are closely related to several other topics of our study, such as each state's election-day experience in using its database of registered voters, and in implementing its choice of voting technology. These factors contribute to the efficiency with which voting occurs, and affect the amount of time that voters spend at the polls waiting for an opportunity to cast a ballot. In analyzing polling place operations, we therefore focus in substantial part on the voters' experience engaging with the democratic process, including how well the election process protects voters' ability to vote freely and without intimidation. One critical subset of voters are those who need accommodation at the polls for a disability, whether mobility impairments, vision impairments, or cognitive impairments, as well as those with limited English proficiency, who may require extra time or assistance in casting their ballots.

The topic of polling place operations also could encompass such matters as safeguarding the ballots, provisional voting, and counting the votes, but as next described we have chosen to treat each of these matters separately (while mindful of the importance of understanding all of these matters as an ecosystem).

7. Ballot security. A crucial step in protecting the integrity of an election is protecting the integrity of the ballots themselves. In today's election environment, ballot security arguably partakes of three distinct components: protecting physical ballots (or other physical records of voting) from tampering, damage, or loss;

protecting electronic voting equipment and records from tampering, hacking, contamination, viruses, damage, or loss; and ensuring that only eligible voters are allowed to cast a ballot.

With respect to both physical voting records and electronic voting equipment and records, a critical component of securing their integrity is maintaining the proper chain of custody, from the time the ballots or equipment are prepared, through the casting of the ballots, and through the post-election counting (and any recounting) of the ballots. Maintaining an impeccable chain of custody is paramount because many forms of tampering or alteration might not be self-evident, and can only be presumed not to have occurred because the ballots have been properly secured. But a state's chain of custody requirements also should protect against accidents that would undermine or invalidate an election. Protecting electronic equipment also may include various kinds of tests and audits, before, during, and after an election, as well as steps taken at the design or procurement stages to develop and select a voting system with lower risks of security problems.

As a third aspect of ballot security, we have also chosen to address the steps that states take on Election Day to confirm the eligibility of those who desire to vote. Although these steps are closely related to the way in which states conduct their voter registration process, the registration process itself has no direct implication on ballot security until a voting official makes a decision about whether to give a person a ballot. In states that require advance voting registration, this decision often involves asking the person to sign a poll book and then comparing the signature with the signature on file from the time of registration. But increasingly this decision is also turning on whether the person can present some additional form of personal identification.

Including the topic of voter identification in the ballot security category may be somewhat controversial. We have chosen to discuss it here because the principal justification for voter identification requirements is to promote the security of the ballot. But certain types of voter identification requirements may result not so much in enhancing election integrity as in constraining election access. We address these issues in greater detail with respect to individual state systems.

8. Provisional voting. Also closely related both to preventing ineligible voters from casting a ballot, and to polling place operations generally, is the use of provisional ballots. Already in use in some states but required in all states by the Help America Vote Act,[8] provisional ballots permit poll workers to accommodate individuals who present themselves at the polls to vote but whom the poll workers are unable to confirm are proper voters at that poll, by letting them vote special ballots "provisionally." These provisional ballots then are subject to subsequent verification that the voter was eligible and in the right place, in which case they are counted like regular ballots.

Although their obvious purpose is to enhance access to the ballot, they may have the opposite effect if the result of their availability is that election officials fail to ascertain ahead of or on Election Day whether a voter is properly registered and in what polling location. This can lead to the casting of provisional ballots that end up uncounted. The states in our study have a range of experiences with provisional

ballots, including litigation over when provisional ballots must be cast and when they can be counted, and wide variations in the number of provisional ballots cast and counted.

9. Vote counting, recounting, and contests. The final step in administering an election is to determine the result. In most cases, this is a straightforward matter of tabulating the ballots and certifying the outcome. To this end, all states have established procedures by which poll workers either process and report their precincts' totals to supervising officials, or transmit their ballots to regional centers for counting.

Occasionally, however, determining a final result becomes more complicated, either because an outcome is sufficiently close, or because an error occurs that renders the tallies unreliable. In these circumstances, recounts and election contests provide supplemental mechanisms for determining the outcome. Wide variation exists among states in how they conduct both recounts and contests, including whether a recount is automatic when an election outcome is within a certain margin, what tribunal has jurisdiction over an election contest, and what remedies are available for an unreliable election outcome.

In order to better understand these variations and their implications, we have examined how each state in our study would likely handle several prototypical election controversies. These scenarios include: an election in which a number of unverified ballots (or ballots in excess of voters who have properly signed in) are cast; an election in which ballot shortages or equipment failures deprive a number of voters from the opportunity to vote; a controversy over the eligibility of a number of provisional ballots; and evidence that absentee voters were improperly influenced in their votes. Our reflections on these and other scenarios inform this report, and a more detailed discussion is available separately.[9]

THE NOTION OF AN ELECTION ECOSYSTEM

Having described the nine components of our study of election administration, the nature of their interconnectedness merits brief elaboration. We have approached this study from the perspective that a state's processes for administering its elections deserve to be understood as an ecosystem because the choices that a state makes about the procedures and requirements in one area inevitably affect the health and functioning of several other areas as well. For instance, the nature of a state's voter registration process can have a dramatic impact not only on the ease with which the state can maintain its statewide voter database, but also on whether that database is a valuable Election Day tool both for ensuring the integrity of an election, as well as for minimizing the need for provisional ballots. The choice of which type of voting equipment to use affects not only the ease with which voters, including those with disabilities, can vote, but also the way in which recounts will occur, and perhaps the grounds available for an election contest. And obviously the institutional arrangements, at both the state and local levels, will relate to each of the other components of the election administration process.

Furthermore, as previously described, a key component of our study is an examination of each state's implementation of the Help America Vote Act, several critical requirements of which only took effect in 2006. HAVA required states to make significant changes regarding voting equipment, registra-

tion, provisional voting, and identification requirements.[10] This study is one of the first to examine the impact of these newly effective requirements, as well as how they might be improved. Yet such an analysis can only be properly conducted with an appreciation of each state's entire election ecology. It is for this reason that we have studied not only how the requirements of HAVA are being implemented, but how these changes relate to other aspects of state and local election administration.

The chapters to follow will spell out and justify our conclusions regarding the election ecosystems of these five states in greater detail, but we can briefly note here some of the principal findings of our examination of these matters. These include the following: (1) the health of a state's election ecosystem is affected by its underlying political culture; (2) regardless of the underlying culture, an effective statewide elections bureau or administrator can play a crucial role in the smooth operation of an election ecosystem; (3) good communication and trust between levels of election officials is critical to a healthy election ecosystem; (4) to varying degrees, all states are struggling to find and train poll workers; (5) also to varying degrees, all states suffer when they seek or are required to make wholesale changes to their election systems too quickly; (6) statewide consistency in administrative practices and procedures provides a substantial advantage; (7) most states can benefit from improving their processes for handling post-election proceedings; and (8) it is increasingly important that election administration be approached as a professional administrative task, rather than as an adjunct to a political or partisan position.

We discuss each of these conclusions in greater detail in Part III. Some of them are detailed in Chapter 8, which is structured around a set of general observations about election ecosystems. Others are discussed in Chapter 9, which makes specific recommendations for each of the nine areas of election administration that we have studied. Finally, Chapter 10 prioritizes three key reforms for each state, tailored to their particular circumstances. But first, in Part II we consider the current condition and characteristics of the election ecosystems of each of these states.

REFERENCES

1. North Dakota has not had a voter registration requirement since 1951. For a history, see http://www.nd.gov/sos/ electvote/voting/vote-history.html.

2. *See* 42 U.S.C. §15483(a).

3. *See* Raymond Bonner, *Counting the Vote: Duval County; Democrats Rue Ballot Foul-Up in a 2nd County*, N.Y. TIMES, Nov. 17, 2000, at A1.

4. *See* Election Data Services, *Almost 55 Million, or One Third of the Nation's Voters, Will Face New Voting Equipment in 2006 Election*, Oct. 2, 2006, *available at* http://www.edssurvey.com/images/File/ve2006_nrpt.pdf.

5. *See* 42 U.S.C. §15302.

6. *See* Daniel P. Tokaji, *The Paperless Chase: Electronic Voting and Democratic Values*, 73 FORDHAM L. REV. 1711 (2005).

7. In a state that allows anyone to vote an absentee ballot, the distinction between absentee and early voting may blur. For a thoughtful discussion of recent developments in both early and absentee voting, see John C. Fortier, ABSENTEE AND EARLY VOTING: TRENDS, PROMISES, AND PERILS (2006).

8. *See* 42 U.S.C. §15482(a).

9. For a more extended discussion of how the five states might handle these kinds of problems, see Edward B. Foley, *The Analysis and Mitigation of Electoral Errors: Theory, Practice, Policy*, 18 STAN. L. & POLY REV. 350, 361-74 (2007).

10. *See* 42 U.S.C. §15302 (equipment); §15483(a) (registration); §15482(a) (provisional voting); §15483(b) identification.

PART II: ELECTIONS IN THE FIVE STATES

Chapter 3:   Ohio's Election Ecosystem
             A Poster Child For Reform

Chapter 4:   Illinois' Election Ecosystem
             From Illegalities To Inconsistencies

Chapter 5:   Michigan's Election Ecosystem
             Statewide Stability, But Local Vulnerabilities

Chapter 6:   Wisconsin's Election Ecosystem
             Progressive Reform And Decentralized Administration

Chapter 7:   Minnesota's Election Ecosystem
             A Model Today, But Will It Last?

CHAPTER 3: OHIO'S ELECTION ECOSYSTEM
A POSTER CHILD FOR REFORM

OHIO'S RECENT HISTORY exhibits a variety of moderate to serious difficulties in most areas of election administration. These difficulties include: the mishandling of ballots, voting equipment, and recount processes in one of its largest urban counties; concern over partisan and political activities by its secretary of state, who serves as the state's chief election officer; confusion about its voter identification requirements, as well as its provisional balloting rules; misallocation of election equipment and associated long lines at the polls, reported to be as long as ten hours in some places; and controversy over its regulation of third-party voter registration groups. Indeed, in the 2004 presidential election, problems in virtually all of these areas of election administration occurred in Ohio. Perhaps as a result, almost 160,000 Ohio voters, or about 2.8% of those who made it to the voting booth, cast a provisional ballot in 2004, a rate well above the national average of about 1.6%. In the 2006 election, while most states were reducing their proportion of provisional ballots, Ohio saw this percentage grow to 3%.[1]

An especially troubling example of Ohio's recent difficulties is Cuyahoga County, home of Cleveland. In the 2006 primary election, one in five polling places in the county opened late, and equipment malfunctions and supply shortages plagued the county's Election Day operations. Once the polls closed, some seventy voting machine memory cards were initially missing.[2] Later, in the 2006 general election, Cuyahoga County largely avoided these specific problems, but it instead allowed almost 12,000 voters to cast ballots without properly verifying their eligibility.[3] To add insult to injury, in early 2007, two Cuyahoga County election officials were convicted of criminal misconduct in the canvass of the 2004 election (although they are now awaiting retrial after the chief justice of the state supreme court ordered the trial judge removed from the case because of a conflict of interest).[4]

The preceding examples are only a partial list of the miscues that have plagued Ohio elections in recent years. Indeed, even before Cuyahoga County's 2006 difficulties, the League of Women Voters filed a federal lawsuit in July 2005 charging that Ohio's voting system violated the U.S. Constitution and other provisions of federal law. The complaint alleged that, both in 2004 and in many prior years, a litany of inconsistencies in election administration – from the way in which poll workers were trained, to how they handled provisional balloting in different precincts, to the processes used to administer absentee ballots, to the way in which counties allocated voting machines among precincts, among other things – deprived Ohio voters of their rights to Equal Protection of the law.[5] This case remains pending. Moreover, it is only one of a score of recent cases challenging various aspects of Ohio's election system.

The state has made some significant adjustment, both as a matter of governing law and as a matter of administrative practice. After the 2004 election, the state legislature enacted an extensive revision to Ohio's election code, intended to address many of the issues that arose in that election – although there is some disagreement as to whether the law made things better or worse. Furthermore, since January 2007, a new secretary of state has been actively pursuing a reform agenda intended to correct a number of deficiencies in the state's election processes. She also has been hoping to settle many of the outstanding election administration lawsuits facing the state. Thus, whether as a result of settlements or of court judgments, further changes to Ohio's election ecosystem are likely in the near future.

For now, with the 2008 elections just months away, the dominant features of Ohio's current election ecosystem are: (1) the significance of the role that the elected secretary of state plays in election administration and coordinating the work of the state's eighty-eight county boards of election; (2) a statewide database of registered voters, implemented pursuant to the Help America Vote Act, that falls short of its full potential; (3) continuing flux in the technology and procedures used to vote; (4) concerns about the serious problems that have repeatedly plagued Cuyahoga County in recent elections; and (5) an ongoing history of litigation over election processes, only partly explainable by the political battleground nature of the state.

THE SETTING

Relevant to all of the features of Ohio's election ecosystem are the state's history, traditions, and demographic circumstances. Ohio has long held a position of influence in national politics. Admitted to the Union in 1802 as the seventeenth state, by the mid-nineteenth century Ohio had the country's third largest population,[6] twenty-one presidential electors (down to twenty today, even as the nation's total number of presidential electors has grown),[7] and a diverse citizenry that mirrored much of the growing nation. In the final decades of the nineteenth century, five of the country's six presidents hailed from Ohio,[8] as did two more elected in the early twentieth century.[9] Since 1900, the winner of twenty-five of the twenty-seven U.S. presidential elections has carried Ohio,[10] underscoring the political saying that "as Ohio goes, so goes the nation."

In part, this reflects the fact that Ohio's demographics tend to approximate the nation's. For instance, Ohio's per capita income today is near the median among U.S. states, and it has been in a similar position for some time.[11] The state's proportion of African American citizens – about twelve percent – also is close to the national average, although Ohio has somewhat fewer members of several other racial minorities (and slightly more Caucasians) than the national average.[12] Also like the nation as a whole, Ohio today is a mix of urban and rural areas, accompanied by a rapidly expanding suburban landscape. More than six million of its 11.5 million residents live in the metropolitan areas of ten of its eighty-eight counties,[13] yet no single city dominates the state's culture, and the remaining seventy-eight counties are predominantly rural.

Historically, Ohio's population grew primarily along the series of highways, canals, railroads, and rivers integral to the settlement of the country's western frontier during the early nineteenth century. These include the National Road, which bisected the state from east to west (and which eventually became U.S.

Highway 40, roughly paralleled today by Interstate 70), as well as along routes of the Underground Railroad.[14] The southern part of the state, bordering Kentucky and West Virginia, was especially shaped by the Ohio River, and partakes of certain elements of the country's southern culture, while the northern portion shares more of a kinship with the northeast United States. Today, U.S. Highway 40 (or alternatively Interstate 70) is often described as the dividing line between a more liberal north and a more conservative south.[15]

Ohio's economy also has epitomized core elements of the national economy. For most of the twentieth century Ohio was an important manufacturing state, with a variety of industries clustered around its major metropolitan centers of Cincinnati, Cleveland, and Columbus, and other urban communities of Akron, Canton, Dayton, Toledo, and Youngstown. But Ohio is among the "Rust Belt" states recently experiencing a decline in manufacturing, and large portions of its economy are transitioning to the service sector. Today it has a mix of blue collar and white collar employment. As in many other states, Ohio's number of family farms is dwindling. In addition, almost thirty of Ohio's eighty-eight counties belong to Appalachia, and share that region's history of economic struggle.[16]

Ohio's county structure has been in place since 1851, when the state legislature created the eighty-eighth county.[17] These counties served as the locus of government and civic participation for most Ohioans as the state's population expanded. Today, Ohio administers its elections primarily at the county level, with an evenly bipartisan Board of Elections in each county (with ties broken by the secretary of state) responsible for hiring an elections director and staff, structuring its election precincts, maintaining and operating its polling equipment and polling places, and processing its ballots. In the early 1970s, several decades before the current national interest in election administration, three of Ohio's larger urban counties attracted national attention for their election failures. Specifically, Hamilton County (home of Cincinnati), Summit County (home of Akron), and Cuyahoga County (home of Cleveland) experienced serious difficulties in opening and operating their polling places in 1971 and 1972, including supplying a number of precincts with insufficient equipment and poorly trained poll workers.

Given its mix of urban and rural, liberal and conservative voters, it is not surprising that the state's political traditions include a history of swings of control. For instance, during the twentieth century, party control of the state senate changed hands more than a dozen times, while control of the state house of representatives changed almost as much.[18] In the fifty years since Ohio lengthened the term of office for its governor from two to four years in 1958, Republicans have won eight gubernatorial elections and Democrats five.[19] Ohio's voters also have often split their tickets, voting for individuals more than party or ideology. For instance, in 1980, at the same time that they were re-electing U.S. Senator Howard Metzenbaum, a liberal Democrat, they also favored conservative Ronald Reagan more strongly than did the nation as a whole.[20] Similarly, in 1990 Republicans won the races for governor and secretary of state, while Democrats won the races for state auditor, state treasurer, and attorney general. More recently, Republicans have controlled all five statewide offices, until Democrats retook four of them in 2006. Ohio also has seen a number of close elections, a few of which have been settled in court, most prominently its 1990 race for attorney general, discussed below, decided by a little over a thousand votes out of over three million cast.

Although Ohio's relative population has been shrinking in recent decades, it remains the seventh largest state in the country.[21] Given the state's size, demographic diversity, and its past and current political balance, it has remained a battleground state in national politics. Unsurprisingly, its election system has received close scrutiny of late. It also has come under tremendous pressure.

Many observers of the nation's electoral processes well remember the controversy and litigation surrounding the 2004 presidential election in Ohio. They will recall the fight over whether the new federal Help America Vote Act of 2002 ("HAVA") required the state to count provisional ballots cast in a precinct other than the voter's own – the so-called "wrong precinct" issue – a fight that ultimately was resolved in favor of the state's position against counting the ballots by the U.S. Court of Appeals for the Sixth Circuit, which sits in Cincinnati.[22] They will remember, too, the former secretary of state's short-lived but much-maligned requirement that voter registration cards be submitted on eighty-pound card stock. More serious was the litigation that surrounded challenges to the eligibility of newly registered voters, first in the form of "pre-Election Day challenges" to some 35,000 new names, and then, after the federal courts enjoined that practice, the threat of polling place challenges on Election Day (a threat that never

materialized as a result of a last-minute stand-down called by Ohio's then-Governor Bob Taft). Some may also remember the effort to contest the result of the presidential election in Ohio, as a small but vocal minority of the populace insisted that the outcome was erroneous or, worse, rigged (a position fueled by a Robert F. Kennedy, Jr. article for *Rolling Stone* magazine[23]). The Ohio Supreme Court ultimately dismissed that contest, joining the view of most observers that the electoral process in the state in 2004, while deeply flawed, did not affect the result.[24]

What many who retain these memories of 2004 may not remember is that Ohio's 2006 general election was also marked by contentiousness and litigation, albeit it over different issues. In 2006, the lawsuits attacked a new law concerning challenges to voter eligibility, new rules regulating voter registration drives conducted by third-party groups, and new voter identification requirements enacted by the state legislature. The U.S. Court of Appeals for the Sixth Circuit once again was called upon to intervene in late October, to resolve a dispute over new identification requirements for absentee voters, deciding to let the requirements take effect.[25] In the wake of this court order, the threat of renewed litigation over the provisional voting process loomed large, but this threat was avoided in part by a pre-Election Day consent decree (a kind of "cease fire" in this litigious battle), and in part because the margins in the vote tallies of the elections themselves were slightly beyond worth fighting over. The congressional race between incumbent Deborah Pryce and challenger Mary Jo Kilroy came closest to litigation, and during the time in which an automatic recount was conducted there was considerable jockeying over the treatment of the provisional ballots among attorneys for those parties interested in the outcome of this race. But ultimately Pryce's margin of victory of about 1,000 ballots proved too great, with only about 2,500 uncounted provisional ballots for Kilroy to dispute.

A lesson from the litigation over Ohio's 2006 general election is that there will be renewed disputes over the state's voting process in 2008, unless either the elections themselves are not considered close enough to justify a legal dispute, or significant reforms are adopted. The particular issues that are disputed in 2008 may differ from those raised in 2006, or back in 2004, although some issues that remain unresolved may resurface. But the candidates, political parties, and interest groups will again "lawyer up" in Ohio, as they will to a lesser extent in other battleground states. Voting rights advocates will challenge practices that they believe are harmful, while the parties will look for legal issues that will help tilt the electoral battlefield in their favor and increase their odds of victory.

In light of this prospect, it is worth examining the current status of Ohio's election administration system, to see how robust it may be in the face of strategic efforts to identify weaknesses it in. To that end, we should begin by describing a 2006 legislative enactment popularly known as House Bill 3, which was the state legislature's effort at a major overhaul of the state's electoral system after 2004.

HOUSE BILL 3

House Bill 3 is a comprehensive amendment to Ohio's election code enacted in January 2006, most of which became effective after Ohio's primary election in May 2006.[26] House Bill 3 ostensibly sought to respond to issues that surfaced in the 2004 election, while continuing to bring Ohio law into compliance with provisions of the federal Help America Vote Act, particularly HAVA's statewide voter database and provisional balloting requirements. House Bill 3 also imposed additional constraints on the voter registration process; adopted new voter identification requirements; adjusted provisions enacted the prior year to permit no-excuse absentee voting; limited the ways in which challenges to a voter's eligibility could occur; required naturalized citizens to produce a certificate of naturalization if their eligibility was challenged at the polls; and enhanced the options and assistance available to disabled voters.[27]

Despite its comprehensive scope, House Bill 3 left a variety of interpretive issues for Ohio's chief election officer, the secretary of state, to address through implementing regulations and administrative guidance. In some instances, controversy erupted over regulations promulgated by then-Secretary of State Kenneth Blackwell, who at the time was also running as the Republican candidate for governor. In other instances, Secretary Blackwell did not promulgate any interpretive guidance.

For example, under the new voter registration requirements of House Bill 3, individuals who submit their own voter registration forms may return their forms to a variety of public offices, including schools and libraries, but paid voter registration drive workers who are returning other individuals' completed registration forms must return them within ten days of collection and only "to any board of elections or to the office of the secretary of state." Registration drive workers are criminally liable if they fail to do so.[28] This requirement gave rise to an interpretive issue in the spring of 2006 when several national voter registration groups, including the Association of Community Organizations for Reform Now ("ACORN") and Project Vote, descended on Ohio to recruit new voters. These groups asked Secretary Blackwell to confirm their interpretation that while these provisions limited the offices to which paid registration collectors could return the forms and required that they ensure that this return occurred or face criminal punishment, they did not limit the manner in which they accomplished the return.

However, in his implementing regulations of May and June 2006, the secretary of state interpreted these provisions to require that paid registration drive workers *personally* return the forms that they collected, rather than letting their employers or colleagues accomplish this return for them. Thus, an advisory from the secretary of state to county boards of elections stated that any person "being compensated to register voters must . . . [r]eturn an applicant's completed voter registration form directly to the office of a county board of elections or the secretary of state and shall not, under penalty of law, return the completed form to any other person, group, organization, office, or entity."[29] While some viewed this requirement as properly effectuating a statutory purpose of reducing the likelihood of registration fraud, others perceived the secretary's interpretation as disproportionately hindering the work of organizations registering voters in communities that historically favored Democrats. In response, Project Vote, ACORN, and other groups sued the secretary of state in July 2006, arguing that this interpretation would se-

verely restrict their ability to conduct voter registration drives in Ohio.[30] In early September 2006, the state trial court issued a preliminary injunction against enforcing the "personal return" requirement during the 2006 election season, pending the court's final disposition of the legal issues the case raises.[31] The case remains pending, with its final disposition delayed in part by the efforts of Secretary Blackwell's successor to settle the matter.

Equally significant uncertainties emerged over the meaning of various other provisions of Ohio's newly revised election code. For instance, despite the detailed nature of the state's new voter identification rules, they left important practical questions unanswered, including: (1) which of two numbers that appear on an Ohio driver's license number qualify as appropriate identification, (2) how "current" must a utility bill be to qualify as valid identification, and (3) does an identification card issued by one of Ohio's many public universities qualify as a form of "government" issued identification? While local election boards and various advocacy organizations clamored for the secretary of state to issue interpretative regulations resolving these ambiguities, he and his office refused to do so, either because he was preoccupied with his own gubernatorial campaign, for fear of greater public criticism from action rather than inaction, or for some other reason. This led to more litigation, the case that wound up before the Sixth Circuit in late 2006 and remains pending today.

The provision of House Bill 3 requiring naturalized citizens to produce their certificate of naturalization if their eligibility to vote was challenged at the polls also generated a lawsuit. The suit, *Boustani v. Blackwell*, alleged that this requirement impermissibly discriminated between naturalized and native-born citizens in violation of the Equal Protection Clause of the U.S. Constitution.[32] Secretary Blackwell agreed that this provision was unconstitutional, resulting in a federal court order prohibiting the state from giving effect to this portion of the law.[33]

ROLE OF THE SECRETARY OF STATE

As the preceding examples suggest, the Ohio Secretary of State has substantial influence on the state's election system. Ohio is far from unique in assigning to its secretary of state the primary responsibility for administering government elections at the state level. Among the five states in this study, Michigan and Minnesota also do so, along with a total of thirty-nine states.[34] Nevertheless, Ohio in particular has attracted national attention for actions of its immediate past secretary of state, Kenneth Blackwell, and for those of its current secretary of state, Jennifer Brunner.

Secretary Blackwell's history of drawing attention to his role as Ohio's chief election officer predates his interpretation of the voter registration provisions of House Bill 3 in 2006. Indeed, his actions in connection with the 2006 election undoubtedly received greater critical scrutiny because of Secretary Blackwell's activities during the 2004 election. That election left him vulnerable to claims that he had indulged in partisan behavior inconsistent with his election administration role. His two most prominent political involvements in 2004 were his role as a state co-chair of President Bush's re-election campaign in Ohio and his leadership of the successful effort to pass a defense of marriage ballot initiative, known as Issue One.

Both of these activities raised concerns about the impartiality of his execution of his duties as the state's chief election officer.

In Blackwell's partial defense, his role as a co-chair of President Bush's Ohio campaign was an honorary role with no specific responsibilities, a role apparently also bestowed on all statewide Republican incumbents.[35] It was also a type of role that previous Ohio secretaries of states of both parties had sometimes held. At the same time, however, Blackwell repeatedly invoked this role and also engaged in a variety of public activities supportive of President Bush's re-election.

Perhaps most significant was his leadership of the effort to enact Issue One, a defense of marriage amendment widely seen as having at least a secondary, if not primary, purpose of boosting conservative turnout on Election Day in order to assist Bush in what was accurately predicted would be a close presidential race in Ohio. Blackwell appeared in a statewide radio advertisement promoting the defense of marriage amendment. He also recorded the following automated telephone message dialed to individual voters in the days before the 2004 election:

> Hi. This is Ohio Secretary of State Ken Blackwell. Voting "yes" on Issue One to keep marriage between one man and one woman is just common sense. . . . This is Ken Blackwell. For the future of Ohio, please join me in voting "yes" on Issue One.[36]

Voter alarm over these advocacy efforts by the person responsible for overseeing the election was only compounded by another automated phone message a few days later. That message invited voters to do their civic duty by voting on Election Day. Taken together, the way these messages conflated the roles of advocate and neutral is troubling.[37]

Largely as a result of these activities, Secretary Blackwell lost the trust of at least some portions of the state's electorate, and several aspects of his administration of the 2004 election came under increased scrutiny. For instance, he was criticized for his interpretation of the state law permitting political parties to designate polling place "challengers." In circumstances in which several precincts are combined in one polling place, Blackwell interpreted the statutory language authorizing one challenger per "polling place" to permit one challenger for each precinct. His directive in this regard was the predicate for several lawsuits on the eve of the 2004 election charging that both the Election Day challenge process and the pre-election challenge process were being misused for partisan gain.[38]

Blackwell also was pilloried for a ruling that voter registration applications must use at least a certain weight of white paper to be valid,[39] a ruling he subsequently reversed under pressure. Additionally, he was criticized for his decision that provisional ballots would be invalid if cast in the wrong precinct, a decision ultimately sustained by a federal appeals court as consistent with (although not required by) HAVA, as discussed further below. However, despite the existence of neutral, statutory justifications for both rulings, some observers perceived these rulings as disadvantaging Democratic candidates more than Republicans and therefore as potentially influenced by Secretary Blackwell's avowed commitment to conservative issues and candidates. Meanwhile, other problems in the

2004 election, such as an insufficient number of voting machines in some urban areas, which led to waiting times of several hours or more,[40] and errors in vote counting in certain counties[41] were also imputed (unfairly) to partisanship by Secretary Blackwell, even though the responsibility for these decisions was at the local level.

Thus, when the 2006 election arrived, Secretary Blackwell was already fighting the perception in some quarters that he was a partisan chief election officer. The fact that he himself was competing in the top race on that year's ballot further compounded his difficulties in overseeing the election and making tough decisions about its administration. The result, as the election neared, was a form of paralysis in the state's election ecosystem, even though (or perhaps partly because) Blackwell delegated his election administration responsibilities to his assistant secretary of state.

For instance, local election officials described a state elections division within the secretary of state's office that was frequently unresponsive to their questions and concerns and that often expected them to rely on their own county attorneys for legal advice and interpretation, advice that often varied from county to county. With just over three months remaining before the election, the president of the Ohio Association of Election Officials, Steven Harsman, went on record stating that election officials throughout the state were concerned about Secretary Blackwell's disengagement from his election administration duties, particularly in light of the number of major changes to election administration wrought by HAVA and House Bill 3. "These are critical times, and we need that leadership from Mr. Blackwell," the *Columbus Dispatch* quoted Harsman as saying.[42] Yet months earlier, Democratic leaders in the state had called for Blackwell to recuse himself from an investigation he ordered into problems that occurred in the primary election in Cuyahoga County,[43] where Cleveland is located, precisely the sort of investigation that an attentive secretary of state should have ordered. Blackwell was caught in an untenable position, unable personally to carry out his election responsibilities in a manner that would build confidence and acceptance among the public generally and among the local election officials who depended upon his leadership.

In light of how estranged and dispirited local election administrators have recently felt about election administration at the state level, one notable aspect of Ohio's election ecosystem today may be the changes that the new Ohio Secretary of State, Jennifer Brunner, seeks to make. Brunner, who began serving in January 2007, has been working to re-establish good lines of communication between her office and local election directors. In the first nine months of her term she has issued written guidance on a variety of election administration issues, addressing a number of matters that her predecessor had largely ignored in his final years.[44] She also paired the attorneys in the elections division of her office with each of Ohio's eighty-eight counties in order to give the counties a consistent primary point of contact in her office and to encourage regular communication.[45] And she has been seeking to settle a range of election related litigation, discussed further below, that was pending against her office when she began her term.

Secretary Brunner also is promoting several new initiatives intended to improve how Ohio administers its elections. One such initiative is a proposal that citizens be called to poll service, much in the way that they are called to jury service.[46] Little legislative or popular support appears to exist for this proposal, but the dialogue around the proposal has been constructive. She also has established a Voting Rights Institute, which aspires to enhance access to voting, address voter concerns, and promote related legislative and policy initiatives.[47] The institute, which is run by a full-time director, with the advice of a thirty-eight-member advisory council, is to serve as a clearinghouse on voting issues in the state. Another initiative involves verification of the accuracy of Ohio's election equipment, through both pre-election testing as well as post-election audits, including a comprehensive test of the security of the state's direct recording electronic ("DRE") and optical scan equipment presently underway.[48] The new secretary of state also has proposed experimenting with mail-in only voting for issue elections,[49] as well as expanding early voting opportunities.[50]

Despite a palpable increase in the trust that Ohio's county election officials now have in the secretary of state and her role as the state's chief election officer, the fact that the chief election officer is a partisan elected position continues to have an impact. Perhaps in part because of the amount of negative publicity that attended her predecessor for publicly campaigning for certain ballot measures and candidates while also serving as secretary of state, Brunner has vowed that she will not participate in any candidate or issue campaigns[51] (and a provision enacted in House Bill 3 now prohibits the Ohio Secretary of State from serving in any official capacity for another candidate's campaign or on behalf of an initiative petition[52]).

Still, in her first months on the job she fired all four members of the bipartisan Board of Elections in Cuyahoga County, which as discussed further below has been the locus of the state's most serious recent election administration problems. Some observers worried that it was an effort to take over the county and remake its election system for partisan gain. But Secretary Brunner moved quickly to empanel replacement board members and to let the board get back to work cleaning up its own shop as quickly as possible, in advance of the 2008 election. She has also been accused of partisanship in other aspects of her job, such as in selecting which counties to include in a pilot voter recruitment project.

In fact, perhaps as a form of payback for all of the attacks on Secretary Blackwell, or perhaps just as a matter of "politics as usual" (whereby it has become standard operating procedure for the leaders of one party to question the motives of the other party's leaders), some Ohio politicians appear intent to undercut Secretary Brunner and instill public doubt about her ability to administer the 2008 election fairly. Whether the specific criticisms of Brunner are justifiable or not, the dynamic that has developed is troubling. Whereas the leaders of both parties should be looking for ways to build a bipartisan structure that can handle any problems that might arise in the 2008 presidential election, their instinct for attacking one another is a byproduct of the poisonous atmosphere that existed in 2006 and 2004, if not before.

Thus, as we look ahead to the 2008 election, Ohio remains tethered to an administrative structure – an elected chief election officer – in which political activities or allegations of parti-

san election administration at the top could continue to undermine public confidence. Nevertheless, if the new secretary of state successfully follows through on her efforts to reestablish effective leadership in her office, there is reason to hope that in 2008 Ohio's election ecosystem will be better managed from the top down. This includes realistic hopes that the system will operate with greater statewide consistency, and that local elections officials will benefit from additional state-sponsored training, guidance, and other state resources. Preparing for and conducting an election is a massive undertaking, and it takes conscientious dedicated efforts at all levels of election administration to protect adequately against potential problems.

THE FUNCTIONING OF OHIO'S STATEWIDE VOTER DATABASE

The provisions of Ohio's House Bill 3 concerning voter registration drives had two stated purposes: reducing the number of eligible voters who were prevented from voting because of failures or errors in the registration process, and reducing voter registration fraud and the accompanying prospect that ineligible voters would be able to cast ballots. Similarly, the HAVA requirement that by 2006 (originally 2004) each state develop a single computerized database of its voters was intended both to help purify the registration lists, thereby avoiding erroneous purges, and to enhance a state's ability to detect ineligible voters. To further these purposes, states were required to develop a database of voters' names and registration information that permitted comparisons throughout the state and that could be rapidly updated based on information gathered by local election officials.

Although some states already had such a database prior to HAVA, many states, including Ohio, instead allowed each county independently to maintain its own list of registered voters. Each county made its own decisions about how to create and maintain this list, consistent with provisions of state and federal law, including the National Voter Registration Act. Although each county updated its list monthly in light of information concerning death, felony conviction, or mental incompetency of a voter received from other county agencies (and although every two years the state submitted all county lists to a national change of address service),[53] across counties there was little systematic effort to identify or eliminate duplicate registrations, as could result either incidentally when a voter moved from one jurisdiction to another or through deliberate fraud.

To comply with the HAVA requirement, Ohio chose to construct its statewide database from the bottom up, working to link together its existing county databases, rather than to build a new single statewide database from the top down. But getting all the existing county lists to talk to each other electronically has not been as simple as hoped, as county lists varied in the way that the data was organized and formatted, and the software from several vendors has had to be upgraded to permit the exchange of data in a uniform manner. Although the secretary of state's office worked diligently to meet the January 2006 deadline, and now has in place a web-accessible statewide database, organized by county and updated every 24-hours in the height of election season,[54] county election officials describe a system that at least in the 2006 election was useful primarily to coordinate corrections to the list after the election, not in helping on Election Day.

Moreover, at least in 2006, integrating the county registration lists into a statewide compendium did not eliminate a variety of problems with the accuracy of the statewide list. For instance, tens of thousands of "errors" appear in the state list for Hamilton County (Cincinnati) alone, although county officials are confident that their local database is accurate and that the problem is the interface between the county data and the state list.

In some cases the new system appears to have caused errors. While creating a single statewide master file does permit counties to eliminate duplicate registrations in the name of the same individual, issues of how to determine just what constitutes a duplicate registration have not yet been resolved. It remains each county's responsibility to manage its own piece of the database at the county level, but in the 2006 election counties lacked uniform statewide standards for how they were to do so, including the steps they should take to determine whether similar but not identical names (such as Ted Jones and Edward Jones) represented the same individual and whether identical names in fact represented different individuals. When two such names are mistakenly identified as duplicates, as apparently happened in a number of instances in 2006, one voter's registration information is deleted from the database.

The secretary of state's office has declared that it will have developed appropriate and uniform standards in time for counties to implement them for the 2008 election. As one piece of this effort, the secretary of state issued a directive earlier this year with guidance about the standards that counties were to use for purging the names of voters who had moved.[55] Meanwhile, Ohio also continues to rely on each county to identify incarcerated felons, as well as to identify individuals found incompetent and to remove them from the list of registered voters. But even with statewide standards in these matters as well, some county-by-county variation in the implementation of these standards is likely to persist.

Of course, the efficiency and accuracy with which Ohio's counties update and correct their voter lists, both within each county as well as through electronic coordination with the remaining eighty-seven counties, has a di-

rect impact on the provisional voting process in Ohio. A sound statewide voter database should reduce those instances when provisional ballots must be used by voters whose names or addresses do not match those on the voter list. At this point it is premature to conclude whether Ohio's statewide database in fact is having such an impact, although an early signal was not encouraging. Ohio saw widespread use of provisional ballots in 2004, and still greater use in 2006, measured as a percentage of voter turnout. Table 1 displays comparative data about the provisional balloting experiences of not only Ohio but also Illi-

TABLE 1
STATE PROVISIONAL VOTING DATA

November 2004

	Total Ballots Cast	Provisional Ballots Cast	% PB Cast	PB Counted	% PB Counted	PB Counted/ Total Cast
Ohio	5,722,443	158,642	2.772%	123,548	77.878%	2.159%
Illinois	5,350,493	43,464	0.812%	22,238	51.164%	0.416%
Michigan	4,875,692	5,610	0.115%	3,227	57.522%	0.066%

November 2006

	Total Ballots Cast	Provisional Ballots Cast	% PB Cast	PB Counted	% PB Counted	PB Counted/ Total Cast
Ohio	4,186,207	129,432	3.092%	104,581	80.800%	2.498%
Illinois	3,587,676	15,875	0.442%	5,874	37.002%	0.164%
Michigan	3,852,008	2,426	0.063%	952	39.242%	0.025%

Differences Between 2004 and 2006

	Change in % Cast	Change in % Counted	Change in PB Counted/Total Cast
Ohio	11.528%	3.751%	15.71%
Illinois	-45.529%	-27.681%	-60.61%
Michigan	-45.264%	-31.780%	-62.66%

Source: Data from Ohio Secretary of State, Michigan Secretary of State, and Illinois State Board of Elections

nois and Michigan. As this table reflects, in 2004, Ohio issued over 158,000 provisional ballots, representing 2.77% of those who went to the polls.[56] In 2006, Ohio issued approximately 130,000 provisional ballots, a smaller absolute number but one representing 3.09% of those who turned out that year.[57] Of course, even adjusting for variations in turnout across elections, comparing these figures is difficult given the changes that House Bill 3 made to Ohio's provisional balloting process in the interim.

Ohio's provisional ballots tell another story as well, this one about potential variations in election administration between counties. In 2006, the county-wide rates at which provisional ballots were cast varied from a high of 8.5% in semi-rural Athens County, home to Ohio University and a high student population, to a low of 0.4% in rural Harrison County.[58] With Athens County as an aberration, rural counties generally had much lower rates of provisional voting than urban ones. Of course, demographics – and the greater transiency of urban voters – likely explain much of this variation. But one curious feature is the difference in provisional voting rates even between just the state's most urban counties. For instance, in Cuyahoga County (Cleveland area), the provisional voting rate was 3.76% in 2006, while in Franklin County (Columbus area), the rate was 5.08%, more than 30% greater. More details about Ohio's provisional voting, with additional discussion of county variations, are presented in the Supplement on Provisional Voting at the end of this chapter.

These variations at least raise the question of whether poll workers applied provisional voting requirements inconsistently from county to county. To the extent that such inconsistency is to blame, it may reflect the difficulty in adapting to the rapid changes in the legal framework surrounding election administration that occurred in the run-up to the 2006 election. Precisely this circumstance gave rise to the ongoing *NEOCH v. Blackwell* case, described more below, over inconsistencies in the counties' applications of the state's complicated new voter identification rules. But voter identification requirements were not the only area of Ohio election administration to undergo rapid change for the 2006 election.

RAPID CHANGES IN VOTING EQUIPMENT AND PROCESSES

Until 2006, Ohio had relied heavily on punch card voting. By one estimate, seventy-two percent of the state's voters were using punch card machines in 2002, about twice the proportion of voters nationally.[59] Although by 2004 many other states had upgraded their voting equipment, most Ohio counties continued to use essentially the same equipment that year as well. Yet by 2006, Ohio's punch card machines were all but nonexistent, replaced by a combination of optical scan and touch screen or other direct recording electronic ballots. The rapid change in equipment did not come without transition problems, and lingering concerns remain over the security of electronic voting.

In exchange for federal funds, HAVA required states to replace their punch card and lever machines by the first federal election of 2006 with voting systems satisfying specific standards of security, accuracy, accessibility, and privacy. Many Ohio counties at first had hoped to upgrade by the 2004 election, and the secretary of state had authorized counties to select from among both DRE and optical scan systems. But as in other states, controversy then arose over whether all acceptable voting systems should generate a paper audit trail, something that most DRE systems readily available in 2004 did not generate (but which optical scan ballots inherently provided). By the time that the legislature had resolved the controversy by requiring a paper audit trail, which was to be the official ballot in the event of a recount, it was too late for most counties to safely implement new machines for the 2004 election.[60]

In January 2005, the secretary of state concluded that evolving DRE systems with paper trails were still too unreliable and expensive and informed all Ohio counties that in order to meet the HAVA and state requirements they would have to use precinct count optical scan systems.[61] Objections and threatened litigation from a number of counties, including several of Ohio's largest, that desired to use newer DRE equipment with paper audit trails eventually led the secretary to reverse his directive in the spring of 2005.[62] The result was something of a rushed scramble from that point to prepare for the 2006 election. Counties upgraded their voting systems by independently contracting with the limited number of vendors of approved equipment, vendors who were heavily overworked by national demand for HAVA-compliant equipment. In the end, almost two-thirds of Ohio's counties elected to use touch screen or other DRE equipment with a paper audit trail, and the remainder chose optical scan ballots, completely replacing punch card ballots in Ohio.[63] In turn, one of a number of recent lawsuits now pending against the Ohio Secretary of State argues that the DRE equipment presently in use in Ohio does not satisfy the legal requirements.

The hurried equipment upgrades may partially explain a variety of implementation problems experienced in 2006. As discussed below, Cuyahoga County had by far the most serious issues, although other Ohio counties also experienced equipment problems or delays in voting in 2006. Many of these problems resulted from a combination of inexperience in using new voting technology and inadequate training of volunteer poll workers. Indeed, a number of Ohio election officials have expressed frustration at the increasing complexity of their responsibilities and the ever-changing nature of their duties, occasioned primarily by continuing fallout from the 2000 presidential election and HAVA.[64]

Specifically, local officials point to the complexity of a voting system that must produce a contemporaneous paper record, alert voters before a ballot is cast that the ballot contains an overvote, and allow voters with disabilities to vote without assistance. DRE systems can more easily satisfy the demands of many disabled voters, but optical scan ballots generally provide a more reliable form of paper record, although one that may give rise to ambiguous markings and difficult problems of determining voter intent. Optical scan systems also can be scaled to accommodate wider swings in turnout more readily simply by supplying extra ballots and providing more surfaces for voters to mark them (rather than needing to have extra DRE machines on hand). Meanwhile, the processes of securing the voting materials, including the machines as well as the ballots and data memory cards or other storage devices, are also more involved, and the training required to operate and troubleshoot the electronic equipment is also increasingly complex.

On top of these issues surrounding the voting equipment itself, local election workers must deal with ever more complicated rules concerning a variety of matters, including what identification voters must show at the polls; who can vote a regular ballot and who must vote a provisional ballot; and how to resolve a challenge to a voter's eligibility. A frequent refrain from county elections directors is to leave the system alone for a few elections and let them refine their ability to implement it. Instead, election officials have been required to implement many changes in procedures and technologies in a relatively short time span in each of the past three election cycles. The constant flux in election equipment and processes not only destabilizes the system but also damages public confidence in election integrity and demoralizes both the paid county elections staff and the increasingly hard-to-recruit cadre of volunteer poll workers. In partial acknowledgement of the growing sophistication of election administration, Secretary of State Brunner issued a directive in early 2007 setting minimum qualifications for county election directors.[65]

TROUBLES IN CUYAHOGA COUNTY

Ohio's most serious local election administration problems of recent years have occurred in Cuyahoga County. The largest problems surfaced in the May 2006 primary election, when the county was using its new DRE machines for in-precinct voting and new optical scan machines for absentee ballots for the first time. Many poll workers were inadequately prepared to use the new equipment, a problem compounded when many other poll workers simply failed to report to work at the polls. As a result, approximately twenty percent of the county's

polling places opened late, one not until early afternoon. In addition, equipment and procedural problems – including DRE machine malfunctions, failures of the verified paper trail devices, missing security seals on equipment, and shortages of supplies – plagued poll workers throughout the day. Many poll workers not only lacked training to handle these contingencies, but lacked even a basic understanding of their responsibilities, evidenced most dramatically by the fact that after the polls closed, some seventy memory cards from DRE equipment were missing. Although the county board of elections eventually recovered all but twelve of the cards, even their disappearance is worrisome. A number of poll workers obviously did not know or follow proper procedures for handling the equipment.[66]

In part, the preparation gap resulted from pre-election difficulties in implementing a new voter registration system that the county adopted to coordinate with the statewide network, difficulties that consumed the attention of county elections officials for many weeks in the run-up to the primary election. Meanwhile, county officials also were having repeated difficulties preparing and testing the optical scan ballot readers to be used for absentee ballots, which led the county elections director early on the morning of the primary to order a time-consuming hand count of the 15,000 absentee ballots instead. The combination of these and other problems, which occupied the attention of a 220-page post-mortem report that Cuyahoga County commissioned,[67] delayed the county's primary election results for five days and created numerous potential security and accuracy issues that would have seriously undermined the outcome had the results been close.

Cuyahoga County also was the scene of problems in the November 2006 general election, when many polling places once again did not open on time or were otherwise not prepared for voters to use the DRE equipment. Voter unfamiliarity with DRE equipment probably contributed to longer waiting times for some voters. As DRE problems persisted into Election Day, poll workers in some locations eventually began distributing optical scan ballots for voters to mark instead. But problems also occurred in connection with the optical scan ballots, primarily in their counting, including scanning some batches of ballots twice and inadvertently deleting the tallies of other ballot batches from the results. And inadequate poll worker training or execution apparently resulted in some 12,000 Cuyahoga County voters casting ballots without properly verifying their eligibility to vote.[68]

In early 2007, Cuyahoga County's election-related embarrassments grew, when two county election officials were convicted and sentenced to eighteen months in prison for charges related to their conduct of the 2004 election.[69] Specifically, they were found to have pre-selected the precincts included in what was supposed to have been a random sample for a hand recount of the punch card ballots used that year for the presidential race. If the sample hand recount matched the machine totals, then a full hand recount would not be required. The county officials apparently pre-selected the precincts in order to ensure that the sample hand count matched the machine totals, and thereby avoid the burdens of a full hand recount. No evidence suggested that they rigged the recount for political reasons. Instead, at trial they maintained that they were doing what

the county had traditionally done and what they believed was proper recount procedure. (After their trial, the chief justice of the state supreme court concluded that the trial judge who had handled their case had a conflict of interest. The case was reassigned to a new trial judge, who then ordered a retrial, which remains pending.[70])

The upshot of the accumulation of all of Cuyahoga County's election problems was that in February 2007, the county elections director resigned, and then in March 2007, Secretary of State Brunner asked the four members of the county board of elections also to resign, which they ultimately did. Brunner then empanelled a new board of elections, which in turn chose a new elections director and deputy director.[71] They and the board of elections have their work cut out for them in preparing for the impending 2008 election season and continuing to manage a hybrid system consisting of DRE equipment for in-precinct voting and optical scan ballots for absentee voting. (In late 2006, the former board of elections briefly considered but abandoned the idea of scrapping the county's new DRE equipment and moving exclusively to optical scan ballots.) This will require stronger poll worker recruiting and training programs, effective processes for managing voting equipment and materials, and thorough preparation to respond to election-week and election-day problems, including potential last-minute litigation about voting administration matters.

ELECTION LITIGATION

The above difficulties have all provided grist for a number of recent lawsuits over election administration in Ohio. Indeed, when new

Ohio Secretary of State Jennifer Brunner took office in January 2007, she identified some twenty active suits then pending against her office.[72] Many of these suits are now being held in abeyance pending settlement discussions with Secretary Brunner's office. Perhaps most significant is *League of Women Voters v. Blackwell*,[73] the wide-ranging litigation referenced earlier that challenges many aspects of Ohio's election processes. It is difficult to anticipate how this case will be resolved, but it merits additional discussion because of its scope and complexity.

The complaint in the *League of Women Voters* case, filed prior to the enactment of House Bill 3, alleges that for decades Ohio's system of election administration has infringed on individuals' rights to vote and violated the federal constitution's guarantees of Equal Protection and Due Process of law. In support of this allegation it claims that, over many years, the state has failed to process voter registration and absentee applications adequately or accurately; has not done enough to ensure that counties provide their polls with adequate supplies and equipment and otherwise prevent unreasonable delays and other burdens on voters; has failed to provide adequate training programs for poll workers; has not enforced its provisional balloting and other polling place requirements uniformly across jurisdictions; and has generally maintained an election system that is unequal across the state, disproportionately infringing on some voters' rights. It focuses on circumstances of the 2004 election, including allegations that a number of registered voters were unable to vote that election because their names had erroneously been removed from the voter rolls, and that many voters had to wait in voting lines for up to ten

hours in some precincts, arguably because voting machines were maldistributed. The complaint also alleges a number of deficiencies in poll worker training and behavior, including errors in handling the provisional voting process. As a remedy, the lawsuit seeks federal-court supervision over the administration of the voting process throughout the state.

These are serious accusations based on real problems that Ohio has historically had. Whether they amount to legally actionable problems remains to be seen, both as a matter of fact and law. Specific facts regarding plaintiffs' claims are still to be developed through the yet incomplete discovery process. Moreover, the law regarding the applicability of the U.S. Constitution's Equal Protection guarantee to election administration is still developing, since the Supreme Court's use of the Equal Protection guaranteee in its 2000 decision in *Bush v. Gore*. Among the issues in play is the extent to which the problems in one area of election administration affect the entire election ecosystem.

The *League of Women Voters* complaint did survive a motion to dismiss – meaning that the federal district court found it legally sound, assuming that its factual allegations are true. That ruling is now on appeal, even as settlement discussions continue. In rejecting the motion to dismiss, the district court specifically relied upon the Equal Protection holding of *Bush v. Gore*, and given the scope of the complaint, the court's opinion may be the most significant use of that precedent to date.[74]

To the extent that the court ultimately finds any of the allegations meritorious – assuming that the parties do not settle and the court of appeals permits the case to go forward – it also may find the question of appropriate relief to be complicated by the interposition of House Bill 3. That law significantly altered the election ecosystem in ways that have yet to fully understood. In addition, some of Secretary Brunner's recent directives may moot some of the complaint's grounds for seeking judicial relief.

Another significant piece of litigation is *Northeast Ohio Coalition for the Homeless (NEOCH) v. Blackwell*,[75] brought in federal court in 2006 to challenge the state's new voter identification requirements and the secretary of state's rules for determining which provisional votes could be counted. The complaint alleged that the identification requirements were vague and confusing, citing the fact that counties were applying them inconsistently. The federal district court entered a consent order in the case, clarifying the identification and provisional balloting requirements applicable to the November 2006 election. But inconsistent adherence to this order – and difficulties in even ensuring that all poll workers knew of its substance – may account for some of the surprising variation in provisional voting rates across counties in 2006, described above. What requirements will be applicable in future elections remains uncertain, pending the outcome of the lawsuit. There also remains the more general question, with regard to both voter identification and provisional voting, whether in actual practice local officials and poll workers will follow the rules laid down in the new directives of Secretary of State Brunner, or whether, because of either mistake or disobedience, they will instead substitute their own preferred practices.

Among dozens of additional lawsuits concerning Ohio election administration filed in recent years, several others deserve brief comment. Another federal court suit, *King Lincoln Bronzeville Neighborhood Association v. Blackwell*,[76] argues that problems in the 2004 election in Ohio had a disproportionate impact on some voters, and specifically alleges that election resources were allocated in a racially discriminatory matter. This suit, which also seeks to put supervision of Ohio elections in the hands of a federal judge, is being held in abeyance pending settlement efforts. In an alarming development in this case, in the summer of 2007 the Ohio Secretary of State's office disclosed that almost two-thirds of Ohio's counties had failed to comply with the federal court's order to retain their ballots and other records from the 2004 presidential election while this litigation proceeded.[77] Although the plaintiffs in the suit have suggested that at least some of these records may have been intentionally destroyed to conceal irregularities, even the inadvertent loss or destruction of these ballots and other materials, contrary to court order, is extremely serious. It also appears to be emblematic of the difficulties that some local jurisdictions have had in following established rules and procedures.

Two more suits concern Ohio's voter registration process. One of these is *Project Vote v. Blackwell*,[78] the previously discussed litigation concerning the requirement that paid voter registration drive workers personally return the registration applications they collect. Although the trial court granted the plaintiffs request for a preliminary injunction prohibiting the enforcement of this requirement,[79] the court has yet to issue a final order.[80] Resolution of the case likely has been delayed primarily because of the efforts of Secretary Brunner's office to develop settlement agreements for this and many other suits. The other is *Harkless v. Blackwell*,[81] which alleged that Ohio was not complying with the National Voter Registration Act requirements for facilitating voter registration at offices of the state's Department of Job and Family Services. This case also has been delayed because of settlement efforts.

Additional lawsuits have concerned a variety of other matters, including limitations on the media's or partisan observers' ability to monitor polling places.[82] This is an issue likely to recur and, given the importance of building confidence in our election ecosystems, an issue that also deserves careful resolution. Election administrators understandably want to limit access to polling places in order to protect the integrity of the process, but it is critical to public acceptance of that same integrity that public representatives have adequate opportunity to observe polling place operations.

In 2006, litigation over the *outcome* (rather than the *processes*) of the congressional election between incumbent Deborah Pryce and her opponent Mary Jo Kilroy was narrowly avoided after Kilroy decided that the final margin of victory of 3,500 votes (or 1.77%) was too large to overcome, despite various problems identified on Election Day, including concerns about the circumstances in which provisional ballots were issued. In fact, in December 2006 the Kilroy campaign briefly went to court seeking an order that the Franklin County (home of Columbus) Board of Elections release to the campaign the names of those voters whose provisional ballots were not counted, which state law appeared to require, but which Franklin County construed HAVA to prohibit.[83] However, the campaign withdrew this lawsuit when it concluded that the margin re-

mained insurmountable. Had Kilroy proceeded with an effort to challenge the official results, it might have tested the meaning of a new provision in state law enacted as part of House Bill 3, also discussed further below, that deprives state courts of jurisdiction to hear contests of federal elections. For now, however, what merits the closest attention is the ongoing litigation over central elements of Ohio's election administration, including its voting equipment, registration processes, identification requirements, poll worker training programs, and lack of statewide uniformity.

The number and scope of these lawsuits may partially reflect the battleground nature of Ohio politics today, and the fact that the state's election ecosystem is therefore under great pressure. But they also reflect some historical weaknesses in Ohio's system of election administration, as well as some difficulties confronting American elections generally. Central among these weaknesses is the tension inherent in placing ultimate authority over election administration in a partisan elected official. Additionally, in contrast to Ohio, other states have derived substantial strength from imposing much greater statewide uniformity over matters of election administration, even while relying on local implementation. And Ohio, like all states, is struggling with issues of evolving election technology.

LOOKING AHEAD

Seven years after troubles in Florida gave new prominence to matters of state election administration and less than one year before the 2008 election, it is perhaps disheartening to conclude that the potential for serious electoral difficulties persists in Ohio. Among other issues, the state is likely to continue to face concerns about the security of voting technology, at least in the short term. The challenge for state and local election administrators is to be nimble in responding to technological developments without being alarmist. Adaptability is essential, but at the same time the election ecosystem must strive for as much stability as it can.

Furthermore, as election administration becomes increasingly complex, the need for reliable and well-trained staff and poll workers also becomes more critical. In the years to come, Ohio, like most states, is likely to struggle to recruit and train poll workers. These personnel will depend on improvements in both the state-developed formal training programs as well as on enhanced communication with the secretary of state's office. But they would also benefit from system stability, which would reduce their need for frequent retraining. The lack of enough well-trained personnel is frequently a contributing cause to many Election Day miscues.

As poll workers (and polling venues themselves) come under increased pressure, one relief valve will be to increase the proportion of voters who vote non-traditionally. In future elections Ohio is likely to see even more voters take advantage of their new (since 2006) ability to vote an absentee ballot without cause, whether by mail or in-person at county election headquarters, in the state's version of an "early voting" option. Meanwhile, the state appears poised to begin experimenting with voting by mail for some elections involving only ballot issues, not candidates.[84]

Given the importance to smooth election administration of some long-term stability, it would be regrettable if ideological fights over

such matters as voter identification, voter registration processes, and provisional voting continue to seesaw back and forth. This will reduce the degree to which the state's election ecosystem can steady itself and re-establish a sense of constancy. To the extent that the state legislature (and Congress) can settle on a satisfactory approach to these matters and then leave election officials to develop experience and expertise in implementing that approach, the system will be strengthened.

On the other hand, if the election ecosystem instead remains in flux, more matters are likely to be fought over in court. Every change provides both another target for a constitutional claim and another opportunity for the sort of implementation failures that tend to arise during transitions to a new technology or administrative process (which failures in turn can themselves lead to legal claims). The foregoing section has already detailed a variety of existing lawsuits concerning the state's current election structure, and given the state's history it seems more than plausible that analogous litigation would arise in response to future major changes to the state's election ecosystem. Even without those changes, we can anticipate litigation in 2008 for reasons discussed previously. There may be little ability for the state to forestall such litigation, beyond the clarifying directives that the secretary of state is in the process of issuing.

Ohio is fortunate, however, in that the vast majority of its recent election litigation has involved issues identified and raised prior to an election, rather than after the fact. Post-election litigation seeking to challenge or overturn the results of Election Day voting is much more destabilizing, because it puts courts in the position of specifically deciding the actual victors of a political contest, rather than merely clarifying the rules of that contest in advance. Before concluding our evaluation of Ohio's ecosystem, it is worth a brief comment on how Ohio courts would respond should such a post-election contest arise in the near future.

Ohio's most significant post-election court contest involved the 1990 race for attorney general. In that race, Lee Fisher defeated Paul Pfeiffer by 1,234 votes out of over 3.3 million votes cast. Pfeifer was able to establish that almost 100,000 ballots were flawed, in that they did not comply with state law requiring the rotation of the order of candidate names on the ballots. Nevertheless, after hearing expert testimony about the effect of this flaw on the vote totals, the state supreme court concluded that Pfeifer had not shown by "clear and convincing evidence" that, were it not for this ballot flaw, Fisher would not have received the most votes.[85]

This case demonstrates two significant principles of Ohio election law. The first is that official election results are presumptively valid and "will not be disturbed except under extreme circumstances that clearly affect the integrity of the election."[86] The second, which follows directly from the first, is that a party challenging an election outcome must establish by clear and convincing evidence – an evidentiary standard substantially higher than the legal system's typical requirement in civil cases of proof by a mere preponderance of the evidence – that the outcome is not reliable.[87] These are difficult hurdles for a person contesting an election outcome, and they mean that a successful election contest is likely to require more than just a speculative possibility that the outcome is flawed.

Notwithstanding these high hurdles, in a sufficiently close race an election contest remains highly likely, with the trailing candidate exploring all aspects of the election's administration in search of grounds to overturn its outcome. In Ohio's current election system, it is provisional ballots that are most likely to offer a candidate a fruitful source of specific, non-speculative grounds to challenge an official election result. The high number of these ballots, coupled with the fact that each ballot can be individually reviewed to determine whether it should or should not be counted, make them an obvious focus of an election contest. Furthermore, variations in how counties process provisional ballots, as the Supplement to this chapter notes occurred in 2006, would compound the grounds for litigation. Absentee ballots are also inviting – and perhaps increasingly so as their numbers swell under Ohio's new "no-reason" absentee voting option – although typically by the time that the validity of a particular absentee voter's ballot can be questioned the vote itself has already been irretrievably commingled with the official results, perhaps compromising a court's ability to find clear and convincing proof that the outcome would have been different.

Although definitely more speculative, it also remains conceivable that any number of errors in polling place operations could themselves lead to grounds for an election contest, if a contestant can convincingly establish that these errors have in some way deprived a critical number of voters of the opportunity to cast their desired vote. Of course, in such a case it is unlikely that the contestant could establish by clear and convincing evidence which candidate would have won, had the errors not occurred. Instead, the proof likely would only be that the election outcome is uncertain or unreliable. In this circumstance, Ohio election law allows the courts only to set aside the election, not to play any role in calling a new election, in which case the position becomes vacant and is filled according to the process applicable to filling a vacancy in that particular office.[88]

Finally, we point out that one little-noticed provision in House Bill 3 amends Ohio law to deprive Ohio courts of jurisdiction over contests involving elections to federal offices. In other words, candidates for U.S. president or Congress may no longer challenge the outcome of their race under the same Ohio election contest provision available to candidates for state and local offices. Instead, the amended law provides that contests for such offices "shall be conducted in accordance with the applicable provisions of federal law."[89] Federal law provides only that the Senate and the House are to be the judges of the elections of their own members, and one federal statute – the Federal Contested Election Act, 2 U.S.C. chapter 12 – establishes some procedures to govern an election contest in the House (but not the Senate). Typically, both the Senate and the House of Representatives have relied on state courts first exhausting their factual inquiry into an election dispute. But Ohio's new provision means that no such state judicial inquiry can occur, perhaps leaving a federal candidate to seek to challenge an election outcome in federal court, if the candidate can allege deprivation of some constitutional right. However, most election administration problems, even including fraud, are not likely to rise to the level of a constitutional claim, leaving federal candidates in Ohio with only the U.S. Congress to adjudicate whether to invalidate an election in light of either electoral fraud or mistakes in election administration.

In the case of a presidential election, when what is technically at stake is which candidate's slate of presidential electors will represent Ohio in the Electoral College, it is even more unclear what would transpire. A candidate might attempt to go to state court using procedures other than a formal election "contest" specifically contemplated in Ohio's election code. The receptivity of the state judiciary to that form of lawsuit may depend, or at least appear to depend, on the political leanings of Ohio's elected supreme court. Currently, all seven members of the Ohio Supreme Court are themselves elected Republicans, although they nominally run for judicial office without a party label appearing on the ballot. The seven hardly see eye-to-eye ideologically on all issues, and they could be expected to fracture on some issues of election law. It is possible that they unanimously would throw out any effort of even a Republican presidential candidate to overturn judicially the result of the state's presidential vote, ruling the attempt to be a now-forbidden "contest" masquerading under another label. Nonetheless, it is at least conceivable – based on the Ohio Supreme Court's rulings in other politically charged cases – that a majority of the justices would permit such a lawsuit to go forward, if they thought the factual allegations were meritorious (for instance, if provisional votes were counted that, by law, should not have been – or evidence existed of widespread and systematic absentee ballot fraud, of the kind that occurred in the Miami mayoral election of 1997[90]).

Indeed, looking forward, one way in which the risk of future election-related litigation in Ohio differs from the litigation that occurred in 2004 and 2006 is that the candidates, parties, and interest groups with an incentive to litigate are likely to be the opposite of those who have recently litigated. The litigation in 2004 and 2006 largely involved voting rights organizations or groups allied with the Democratic Party, who were mostly challenging the alleged deficiencies of Secretary of State Blackwell's administration of the voting process. Now that Democratic Secretary of State Brunner is in office, the dynamics of potential litigation have shifted. It is now more likely that groups associated with Republican interests will go to court in an attempt to challenge enforcement of Brunner's policies.

Litigation over election administration is sometimes necessary to prevent voters' rights from being violated. But litigation can also have a corrosive effect, exacerbating the public's distrust in the process' integrity. Perhaps down the road the time will come when the risk of litigation over Ohio's voting process is diminished. But that time does not appear to be now.

REFERENCES

1. Provisional voting data for 2004 and 2006 are available on the Ohio Secretary of State's website, at http://www.sos.state.oh.us/SOS/ElectionsVoter/results2006.aspx.

2. *See* Cuyahoga Election Review Panel, *Final Report*, July 20, 2006, at 5–6, 30-31.

3. *See* Joan Mazzolini, *Thousands Voted Illegally; Cuyahoga Failed to Ensure Signatures*, (CLEVELAND) PLAIN DEALER, Dec. 5, 2006, at A1.

4. *See* James F. McCarty, *Election Ex-Officials Get 18-Month Sentences; Convicted of Rigging '04 County Recount*, (CLEVELAND) PLAIN DEALER, March 14, 2007, at B1; James F. McCarty, *Judge Orders New Trial for Election Workers*, (CLEVELAND) PLAIN DEALER , Aug. 7, 2007, at B2.

5. *See Complaint, League of Women Voters v. Blackwell*, No. 3:05-CV-7309 (N.D. Ohio, filed July 28, 2005).

6. *See* Ohio, ENCYCLOPEDIA BRITANNICA, 2007, *available at* http://www.britannica.com/eb/article-218797.

7. *See* The National Archives and Records Administration, *U.S. Electoral College, available at* http://www.nara.gov (showing that Ohio had twenty-one presidential electors in 1832, twenty-three in 1844, and twenty-one again by 1864).

8. *See Ohio Presidents*, 9 OHIO HISTORY: THE SCHOLARLY JOURNAL OF THE OHIO HISTORICAL SOCIETY 531-32 (1901).

9. *See* Michael F. Curtin, THE OHIO POLITICS ALMANAC 19-22 (1996).

10. *See id.* at 7 ("From 1900 through 1992, the presidential candidate who carried Ohio has won the presidency twenty-two of twenty-four times."). Most recently, President Clinton carried Ohio in 1996 and President Bush carried Ohio in 2000 and 2004. Ohio Official Election Results, *available at* http://www.sos.state.oh.us/sos/ElectionsVoter/electionResults.aspx.

11. *See* Ohio Department of Development, Office of Strategic Research, *Per Capita Income, available at* http://www.odod.state.oh.us/Research/files/E200/e200000001.pdf (showing that in 1980 Ohio's per capita income was nearly 100% of the U.S. figure; from the early 1980s through 1999, Ohio hovered between 96% and 98% of the U.S. figure; and since 2000, Ohio has typically been 92% to 94% of the U.S. figure).

12. *See* U.S. Census Bureau, State and County Quick Facts: Ohio, *available at* http://quickfacts.census.gov/qfd/states/39000.html.

13. *See* U.S. Census Bureau 2005 population estimates *available at* http://www.census.gov/popest/counties/tables/CO-EST2005-01-39.xls.

14. *See* Alfred J. Wright, *Ohio Town Patterns*, 27 GEOGRAPHICAL REVIEW 615-24 (1937).

15. *See* Michael F. Curtin, *supra* note 9, at 3.

16. *See* Office of Strategic Research, *Ohio County Profile: Appalachia, available at* http://www.odod.state.oh.us/research/files/s0/appalachia.pdf.

17. The last Ohio county created was Noble County, established on April 1, 1851, several months before the Constitution of 1851 went into effect. *See* Ohio History Central Online Encyclopedia, *Ohio Constitution of 1851, available at* http://www.ohiohistorycentral.org/entry.php?rec=1457.

18. *See* Michael F. Curtin, *supra* note 9, at 66.

19. *See* Ohio Public Library Information Network, *Ohio Governors, available at* http://www.oplin.lib.oh.us/page.php?Id=63-24-97&msg=.

20. The rounded percentage of the popular vote for Reagan in Ohio in 1980 was 52%. *See* U.S. Presidential Election Maps: 1860-1996, University of Virginia, Geospatial and Statistical Data Center, http://fisher.lib.virginia.edu/collections/stats/elections/maps/. The U.S. percentage was 50.75% for Reagan. *See* David Leip's Atlas of U.S. Presidential Elections, *available at* http://www.uselectionatlas.org/RESULTS/.

21. *See* U.S. Census Bureau, Table 21, State Population – Rank, Percent Change, and Population Density, *available at* http://www.allcountries.org/uscensus/21_state_population_rank_percent_change_and.html.

22. *See Sandusky County Democratic Party v. Blackwell*, 339 F.Supp.2d 975 (N.D. Ohio), *aff'd in part and rev'd in part*, 387 F.3d 565 (6th Cir. 2004); Daniel P. Tokaji, *Early Returns on Election Reform: Discretion, Disenfranchisement, and the Help America Vote Act*, 73 GEO. WASH. L. REV. 1206, 1228-1230 (2005).

23. Robert F. Kennedy, Jr., *Was the 2004 Election Stolen?*, ROLLING STONE, June 1, 2006, *available at* http://www.rollingstone.com/news/story/10432334/was_the_2004_election_stolen.

24. *See Moss v. Bush*, 820 N.E.2d 934 (Ohio 2005); Mark Niquette, *High Court Grants Request to Dismiss Election Challenges*, COLUMBUS DISPATCH, Jan. 13, 2005, at 8C.

25. *See Northeast Ohio Coalition for the Homeless (NEOCH) v. Blackwell*, 467 F.3d 999 (6th Cir. 2006); Mark Rollenhagen, *Voter ID Rules Change a Third Time in Four Days*, (CLEVELAND) PLAIN DEALER, Oct. 30, 2006, at A1;

Mark Niquette, *Voter-ID Case Remains a Mess as Election Nears*, COLUMBUS DISPATCH, Nov. 1, 2006, at 1A.

26. OHIO REV. CODE § 3506.

27. House Bill 3 also revised several aspects of the state's initiative and referendum processes and changed a number of the state's campaign finance provisions, although these matters are beyond the scope of this report. *See Overview of Substitute House Bill 3 – Elections Reform*, NEOCH v. Blackwell, Document 35, filed 10/31/2006, *available at* http://moritzlaw.osu.edu/electionlaw/litigation/documents/hb3_000.pdf. *NEOCH v. Blackwell, id.*, which in part concerns the provisional voting requirements of HB 3, is only one of several court proceedings challenging specific provisions of HB 3.

28. OHIO REV. CODE § 3503.19 B(2)(c).

29. Kenneth Blackwell, Ohio Secretary of State, Advisory No. 2006-05, at 2 sec. I(A)(3).

30. *See Project Vote v. Blackwell*, 455 F.Supp.2d 694 (N.D. Ohio 2006).

31. *See id.*

32. The Complaint and other documents from this case may be found on the *Election Law @ Moritz* website, at http://moritzlaw.osu.edu/electionlaw/litigation/boustani.php. One of the co-authors of this report, Professor Tokaji, served as an attorney for the plaintiffs in this case.

33. *Boustani v. Blackwell*, 460 F. Supp. 2d 822, 825 (N.D. Ohio 2006) (concluding that Ohio Rev. Code § 3505.20(A)(2),(3) & (4) "discriminates against naturalized citizens with respect to the fundamental right to vote").

34. *See* National Association of Secretaries of State, *New Millennium State Practices Survey*, Aug. 2005, at 2, *available at* http://www.votetrustusa.org/pdfs/NASS/New%20Mill%20Survey%20Update.pdf.

35. *See Bill Seeks Ohio Election Reforms*, AKRON BEACON JOURNAL, Dec. 6, 2005, at B4.

36. *See* Steven F. Huefner, *Independent Election Administration*, *Election Law @ Moritz Weekly Comment*, Feb. 15, 2005, http://moritzlaw.osu.edu/electionlaw/comments/2005/ 050215.php.

37. *See id.*

38. *See* Daniel P. Tokaji, *supra* note 22, at 1234-38.

39. *See* Kenneth Blackwell, Ohio Secretary of State, Directive No. 2004-31, Sept. 7, 2004 ("The form prescribed by the Secretary of State must be printed on white, uncoated paper of not less than 80 lb. text weight. Any Ohio form not printed on this minimum paperweight is considered to be an application for a registration form.").

40. *See* Adam Liptak, *The 2004 Election: Balloting; Voting Problems in Ohio Set Off an Alarm*, N.Y. TIMES, Nov. 7, 2004, at sec. 1, p. 37.("'There is a feeling here that the long-line problem was a problem of disparity that fell along socioeconomic lines,' Professor Foley said. 'There were isolated instances of long lines here in the seven- to nine-hour range, and the common lines were two to three hours. When your line gets to two or three hours, it's system failure.'").

41. *See id.* ("Voting machines in Ohio failed to register votes for president in 92,000 cases over all this year, a number that includes failure to cast a vote, disallowed double votes and possible counting errors. An electronic voting machine added 3,893 votes to President Bush's tally in a suburban Columbus precinct that has only 800 voters.").

42. Mark Niquette, *Blackwell Delegates Jobs to Deputy: Top Aid Issues Rulings While Secretary of State Campaigns*, COLUMBUS DISPATCH, July 30, 2006, at 1A.

43. *See* M.R. Kropko, *Democrats: Blackwell Has Conflict of Interest*, CINCINNATI POST, May 9, 2006, at A2.

44. Directives for 2005, 2006, and 2007 can be found at http://www.sos.state.oh.us/sos/ElectionsVoter/OhioElections.aspx?Section=1234.

45. *See* Erin McPike, *Brunner Commits to Building Confidence in Buckeye State Elections*, OHPOLS.COM, July 31, 2007, http://www.campaignsandelections.com/oh/articles/?ID=443.

46. *See Election Day Conscripts?*, (CLEVELAND) PLAIN DEALER, Feb. 5, 2007, at B7.

47. *See* Jennifer Brunner, Ohio Secretary of State, *Press Release: Secretary Brunner Kicks Off Key Voting Advisory Group*, Mar. 13, 2007, *available at* http://www.ohvotes.org/wp~content/uploads/2007/03/VRI%20Press%20Release.doc.

48. *See* Bob Driehaus, *Ohio to Test Its 5 Voting Systems Before Primary in March*, N.Y. TIMES, Sept. 27, 2007, at A26; Ohio Secretary of State Jennifer Brunner, *Press Release: Brunner Seeks Proposals to Test Voting Systems*, June 18, 2007.

49. *See* Jo Ingles, *Low Turnouts with High Costs Have Secretary of State Considering Other Primary Options*, Statehouse News Bureau, May 11, 2007, http://www.statenews.org/story_page.cfm?ID=10169&year=2007&month=5.

50. *See* Mark Rollenhagen & Joan Mazzolini, *Can We Count on Our Votes? Official Worried About Machines*, (CLEVELAND) PLAIN DEALER, Mar. 13, 2007, at B1.

51. Jennifer Brunner, Ohio Secretary of State, *About the Ohio Secretary of State's Office: Jennifer Brunner*, Aug. 8, 2007.

52. OHIO REV. CODE § 3501.052.

53. OHIO REV. CODE §§ 3503.18, 3503.21(D).

54. *See* Mark Niquette, *New Statewide Voter Registration Database Implemented: Project Ordered by Congress Meets Deadline*, COLUMBUS DISPATCH, Dec. 12, 2005, at 11B.

55. Jennifer Brunner, Ohio Secretary of State, *Directive No. 2007-11: General Voters Records Maintenance Program*, July 23, 2007, *available at* http://www.sos.state.oh.us/sos/electionsvoter/directives/2007/Dir2007-11.pdf. For a full set of Brunner's directives, see http://www.sos.state.oh.us/sos/ ElectionsVoter/OhioElections.aspx?Section=2476.

56. *See* Jennifer Brunner, Ohio Secretary of State, *Provisional Ballots, Official Tabulation: November 2, 2004, available at* http://www.sos.state.oh.us/sos/ ElectionsVoter/results2004.aspx?Section=148.

57. *See* Jennifer Brunner, Ohio Secretary of State, *Absentee and Provisional Ballot Report, Official Results: November 7, 2006, available at* http://www.sos.state.oh.us/SOS/ElectionsVoter/results2006.aspx?Section=1840.

58. Percentage figures in this paragraph are derived from data in *Absentee and Provisional Ballot Report, Official Results: November 7, 2006, id.* For additional discussion of the impact of provisional voting, see Edward B. Foley, *Uncertain Insurance: The Ambiguities and Complexities of Provisional Ballots, in* 4 VOTING IN AMERICA: AMERICAN VOTING SYSTEMS IN FLUX: DEBACLES, DANGERS AND BRAVE NEW DESIGNS (Morgan E. Felchner ed., forthcoming 2008).

59. *See* Ohio State Plan Committee, *Changing the Election Landscape in the State of Ohio: A State Plan to Implement the Help America Vote Act of 2002 in Accordance with Public Law 107-252, §253(b),* at 10 (revised Jan. 12, 2005), *available at* http://www.sos.state.oh.us/sos/hava/ statePlan011205.pdf.

60. *See* John McCarthy, *Ohio Election Board Not Concerned, But Ready For Trouble*, USA TODAY, Jul. 9, 2004, *available at* http://www.usatoday.com/tech/news/techpolicy/ 2004-07-09-ohio-evote_x.htm.

61. Kenneth Blackwell, Ohio Secretary of State, *Directive No. 2005-01: Deployment of Voting Systems*, Jan. 12, 2005.

62. Kenneth Blackwell, Ohio Secretary of State, *Directive No. 2005-07: Selection of Voting Systems*, Apr. 14, 2005; *see* Mark Naymik, *Ohio Picks Computer Voting With Paper Trail: Diebold To Benefit From State Decision*, (CLEVELAND) PLAIN DEALER, Apr. 15, 2005, at A1.

63. *See* Robert Vitale & Mark Niquette, *Voters Face New Rules – and New Voting Machines*, THE COLUMBUS DISPATCH, Nov. 5, 2006, at 1D.

64. *See, e.g.,* Lisa A. Abraham, *Voting Machines Too Close To Call: As Decision Nears, Summit Elections Panel Laments Lack of Options*, AKRON BEACON JOURNAL, Aug. 14, 2005, at B1.

65. Jennifer Brunner, Ohio Secretary of State, *Directive No. 2007-01: Minimum Qualifications for Directors and Deputy Directors of Boards of Elections*, Feb. 20, 2007, *available at* http://www.sos.state.oh.us/sos/electionsvoter/directives/2007/Dir2007-01.pdf.

66. *See* Cuyahoga Election Review Panel, Final Report, July 20, 2006, at 5–6, 30-31.

67. *Id.*

68. *See* Joan Mazzolini, *Thousands Voted Illegally*, (CLEVELAND) PLAIN DEALER, Dec. 5, 2006, at A1.

69. *See* James F. McCarty, *Elections Ex-Officials Get 18-Month Sentences Convicted Of Rigging '04 County Recount*, (CLEVELAND) PLAIN DEALER, Mar. 14, 2007, at B1.

70. *See* James F. McCarty, *Judge Orders New Trial for Election Workers*, (CLEVELAND) PLAIN DEALER , Aug. 7, 2007, at B2.

71. *See Cuyahoga Board of Elections Gives Job to Interim Director, Jane Platten Accepts Appointment, Takes Over Often-Criticized Agency*, THE AKRON BEACON JOURNAL, June 12, 2007, at B5.

72. *See Ohio Dems Want to Settle Lawsuits*, THE CINCINNATI POST, Jan. 19, 2007, at A5.

73. *League of Women Voters v. Blackwell*, No. 3:05-CV-7309 (N.D. Ohio, filed July 28, 2005). Pleadings and other documents in this case, including the complaint, are available at http://moritzlaw.osu.edu/electionlaw/ litigation/lwv05.php.

74. *See League of Women Voters v. Blackwell*, No. 3:05-CV-7309 (N.D. Ohio, Dec. 2, 2005) (order denying motion to dismiss).

75. *Northeast Ohio Coalition for the Homeless v. Blackwell*, No. 2:06-cv-896 (S.D. Ohio, filed Oct. 24, 2006). Pleadings and other documents in this case are available at http://moritzlaw.osu.edu/electionlaw/litigation/NEOCHv.Blackwell.php.

76. *King Lincoln Bronzeville Neighborhood Association v. Blackwell*, No. 2:06-cv-745 (S.D. Ohio, filed Oct. 31, 2006). Pleadings and other documents in this case are available at http://moritzlaw.osu.edu/electionlaw/litigation/klbna.php.

77. *See* Mark Niquette, *Many Ballots from 2004 Presidential Election Missing, Brunner Says*, COLUMBUS DISPATCH, Aug. 1, 2007, at 6B.

78. *Project Vote v. Blackwell*, 455 F.Supp.2d 694 (N.D. Ohio 2006). Pleadings and other documents in this case are

available at http://moritzlaw.osu.edu/electionlaw/
litigation/projectvote.php.

79. *See Project Vote v. Blackwell*, No. 1:06-cv-1628, (N.D.
Ohio, Sept. 8, 2006) (memorandum and order granting
plaintiff's application for a preliminary injunction).

80. For the current status on this case, see Election Law @
Moritz – Litigation (Project *Vote v. Blackwell*),
 http://moritzlaw.osu.edu/electionlaw/litigation/
projectvote.php.

81. *Harkless v. Blackwell*, No. 1:06-cv-02284 (N.D. Ohio,
filed Sept. 21, 2006). Pleadings and other documents in this
case are available at
http://moritzlaw.osu.edu/electionlaw/litigation/HarklessvBlac
kwell.php.

82. *See American Broadcasting Companies, Inc. v. Blackwell*,
No. 1:04-cv-750 (W.D. Ohio, filed Nov. 1, 2004). Pleadings
and other documents in this case are available at
http://moritzlaw.osu.edu/electionlaw/litigation/ABCv.Blackwe
ll.php.

83. *See Kilroy v. Franklin County Bd. of Elections*, No. 06-cv-
15963 (Ohio Ct. Comm. Pleas, filed Dec. 5, 2006); Robert
Vitale, *Pryce's Lead Stays the Same in Recount; Kilroy's Camp
Sues Franklin County Board of Elections*, COLUMBUS
DISPATCH, Dec. 6, 2006, at 3B.

84. *See* Jo Ingles, *supra* note 47; Jennifer González, *Voting by
Mail for Special Elections? State Elections Chief Backs
Senator's Plan*, (CLEVELAND) PLAIN DEALER, Aug. 30,
2007, at A1.

85. *In re Election of Nov. 6, 1990 for Office of Att'y Gen. of
Ohio*, 569 N.E.2d 447, 457 (Ohio, 1991).

86. *Id. at 450.*

87. *Id.*

88. *See* OHIO REV. CODE § 3515.14; *Hitt v. Tressler*, 455
N.E.2d 667, 668 (Ohio, 1983).

89. *See* OHIO REV. CODE § 3515.08(A).

90. *See In re Protest of Election Returns and Absentee Ballots
in the Nov. 4, 1997 Election for Miami*, Fla., 707 So. 2d 1170,
1174 (Fla. Dist. Ct. App. 1998).

SUPPLEMENT ON PROVISIONAL VOTING:
WHY ARE PROVISIONAL BALLOTS REJECTED IN OHIO?

IN THE NOVEMBER 2006 general election, just over 23,000 provisional ballots (23,058, according to figures provided by the secretary of state) were rejected in Ohio, or almost 20% of all provisional ballots cast statewide in that election. The predominant reason for rejecting provisional ballots was that they were cast in the wrong precinct: 10,610 statewide, or 46%, were rejected for this reason. The second most common explanation for rejecting a provisional ballot was that the voter was not registered: 7,384, or 32% were rejected on this ground, although there is no available information concerning what steps were taken to determine that the voter – who, after all, as a prerequisite for casting the provisional ballot, signed a statement attesting to the belief that he or she was registered – was in fact not registered.

The third most prevalent reason for rejecting a provisional ballot was that the voter failed to show the required identification: 2,726 statewide, or 12%, were rejected on this basis. Together, these three reasons account for 90% of rejected provisional ballots statewide. No other specific explanation accounted for more than 2% of rejected provisional ballots statewide. Among the miscellaneous other reasons for rejecting a provisional ballot were: not eligible to vote (2%), no signature (1.25%), missing ballot (0.8%), or the person already voted (0.7%). Table 2 summarizes these data.

TABLE 2
OHIO REJECTED PROVISIONAL BALLOTS, NOVEMBER 2006
STATEWIDE FIGURES

Reason Ballot Rejected	Number of Ballots	Percent
Wrong precinct	10,610	46.0
Not registered	7,384	32.0
No ID	2,726	12.0
Not eligible	459	2.0
No signature	290	1.25
Missing ballot	181	0.8
Already voted	163	0.7
Other misc.	1,245	5.4
TOTAL	**23,058**	

[Percentages do not total 100% because of rounding]

Source: Ohio Secretary of State

Focusing on the six counties that contain Ohio's largest cities – Cuyahoga (Cleveland), Franklin (Columbus), Hamilton (Cincinnati), Lucas (Toledo), Montgomery (Dayton), and Summit (Akron) – reveals some interesting differences among them. These counties were the six largest in terms of the number of provisional ballots rejected, and collectively they accounted for 13,171, or 57%, of all rejected provisional ballots. Yet they differed in a number of respects, as Table 3 shows. First, they differed in the aggregate rate at which they rejected provisional ballots, from 13% to 33%. But the primary reason for rejecting provisional ballots – voting at the wrong precinct – does not appear to explain most of this variation. Rather, these six counties are fairly similar in the rates at which they rejected provisional ballots for this reason. Two counties (Hamilton and Montgomery) rejected 10% of their provisional ballots for being in the wrong precinct, and two others (Lucas and Summit) rejected 12% of their provisional ballots for the same reason. One county (Franklin) was a little bit lower in this respect, at 9%, whereas another (Cuyahoga) was somewhat higher, at 16%. (Cuyahoga's outlier status on this point, with more voters showing up at the wrong place to cast their ballots, may be a reflection of the distinctive and significant administrative problems this county had in the 2006 election.)

Instead, the six urban counties diverged somewhat more with respect to the second major reason for rejecting provisional ballots: that the voter was not registered. These six urban counties ranged from a high of 11% (Lucas) to a low of 3% (Franklin) in rejecting provisional ballots for this reason. In other words, over one-tenth of provisional ballots cast in Lucas County were rejected on the ground that the voter was not registered, even though the voter thought he or she was and was willing to sign a statement to that effect. By contrast, Franklin County's rate of rejecting provisional ballots for lack of registration was less than one-third as large as Lucas County's. What explains this difference? Is it that three times as many voters in Lucas County are mistaken in thinking they are registered than in Franklin County, or do the two counties use different procedures in endeavoring to resolve discrepancies about a voter's registration status? Does Franklin County, for example, conduct more rigorous investigative searches to track down missing registration forms, or perhaps resolve doubts more favorably to the voter? (In between Lucas and Franklin, two counties – Cuyahoga and Montgomery – rejected 8% of their provisional ballots for lack of registration, and two others – Hamilton and Summit – rejected 6% for this reason.)

The six urban counties varied even more sharply with respect to rejecting provisional ballots for lack of required identification. Two counties, Lucas and Summit, stand out for rejecting a relatively large number of provisional ballots for this reason, 7.8% and 7.1% respectively. In absolute numbers, Lucas threw out 330 votes for lack of identification, and Summit discarded 349. By contrast, Franklin County *did not reject a single provisional ballot for failure to provide identification as required by Ohio law*, even though Franklin County had far more provisional ballots cast than any other county in Ohio. Over 20,000 provisional ballots were cast in Franklin in 2006, whereas less than 5,000 were cast in both Lucas and Summit. Franklin's refusal to reject any provisional ballots for lack of identification, in contrast to the willingness in

Lucas and Summit counties to reject hundreds of them (amounting to almost one in every dozen of provisional ballots cast), can be attributed only to a difference in policy at the county level in interpreting and enforcing Ohio law.

This county-level variation in applying Ohio's new voter identification rules presumably makes the state vulnerable to an Equal Protection challenge based on *Bush v. Gore*. In 2006, Franklin County may have been more generous to voters failing to provide the identification required by Ohio law in part because of the threat of litigation over rejected provisional ballots that loomed in the context of the Pryce-Kilroy recount. But this kind of local generosity, when absent elsewhere in the state and when not specifically authorized by state law, may create an unjustified inequality in the counting of ballots cast by citizens in equivalent circumstances, in violation of the U.S. Constitution's protection of equal voting rights.

Franklin County's generosity in this regard, while absolute, was mirrored to a lesser extent by Montgomery County, which rejected only eight of its over 6,000 provisional ballots, or 0.12%, for lack of identification. The two remaining counties, Hamilton and Cuyahoga, rejected 0.4% and 1.2% of their provisional ballots for lack of identification. These rates, although somewhat higher than Franklin and Montgomery, were still much lower than Lucas and Summit. In absolute numbers, Hamilton discarded 54 votes for lack of identification, and Cuyahoga threw out 189. Again, differences in administrative practices seem the most likely explanation for these variations, although the topic deserves further study.

One additional anomaly deserves brief mention. Although three of the six urban counties (Hamilton, Lucas, and Montgomery) did not reject any provisional ballots on the ground that the person who cast the ballot was not "eligible" to vote, and Franklin County rejected only two provisional ballots for this reason, Summit County rejected a surprising 128 provisional ballots on this basis. This number amounted to 2.6% of all provisional ballots cast in Summit County. Cuyahoga County rejected 27 provisional ballots on the ground that the voters were ineligible, or 0.17% of provisional ballots cast in that county. While that number separates Cuyahoga from the other four urban counties, it does not come close to the rate at which Summit County rejected provisional ballots on the ground of voter ineligibility – as distinct from lack of registration. One wonders whether Summit County employed a different administrative understanding of the concept of voter eligibility than elsewhere in the state, or whether instead some election officials in Summit County simply confused the two different concepts of eligibility and registration, with some of them reporting a lack of registration as a lack of eligibility instead. If the latter explanation were indeed the case, it would be disappointing but not surprising. It would merely corroborate other evidence that local officials sometimes have difficulty understanding – and therefore enforcing correctly – each of the many requirements of the state's election law.

TABLE 3
OHIO REJECTED PROVISIONAL BALLOTS, NOVEMBER 2006: LARGE COUNTIES

	LUCAS (Toledo)	SUMMIT (Akron)
Total provisional ballots cast	**4,227**	**4,891**
Provisional ballots rejected	**1,379**	**1,525**
Total rejected as percentage of PB cast	**32.62%**	**31.18%**
Number of provisional ballots rejected - wrong precinct	**489**	**601**
Percentage of Total Rejected	35.46%	39.41%
Percentage of Total PB Cast	11.57%	12.29%
Number of provisional ballots rejected - not registered	**475**	**278**
Percentage of Total Rejected	34.45%	18.23%
Percentage of Total PB Cast	11.24%	5.68%
Number of provisional ballots rejected - no ID provided	**330**	**349**
Percentage of Total Rejected	23.93%	22.89%
Percentage of Total PB Cast	7.81%	7.14%
Number of provisional ballots rejected - ineligible to vote	**0**	**128**
Percentage of Total Rejected	0.00%	8.39%
Percentage of Total PB Cast	0.00%	2.62%
Number of provisional ballots rejected - other	**85**	**169**
Percentage of Total Rejected	6.16%	11.08%
Percentage of Total PB Cast	2.01%	3.46%

Source: Ohio Secretary of State

CUYAHOGA (Cleveland)	HAMILTON (Cincinnati)	MONTGOMERY (Dayton)	FRANKLIN (Columbus)
15,917	12,569	6,630	20,322
4,168	2,238	1,249	2,612
26.19%	17.81%	18.84%	12.85%
2,541	1,329	687	1,801
60.96%	59.38%	55.00%	68.95%
15.96%	10.57%	10.36%	8.86%
1,282	784	527	684
30.76%	35.03%	42.19%	26.19%
8.05%	6.24%	7.95%	3.37%
189	54	8	0
4.53%	2.41%	0.64%	0.00%
1.19%	0.43%	0.12%	0.00%
27	0	0	2
0.65%	0.00%	0.00%	0.08%
0.17%	0.00%	0.00%	0.01%
129	71	27	125
3.10%	3.17%	2.16%	4.79%
0.81%	0.56%	0.41%	0.62%

Ohio:
NINE AREAS

INSTITUTIONAL ARRANGEMENTS

Ohio's chief election officer is its secretary of state, responsible for administering state election law, canvassing votes for all elective state offices and issues, investigating election fraud and irregularities, and overseeing all eighty-eight county boards of elections. O.R.C. (Ohio Revised Code) §§ 3501.05, 3505.34. The secretary of state appoints the four members of each county board on an evenly bipartisan basis, and each board in turn hires a professional elections director and deputy director to run elections in that county. O.R.C. §§ 3501.06, 3501.09. The director must be of the opposite political party from both the deputy director and the chair of the county board of elections.

VOTER REGISTRATION/STATEWIDE DATABASE

Eligible voters must submit a registration application at least thirty days before the election, either by mail or in person at any public high school or public library, as well as at their county board of elections, county treasurer's office, offices of the state's bureau of motor vehicles, and other designated state offices. O.R.C. §§ 3503.01, 3503.10, 3503.11. Voters are notified by mail of their registration status, and also can check their status at their local board of elections or through the secretary of state's website. Many Ohio counties also maintain their own websites where voters can check.

Ohio's statewide database matches information on registered voters with information from Ohio driver's license applications. A registered voter can be removed from the registration list upon death, determination of incompetence, incarceration on felony charges, failure to vote over a four year period after being mailed a registration confirmation notice, or moving out of the county. O.R.C. § 3503.21 Local election officials update the database regularly, both by purging names of those no longer eligible to vote and by adding new registrants. The database is used primarily before and after the election, to prepare and update the poll books used on Election Day, rather than on Election Day.

CHALLENGES TO VOTER ELIGIBILITY

Private or citizen challenges of a voter's eligibility are no longer allowed at Ohio polls on Election Day (although special observers may still monitor the election). Instead, only poll workers are allowed to challenge a voter's eligibility at the polls. O.R.C. § 3505.20. However, until twenty days prior to an election, any Ohio voter can file a challenge to the eligibility of any other Ohio voter. If the county board of elections is able to adjudicate the challenge based solely on records it maintains, the board may do so without a hearing. Otherwise, the board must notify a challenged voter and conduct a hearing on the challenge before it can remove the voter from the registration list. When a hearing is required on a challenge filed less than thirty days before an election, a board of elections may postpone the hearing until after the election and permit the voter to cast a provisional ballot. O.R.C. § 3503.24.

PROVISIONAL VOTING

Under Ohio's complex set of provisions governing provisional balloting, voters who must cast a provisional rather than a regular ballot include individuals: (1) whose names are not in the poll books, or whose signatures do not match poll book signatures; (2) who cannot present proper ID; (3) who have requested an absentee ballot but appear at the polls to vote; (4) whose notice of registration was deemed "undeliverable"; (5) who are challenged by an election judge at the polls, or who are subject to a pending challenge by another voter; (6) who have changed their name or moved to a new precinct. To vote a provisional ballot, these individuals must complete a written affirmation that they are registered and eligible to vote, and provide as much identifying information as they can. O.R.C. § 3505.181. In the 2004 general election, 2.77% of those who turned out to vote in Ohio, or over 150,000 voters, cast a provisional ballot. In 2006, the percentage was over 3%. A fuller account of Ohio's provisional balloting is in the accompanying Ohio Supplement on Provisional Voting.

To count a provisional ballot, county officials must determine that the individual: (1) properly completed the provisional ballot affirmation; (2) was registered to vote; (3) was eligible to vote that election in that precinct; (4) provided proper identification to the board of elections within ten days after the election, if failure to provide such identification at the polls was the basis for voting a provisional ballot; and (5) overcame a challenge, if that was the basis for voting a provisional ballot. County boards of election must complete this process, including holding any necessary hearings, within ten days after the election. O.R.C. § 3505.181. Under the election code a board's decision whether to count a provisional ballot is final, although some such decisions still could end up in court in a close race.

EARLY AND ABSENTEE VOTING

Ohio has no "early voting" option as such, but any voter may cast an absentee ballot without cause as many as thirty-five days in advance of an election. Absentee ballots can be requested and voted either by mail or in person at county offices. O.R.C. § 3509.05 The state's first experience with no-excuse in-person absentee voting in 2006 was generally successful, and election officials expect greater numbers of Ohio voters to vote in this manner in 2008. Indeed, some local election officials deem it essential that more voters take advantage of this option in order to reduce the risk of Election Day voting problems associated with identification requirements, new voting equipment, and provisional balloting. Except in cases of Election Day emergencies, the deadline for requesting an absentee ballot is noon on the third day before an election. Ordinarily, the ballot must be received by the close of the polls on Election Day, although ballots cast overseas may be received up to ten days after the election. O.R.C. § 3509.05.

VOTING TECHNOLOGY

Each county board of elections selects the county's voting equipment from among a list of approved vendors and equipment established by the secretary of state. A state law enacted in 2004 requires that all voting systems generate a voter verifiable paper audit trail. O.R.C. § 3506.10. Counties are free to use a combination of equipment, as Cuyahoga County did by selecting optical scan ballots for absentee voters and DRE machines for in-person voting. As a matter of ballot design, since 1949 Ohio law has required rotation of candidate names, so that each candidate in a particular race has an equal advantage in the order in which the candidate's name appears on the ballot. O.R.C. § 3505.03.

POLLING PLACE OPERATIONS

The county board of elections is responsible for finding at least four poll workers, called election judges, for each precinct, no more than half of whom can belong to the same political party. O.R.C. § 3501.22. Poll workers must work the full day, from 6:00 a.m. until they have completed the post-election processes, for which they may receive up to $95. They also are expected to attend a county-administered, state-developed training program within sixty days prior to Election Day. Experienced poll workers must attend this training at least every three years, while the presiding election judge in each precinct must complete the training every other year. O.R.C. § 3501.27. Only official poll workers, voters in the act of voting or waiting to vote, and specially appointed observers are allowed in the polls during the election. O.R.C. § 3501.35. At least one voting machine in each polling location must accommodate visually impaired voters. O.R.C. § 3506.19. Voters are entitled to obtain assistance in physically signing their names and casting absentee ballots, if needed. Voters with disabilities also can request an absentee ballot if they do not feel comfortable voting at their polling place. O.R.C. § 3509.08.

BALLOT SECURITY

Ohio's procedures for handling both voting machines and the media on which the votes are recorded, whether optical scan ballots or DRE voting machine memory cards, have grown increasingly elaborate – from chain-of-custody rules, to requirements to seal voting machines and voting supply containers with tamper-proof seals, to provisions calling for certain steps to be performed only before specified observers. O.R.C. §§ 3501.26, 3505.27, 3505.31. While flawless adherence to them may be difficult, remedies for errors can be problematic.

As another form of ballot security, all Ohio voters must authenticate their eligibility to vote by showing identification at the polls. Ohio's list of acceptable identification is broader than that of some other states, and includes: current government photo identification, military identification, utility bill, government check, paycheck, or another government document. All acceptable forms of identification must have the voter's current address, with the exception of a state drivers' license, which is acceptable even if it shows an old address. Directive 2007-06. Voters who appear at the polls without presenting one of these forms of identification may cast a provisional ballot. O.R.C. § 3505.18.

POST-ELECTION PROCESSES

Although on occasion Ohio election officials still must conduct some true counting of ballots (as when Cuyahoga County officials had to manually count their absentee ballots in the 2006 primary), today ballot "counting" typically involves processing totals generated from electronic equipment. Preparing the results also involves reconciling any discrepancies between the ballot totals and the number of people who voted. Precinct judges must conduct these processes without leaving the polling place, before sealing their voting equipment and materials and transmitting them back to the county board of elections. The board of elections must maintain these records for at least sixty days, or twenty-two months in the case of records of a federal election. O.R.C. § 3505.31.

For a statewide office, Ohio law provides for an automatic recount if the margin of victory is less than 0.25% of the total vote. For other offices, a recount is automatic when the margin of victory is less than 0.5%. O.R.C. § 3515.11. Losing candidates also may apply for a recount within five days after the results are declared, provided they post a bond of $50 per precinct to cover administrative costs. O.R.C. § 3515.03. Recounts for presidential elections must be completed no later than the federal "safe harbor" date (six days before the date specified for presidential electors to meet and cast their votes). All other recounts must be certified by the 81st day after the election. For recounts of ballots cast on DRE machines, the voter verifiable paper audit trail is the official ballot of record. O.R.C. § 3506.18.

Losing candidates and their supporters can also seek to alter the outcome of an election by filing a contest petition challenging some aspect of the election. The contest petition must be filed within fifteen days of the certification of the election, and the hearing on the contest must occur between fifteen and thirty days after the contest commences. O.R.C. §§ 3515.09, 3515.10. The contestant in an election contest bears the burden of proving by "clear and convincing evidence" that one or more election irregularities occurred, and that the irregularity affected enough votes to change or make uncertain the results of the election. *In re Election of Nov. 6, 1990*, 569 N.E.2d 447, 450 (Ohio 1991). This is a high standard, as courts are reluctant to void or overturn an election.

OHIO

CHAPTER 4: ILLINOIS' ELECTION ECOSYSTEM
FROM ILLEGALITIES TO INCONSISTENCIES

WHEN IT ADOPTED its current state constitution in 1970, Illinois transferred responsibility over its elections from the secretary of state to a newly created state board of elections.[1] The secretary of state at the time, Paul Powell, was a colorful figure in state politics with a less than sterling reputation.[2] Illinois of course has a storied history of political corruption, which at least in previous eras has sometimes been accepted as a cost of doing business there.[3] But by taking election administration out of the hands of a powerful central figure, the revised constitution injected two new characteristics into the Illinois election system. First, in doing away with the secretary of state's role as Illinois' chief election officer, the constitution diffused the real power over elections through a patchwork system of county clerks and municipal elections boards, and left the new state board of elections comparatively weak. The result was a highly decentralized system. Second, the absence of a powerful central authority opened the door to inconsistent procedures across jurisdictions, a problem some Illinois election administrators complain about today.

Furthermore, in recent decades the absence of a strong state elections authority to pull local election officials together seems to have allowed a culture of suspicion and lack of cooperation to develop between many individual jurisdictions, encouraged by the state's history of election fraud and abuse. The presence in the state of both Chicago and Cook County – two huge, separate election jurisdictions that face a level of complexity in administering

elections unsurpassed elsewhere in the Midwest – compounds the difficulty of developing consistency in Illinois election administration.

Accordingly, this chapter discusses in turn the following features of Illinois' election ecosystem: (1) decentralized administration, (2) a legacy of fraud that, while diminishing, remains a concern and has helped foster distrust and lack of cooperation among election officials, (3) the presence of mammoth Cook County, as well as Chicago, (4) inconsistencies across jurisdictions, and (5) a substantial risk of litigation attacking these locally divergent practices, as well as other problems that may occur in the state's voting administration. Whether or not any deliberate disregard of established standards or other mismanagement is present in Illinois' current election ecosystem, what is clear is that Illinois needs to achieve greater uniformity in its election administration, built upon improved relationships among its various election administrators. The state's biggest challenge is to find a way to put the past aside and work together to create a consistent experience for every voter and a consistent treatment of every ballot. If Illinois is unable to foster this teamwork and consistency, the state is likely to experience one (or both) of two unfortunate consequences. First, election administrators could be impaired by the financial and management inefficiencies that come from lack of logical coordination. This in turn could lead to concrete problems at the polling places on Election Day. Second, inconsistent election procedures and an uneven quality of election administration across jurisdictions could trigger lawsuits alleging that voters' constitutional rights to Equal Protection have been violated.

DECENTRALIZED ADMINISTRATION

One of the most prominent features of Illinois' election ecosystem is its decentralized administration, coupled with the comparatively weak role played by state election officials. At the state level, the Illinois State Board of Elections ("SBE") is the body responsible for supervising elections.[4] The eight members of the state board are appointed by the governor,[5] subject to the advice and consent of the state Senate.[6] The board must consist of two members from Cook County who are of the governor's political party, two members from elsewhere who are of the governor's political party, and two members from each of these regions who are of the other leading political party.[7] The members serve staggered terms.[8] Five out of eight votes are needed in order for the board to take any action.[9] The board has staff in both Springfield and Chicago.

Nevertheless, the real power in Illinois' election system resides in local jurisdictions, many of which function almost independently of the state board of elections. This is not just because the state board has modest formal power, but also because it has relatively limited resources, as well as little credibility among local administrators of many of the larger jurisdictions. The board has the authority to supervise elections, but its executive director characterized this supervision as "indirect." Its principal power derives from its authority to certify (and decertify) election equipment. As a result, the board functions mainly as a clearinghouse of information for local election officials.

At the local level, Illinois election administration occurs in a few large jurisdictions and about one hundred smaller jurisdictions. In most parts of the state, the county is the primary unit of election administration, and in all counties except DuPage County an elected county clerk is in charge of elections.[10] However, Illinois' "City Election Law" also allows cities to choose to govern their own elections independently of their county.[11] Eight out of Illinois' 110 election jurisdictions, including Chicago, use this system.[12] Cities that have opted into this system govern elections through a three-member board of elections appointed by the county circuit court.[13] At least one representative of each of the two leading political parties must sit on this municipal board.[14] The circuit court may remove board members upon filing of a proper complaint, but the code does not specify what would be sufficient to justify such removal.[15] An appointed executive director oversees day-to-day operations.[16]

Large Jurisdictions. By far, Illinois' two most important election jurisdictions are Chicago and Cook County. Both jurisdictions serve about 1.4 million registered voters,[17] and together represent about thirty-seven percent of the state's registered voters.[18] Though Chicago is in Cook County, it operates elections independently from the county because it has opted to use the state's City Election Law. Chicago and Cook County are both heavily Democratic, and have worked successfully together in many instances, but they also disagree about matters both practical and philosophical, which sometimes has created tension. Their place in Illinois election administration is discussed in greater detail below.

Another important large jurisdiction is DuPage County, a wealthy predominantly Republican jurisdiction west of Chicago. DuPage County, like Chicago, has opted out of the county clerk-based system but, unlike Chicago, uses a county, rather than municipal, board of elections.[19] Historically, DuPage County wielded great influence in state election policy, but it lost much of that influence after Democrats came into power in the 2000 elections. Nevertheless, DuPage County remains a leader in election administration and is particularly strong in the area of election technology. For instance, its executive director explained that it uses a custom-built electronic flow-chart system to help election workers process incoming voters to determine if they are eligible to vote an ordinary ballot or must cast a provisional one. DuPage County also paid to develop a computer system that creates records (not recordings) of incoming election hotline phone calls on Election Day.[20] The system keeps track of who made the call, what election administration question was asked, who handled the call, what solution was provided, and other matters. The system allows administrators to analyze their operations after the election and identify areas for improvement. Most other jurisdictions simply cannot afford this level of technology.

Other large jurisdictions include Lake County, a wealthy suburban area of about 650,000 people just north of Cook County; Will County, with a population of about 500,000 just south of Cook County, and Kane County, just west of Cook County, with a population of about 400,000. The next largest election jurisdiction is McHenry County, northwest of Cook County, with a population of about 260,000. (Winnebago County, in the western part of the state, has about 280,000 residents, but this includes Rockford, which is its own separate election jurisdiction.)[21]

Smaller jurisdictions. While much of Illinois' population is concentrated in Chicago and its immediate suburbs, a significant number of people live in smaller jurisdictions in the more distant Chicago suburbs, as well as farther downstate. While any bright-line distinction between small and large jurisdictions is arbitrary, if we define a small jurisdiction as any county with fewer than 300,000 residents, then approximately 3.2 million registered voters, or forty-three percent, come from such jurisdictions.[22] These jurisdictions are important not only because collectively they represent a significant number of voters, but also because they face different obstacles than those faced by large urban and semi-urban jurisdictions like Chicago and Cook County.

One problem of smaller jurisdictions is a lack of quality control in leadership. As in Cook County, the chief election administrator in most small jurisdictions is an elected county clerk.[23] However, unlike in Cook County, where the clerk position offers comparatively great power and visibility, in smaller jurisdictions the position of county clerk may not attract the same number or caliber of candidates. County clerk candidates are not required to have any training in running elections, or even to be high school graduates. Accordingly, the level of professionalism and experience in election administration varies widely between county clerks. Newly elected clerks are especially unlikely to have any relevant elections experience and, unlike in Cook County, they do not have access to a vast professional elections staff that can get them up to speed. Some state elections officials, although expressing confidence in Illinois election administrators as a whole, are of the view that the lack of any formal check against maladministration at the county level is a notable flaw in the state's election system.

Another problem is a lack of legal sophistication in the smaller jurisdictions. Unlike Chicago and Cook County, most of the state's election jurisdictions do not have in-house legal advisors. Rather, state law designates the local state's attorneys as their legal advisors.[24] In most cases, this means someone with little or no training or experience with election law, and furthermore someone who may be more concerned (perhaps rightly) about bringing an important murder case to conclusion than rendering opinions about such matters as post-election chain-of-custody rules for provisional ballots. There is no guarantee that state's attorneys in different parts of the state will provide the same legal advice, thus opening the door to inconsistency in the administration of state election laws. Additionally, some Illinois election officials expressed the opinion that because state's attorneys are themselves elected officials, they have an interest in staying out of election matters so as not to disturb the system that has brought them and their political allies to office. Yet smaller jurisdictions simply have nowhere else to turn because the SBE does not offer legal advice, and indeed is admonished to avoid doing so by a state attorney general opinion issued in 1987.[25] Accordingly, one obvious reform would be to create a "legal office" within the Illinois State Board of Elections, and require local election administrators to go there, instead of to their local state's attorneys, for legal advice and representation in the conduct of elections.

The resources of these smaller jurisdictions are also limited in other ways. Unlike Chicago, Cook County, and other large jurisdictions, small jurisdictions do not have information technology departments versed in the intricacies of how to configure voting machines and manage the statewide voter registration database. In fact, until Illinois implemented the Help America Vote Act in a way that required the statewide voter registration database to be updated by local jurisdictions, some of these offices did not have even one computer for use in elections.[26]

Devoid of in-house technical savvy and lacking strong leadership from the SBE, these jurisdictions often fall into a condition known as "vendor dependency." When administrations do not have the sophisticated staff necessary to administer technical matters, they rely primarily on vendors to maintain and configure their voting machines. Administrators stuck in this position sometimes find that the vendors, having already sold their machines and service contracts, have little to gain by giving the local officials their utmost attention. Instead, the profit-maximizing strategy is to save costs by providing no more support than is necessary to avoid a lawsuit, leaving the administrators in the lurch. This is particularly a problem with direct recording electronic ("DRE") vendors because DRE machines must be configured and tested before each election to accommodate the numerous ballot styles across all precincts. This problem most affects smaller jurisdictions, whose contracts represent smaller dollar amounts and whose future business vendors decide they can therefore afford to lose.

All of this is not to say that smaller jurisdictions are unable to run procedurally satisfactory elections. In fact, despite their challenges, many smaller communities may have an easier time running elections than their larger counterparts, especially where their county clerk or elections director does possess election administration experience. Smaller communities are typically more tight-knit than larger communities, making it easier to recruit, train, and retain poll workers from year to year. They also tend to be more politically homogenous than larger jurisdictions, creating an environment of trust that frees administrators to implement policies, rather than expending resources in an effort to justify those policies to the media and various stakeholders. Concerns about voter impersonation and double voting are lessened in a small precinct where "everybody knows your name."

Weak State Board of Elections. Statutorily, the Illinois State Board of Elections has the power to disseminate information to and consult with election authorities, prescribe the use of standardized registration and ballot forms, certify voting equipment, require elections statistics from local authorities, make recommendations to the legislature, determine the validity and sufficiency of petitions to amend the state constitution, maintain a public library of elections information with precinct maps, and generally supervise elections.[27] Nevertheless, as a practical matter its power is somewhat limited. One limitation is that the evenly bipartisan eight-member board requires a majority vote of five members in order to act. Therefore, like the Federal Election Commission (which has a similar evenly bipartisan structure), the board is susceptible to partisan deadlock and thus unlikely to adopt any decisive policy that might provoke partisan disagreement. In addition, with the exception of

HAVA funds, it does not have control over the purse strings of local election administrators. It also does not have the ability, like some secretaries of state elsewhere, to remove local officials who do not perform satisfactorily. Without these powers, it is doubtful whether the SBE has the ability to compel the use of correct practices, short of going to court for a writ of mandamus. Moreover, it does not even have adequate resources to monitor the procedures used by local jurisdictions and to identify problems ahead of time. With respect to large jurisdictions, it appears unable to exercise even informal types of power, such as the power of persuasion.

Indeed, almost every large jurisdiction administrator with whom we spoke expressed doubt about whether the state board had either the necessary resources or expertise. Poll worker training affords a good example. Although the SBE currently offers its own free training for poll workers, most of the local administrators whom we interviewed choose not to take advantage of that training, but instead to conduct their own. Part of the reason they reject the free training is that the SBE does not have the detailed, working knowledge of local technology that each jurisdiction has developed from experience. The SBE also offers free training materials on some (but not all) Election Day procedures, but only two of the five jurisdictions whose administrators we interviewed (both from smaller jurisdictions) currently use those materials. One of these jurisdictions had previously used training materials provided by the jurisdiction's voting machine vendor, and only switched to SBE materials after state legal requirements concerning absentee voting made the vendor's manual obsolete.

Furthermore, partially because of past political disputes, the SBE has lost the respect and trust of many if not all of the powerful local administrators, and dialog between them today is in some cases limited. For instance, although the board's power increased slightly as a result of its control over HAVA funds, it subsequently lost a fight to control implementation of the state's voter registration database and, in the process, further alienated itself from the rest of the Illinois election administration community. Local administrators resisted the board's effort to oversee the database in part because they were concerned that if the state were given responsibility for the database, the project would be "dumbed down."

The weakness of the SBE is also suggested by the relative dearth of resources it commands when compared to jurisdictions such as Cook County and Chicago. Cook County has close to 120 employees working on elections and Chicago has about 180, while the SBE has about sixty-five. The budgets are also disproportionate: For the coming year, Chicago is proposing an annual elections budget of about $31 million and Cook County is seeking about $27 million,[28] while the SBE works on a statewide budget ranging from $8.5 to $10.5 million (not counting HAVA funds), depending on whether it is an off-year. Given these limitations, the SBE's former director said the entity is simply incapable of performing the kind of widespread compliance audits that would be necessary to verify that local jurisdictions are following procedures correctly. Part of this lack of resources comes from the fact that SBE staff has been reduced by about forty percent since its creation in the 1970s, while HAVA has only added to its responsibilities.

Moreover, although the state board of elections has the authority to promulgate regulations, as well as to issue other types of guidance for local election administrators, it currently does not have on the books a single administrative regulation concerning provisional voting, early voting, ballot security, recount procedures, or most areas of absentee voting and Election Day polling place procedures.[29] Nor does it have any plans to issue a uniform manual for local administrators. In the absence of any comprehensive written instructions from the board, local authorities have chosen to create their own manuals and procedures, either from whole cloth or using materials provided by voting machine vendors. The SBE does have the power to review these local manuals and require changes, but the SBE's current executive director could not think of a time that the SBE had ever done so. This opens the door to variation in procedures across jurisdictions.

One important power the SBE does have and makes use of is its ability to certify voting machines. Vendors must survive this testing in order to market their machines and services to local jurisdictions in the state.[30] Although the SBE takes pride in its testing, some local election administrators viewed the SBE's testing as neither as rigorous nor as meaningful as the SBE would like to think. Nevertheless, these administrators acknowledged that the SBE's certification power does give it leverage over some aspects of local election administration.

Despite the weakness of the Illinois State Board of Elections compared to the chief elections authorities in other states, the SBE nevertheless does play an essential role for many of Illinois' smaller jurisdictions. Our sense from a relatively small sample size of election administrators from smaller jurisdictions was that the majority of them probably could not function without the SBE's guidance. The executive director of the East St. Louis Board of Election Commissioners, for instance, could hardly have spoken more highly about the SBE or its director of elections information, whom we also found to be highly competent and committed to helping local administrators. Furthermore, some of the criticisms that the larger jurisdictions directed at the SBE may be partly a consequence of policy decisions supported by these same large jurisdictions to limit the funding, staff, and formal power of the SBE, and accordingly may also be a reflection that the larger jurisdictions do not want a stronger central authority.

Indeed, the key problem may be less that Illinois law creates a weak state board of elections than that the state's culture has shaped it to be toothless. While the law on the books also could be improved, it is primarily the culture that needs to change. It is fair to say that Illinois administrators are more independent and individualistic than administrators in a state like Minnesota, for instance, and their politics are more divisive. HAVA implementation only exacerbated those divisions. For instance, problems implementing a joint agreement to cooperate in choosing and administering HAVA voting machines have created significant tension between Chicago and Cook County. Many local administrators also have lingering resentments over the battle with the SBE to determine whether the statewide database would be operated on a top-down or bottom-up basis. The SBE itself undoubtedly could do more to bring people together and create consensus, especially given some administrators' perceptions that the SBE tends

to act unilaterally and without input. The governor and the state legislature also need to provide leadership to make the SBE a more effective institution.

A LEGACY OF SIGNIFICANT BUT DIMINISHING FRAUD

Illinois is a state with a dispiriting history of election fraud and public corruption.[31] Although a powerful statewide elections official may once have provided one set of opportunities for fraud, the lack of a strong central authority since 1970 has created another breeding ground for potentially corrupt elections. According to news reports, in the last twenty-five years some fifty separate election fraud prosecutions have occurred, many of them involving multiple offenders. Although most of these prosecutions occurred in areas in or around either Chicago or East St. Louis, they have affected the entire state.

For instance, after the 1982 gubernatorial elections, widespread allegations of fraud in Chicago led to almost sixty convictions and caused a civil grand jury to conclude that 100,000 illegal ballots had been cast (although one former state election administrator cautioned us that the 100,000 figure might have been overblown for political reasons).[32] When similar allegations surfaced after the 1987 Chicago primary, the then-chairman of the Chicago Board of Election Commissioners estimated that between 36,000 and 52,000 votes had been cast by unregistered voters.[33] In 2003, the Cook County Clerk quashed an apparent attempt to cast some 250 illegal votes in Cicero and Chicago Heights, south of Chicago.[34] In *Qualkinbush v. Skubisz*,[35] an appellate court all but accused a mayoral candidate in Calumet City, south of Chicago, of personally overseeing a program of improperly influencing absentee voters in the 2003 election. In East St. Louis, nine individuals, including some local political leaders, were convicted of vote-buying in the November 2004 general election.[36]

Nevertheless, many of today's Illinois election administrators believe that the state's election ecosystem is so different today than it was twenty-five years ago that it is highly unlikely that Illinois would suffer a repeat of the widespread voting fraud that happened in the 1982 governor's race. According to these administrators, a number of important reforms and changes in voting technology have made election fraud more difficult to accomplish, especially on a massive scale. And the recent prosecutions described above may themselves reflect that the ecosystem has now developed better means of catching the perpetrators.

Illinois election administrators are correct to note that it is much more difficult to accomplish in-person voting fraud today, especially if polling places meet the legal requirement that poll workers from both political parties be present at all times. But we nevertheless are not fully sanguine about the risk of insider fraud committed by an election official determined to steal an election. Meanwhile, absentee fraud is a different issue entirely, as Illinois administrators also acknowledge. It is not a matter of whether such fraud occurs, but how often and in what magnitude. Still, Illinois elections are more secure today than in the past. What follows is a short discussion of developments since 1982 that have helped reduce fraud, and the vulnerabilities that continue to exist.

Improvements in voter registration. Part of the problem in the 1982 gubernatorial race was the Illinois registration system, which left the door wide open for fraud. No identification was required to register to vote,[37] and canvassing for outdated or otherwise invalid registrations was done using a cumbersome door-to-door process that effectively ensured that many such registrations would remain on the rolls.[38] The canvassing had to occur on an unrealistically short timeline, and in many cases required canvassers to get past security into apartment buildings, which they often could not do.[39] Frustrated canvass workers often failed to perform a thorough canvass.[40] Nonperformance was particularly high in areas perceived to be dangerous.[41] Lingering numbers of bad registrations became a vehicle for corrupt election judges and others to cast fraudulent ballots in the polling place at the end of Election Day.

Today, voter registration reforms have reduced the risk of fraud, both by reducing the chance that invalid registrations will make it onto the rolls, and by making the canvassing process more efficient at removing such registrations from active lists. The law now requires two pieces of identification for in-person registration,[42] and HAVA identification for mail-in registration.[43] By late 2007, Illinois anticipates that it will have a fully functioning system for verifying incoming applications against records from the Social Security Administration. It also hopes that its system for verifying registration applications against state motor vehicle databases will be fully implemented in the near future. These systems should further lessen the likelihood of improper registrations reaching the official rosters.

Once the registrations are in the database, officials will continue to remove invalid registrations with the help of improved canvassing procedures. Since 1982, officials have been sending out postcards to all voters automatically once every two years,[44] and to registrants who have not voted for four years.[45] Pursuant to the National Voter Registration Act, when the postcards are returned as undeliverable, the state can begin a process that may lead to these registrations being removed once an additional four-year cycle elapses without any contact or activity by the voter.

Nevertheless, by some estimates Illinois has almost one million "inactive" names on its statewide database, some sizable portion of which certainly reflect voters who have moved or died (a figure comparable to Ohio's number of "inactive" voters).[46] Because the public has a right to see the names of those voters who have not responded to a confirmation notice, potential wrongdoers still have some ability to determine names that could be used to perpetrate fraud.[47] Election judges in each polling place also have the ability to identify inactive voters,[48] and could theoretically use this information to forge ballot applications and cast fraudulent ballots, as in 1982. Although this type of fraud also could be accomplished with active registrations, the inactive registrations could facilitate misconduct both by eliminating the need to wait until the end of the day and by providing more names under which fraudulent votes could be cast, provided election judges have an opportunity to do so (for instance, if real bipartisanship is lacking among the judges at a particular polling place).

Increased prosecutions of vote fraud. Officials also cite heightened law enforcement efforts as a factor reducing the risk of fraud. Election administrators describe both an increased presence of plain-clothed police officers at many polling places, and significant law enforcement support from the state attorney general and local U.S. Attorneys, who since 1982 have been more aggressive in investigating and prosecuting election crimes. In March 2002, for instance, Chicago and Cook County each stationed about 300 investigators in polling places and received support from the local U.S. Attorney, FBI, and U.S. Marshals Service.[49] Officials dispatched over 200 prosecutors and investigators to polling places in the February 2007 election.[50] In 2000, the U.S. Justice Department obtained permission to monitor Cicero, a west Chicago suburb with a reputation for fraud, for a five-year period.[51] DOJ also has made a point over time to target other areas known for fraud.[52] In addition, the state attorney general has sent investigators out into the field to detect election fraud.[53]

Of course, these efforts themselves are some evidence of the continuing need for vigilance in controlling election fraud. Meanwhile, it is not clear how completely potential improprieties observed during an election are pursued by prosecutors and other officials after an election is over. For instance, on at least one reported occasion, the SBE has indicated that it will not investigate suspicious activity unless someone files a formal complaint.[54] Other improprieties presumably go undetected altogether.

Institutional weaknesses as a remaining source of vulnerability to fraud. As discussed above, Illinois' highly decentralized election system heavily depends on the work of more than one hundred county clerks, all of whom are elected, as well as a handful of city officials and appointed local elections directors. Having an elected county clerk run elections presents an obvious potential conflict of interest if that clerk or the clerk's political allies are in a close election. While that risk is present in many states, it is a bigger risk in states with a demonstrated history of fraud. In one recent instance, a county clerk was "opening absentee ballots and replacing ballots in favor of [one candidate] with ballots naming her opponent."[55] The institutional arrangements of the Illinois election system leave it more vulnerable to fraud than it should be.

One current weakness in Illinois's election law is the authority, in most jurisdictions, of a single elected county clerk to compile vote totals received from the various precincts, for the purpose of reporting those totals to the state elections board.[56] This is the result of a recent amendment to the state election code that abolished local canvassing boards because some of the party representatives on these boards often would fail to appear for the canvass. Where the statute used to specify that county clerks should conduct the canvass "with the assistance of the chairmen of the county central committee of the Republican and Democratic parties of the county,"[57] it now provides simply that the "election authorities of the respective counties" are to conduct the canvass.[58]

Despite the administrative convenience of letting the canvass proceed with only the local "election authority," reposing this responsibility in a single partisan official obviously increases the risk that these elected clerks may be tempted to misreport the returns to the state board in order to change the result of an elec-

tion. Party leaders are still entitled to receive copies of the abstracts of votes immediately after the clerk completes them,[59] but to the extent that party leaders were failing to attend the canvass even when they were part of the canvassing board, it would seem that they would be even less likely to be present now. Some argue that the canvass is increasingly ministerial, given that in a recount, an aggrieved candidate could go back and look at the original "tapes" or vote totals from each voting machine to check the validity of the canvass, making any fraud in the canvass obvious. But it is not unrealistic to imagine some daring clerk taking the risk, and seeking to defend the error as a mistake if it is subsequently discovered. In any event, when the canvassing process does not structurally ensure bipartisanship, candidates and the public will understandably have less confidence that the job has been done correctly. In contrast, Michigan,[60] Wisconsin,[61] and Ohio[62] use bipartisan boards to canvass precinct returns.

This particular structural problem does not apply to Chicago, East St. Louis, or the other cities whose "election authority" under state law is a separate multi-member election board, rather than a clerk (although some members of these boards also could choose not to participate in their duties to assist with the canvass). Yet even the few local jurisdictions with bipartisan representation on local election boards may be susceptible to the risk of partisan domination. In East St. Louis, the one Republican board member, who was required by law to vote Republican, nevertheless voted Democratic in a primary, suggesting that the local election board was in fact composed of three Democrats, with no Republican representation.[63] The likelihood that this one board member was truly a Democrat, masquerading as a Republican simply to satisfy the legal requirement that there be Republican representation on the three-member board, is increased by the circumstantial evidence that her husband is a prominent local Democratic leader. Despite the fact that she was eventually removed from the board, this may have been an example of a legal safeguard that arguably is neither sufficiently robust, nor meaningfully enforced even to its limited extent. Illinois needs to consider election law reforms that would do more to assure that the canvassing of vote totals is conducted in a transparently bipartisan or nonpartisan manner.

The system does have some safeguards built into it to decrease the likelihood of fraudulent conduct. In particular, in the wake of the 1982 gubernatorial election Illinois established a mandatory five percent post-election audit of voting machine accuracy, hoping to deter fraud by ensuring that precinct returns reflected the counts recorded on the voting machines themselves.[64] This requirement obligates the SBE to randomly select five percent of precincts for auditing, and local officials then are expected to verify that the precinct vote totals are accurate, either by comparing them against the DRE paper audit trail,[65] or by rerunning optical scan ballots through the machine.[66] Unfortunately, this requirement may not be uniformly followed or enforced, as the SBE could not confirm for us that all jurisdictions are consistently conducting or reporting the results of their audits. A good audit procedure, coupled with bipartisan control and enforcement, can substantially help reduce the risk of fraud.

Another institutional problem is that the ap-

propriate party balance is not present in all polling places, despite improvements in the law governing this issue. In 1982, the law required that election judges from both of the leading political parties be assigned to each polling place,[67] but at that time the judges were required to reside in the precinct in which they served.[68] Because some wards are dominated almost entirely by one political party, this requirement ensured in practice that some polling places could not achieve the appropriate party balance.[69] The law has since been changed to allow importation of poll workers from anywhere in the subject county, and administrators do their best to use this provision to stock polling places with members of both parties.[70] Nevertheless, election officials do not deny that they continue to experience some difficulties in achieving the appropriate party balance. In our opinion, the state needs to do more to ensure that local authorities have the resources to bring polling place operations into compliance with this important legal requirement. The state also needs to do more to ensure that the requirement is monitored and enforced. Noncompliance with this requirement is of particular concern in areas where the election administrator is of the same party as the judges in the imbalanced precincts, and therefore in a position to overlook suspicious activity.

Increased concern about absentee ballot fraud. Given the improvements in election integrity since 1982, absentee ballot fraud is a much more promising way to steal elections today than traditional polling place fraud. Our informal review of the most recent cases of alleged election fraud in Illinois showed that eleven out of fifteen instances since 1990 involved the absentee voting system, while only one clearly involved in-precinct ballot-box stuffing.[71] This is a marked change from the problems in 1982, which mostly consisted of precinct captains, party workers, and election judges looking in the poll book at the end of Election Day for the names of those who had not voted, and then forging ballot applications and casting ballots in the names of those voters.[72]

A number of policies and procedures are designed to discourage absentee ballot fraud. As a primary tool, Illinois continues to limit the grounds for voting by absentee ballot,[73] rather than allowing any voter to vote absentee, as other states have done. With limited exceptions, Illinois then requires that absentee ballots be returned personally by the voter or an immediate family member.[74] In addition, under Illinois law it is a felony to solicit individuals to vote absentee, subject absentee voters to undue influence, tamper with absentee ballots, or return another's absentee ballot without authorization.[75]

To the extent that these legal provisions do not prevent absentee ballot fraud, at least some administrators make an effort to detect the presence of absentee fraud by looking for "spikes" in the number of absentee ballot applications coming from certain precincts or addresses. Cook County targets such spikes and places phone calls to every voter who requests an absentee ballot in the target precinct or address to ensure that the voter is not being manipulated into participating in an absentee balloting scheme. As Illinois' newly created (since March 2006) early voting program picks up steam, it will reduce the number of legal absentee ballots cast and could cause such spikes to stand out in even starker relief. Chicago

makes similar phone calls to some portion of voters who have requested absentee ballots. In addition, state law requires administrators to verify absentee voters' signatures both at the ballot request stage and upon ballot return,[76] and if rigorously enforced these requirements may help to identify some forms of absentee voting fraud.[77] Despite these safeguards, however, the potential for absentee ballot fraud remains more than just theoretical.

CHICAGO AND COOK COUNTY

As suggested above, Chicago and Cook County dominate the world of Illinois election administration. Not only do they represent roughly thirty-seven percent of registered voters, but they also carry the greatest weight with the legislature and have substantial influence over what state election laws are adopted. In addition, Illinois has a history of treating Chicago and its suburbs as separate from the rest of the state in most matters, and that treatment also applies to election administration. Indeed, the law itself exempts the giant Chicago suburbs from the ordinary voter registration laws,[78] and Chicago has opted out of the general election laws by adopting the City Election Law.

Cook County, like most Illinois jurisdictions, runs elections through an elected county clerk, presently David Orr. Orr is a popular, progressive Democrat who started his political career as a Chicago alderman and has been the Cook County Clerk since 1990.[79] His office consists of approximately 120 employees in its elections division. Currently, Orr's division of elections operates on an annual budget of about $21 million and is seeking about $27 million for the coming fiscal year.[80] Among other policies, Orr supports expanded access to voting and aggressive reporting of potential voting fraud.

By comparison, the Chicago Board of Elections has about 180 employees (including some forty who are seasonal) and expects to have a budget of $31 million for the upcoming fiscal year.[81] Chicago's current elections director is Lance Gough, an expert in voting technology who has been with the board since 1988.[82] Like David Orr's office, the Chicago board is Democratic,[83] but with a more conservative orientation focused less on expanding voter participation than on running smooth elections. According to Gough, the history of fraud in Chicago pushes the board to work hard to maintain a clean, professional image, and the board will go to great lengths to avoid embarrassment. Indeed, as another board official related to us, the board once persuaded the local fire department to use a fire engine to rip the doors off of a polling place when its owner failed to show up on time to unlock them.

By themselves, both Chicago and Cook County are more populous than many states,[84] and the scale of their elections operations is commensurate. The difference in these jurisdictions' operations and those of smaller jurisdictions therefore is not merely one of degree, but becomes a difference in kind. For instance, Chicago has 2,600 precincts and 3,000 DRE voting machines, which can take up to four hours each to calibrate and test. The logistics of such an undertaking are immense, as are the logistics of storing and delivering this equipment to thousands of precincts, all in a secure process that protects against tampering. Cook County's operations are similarly complex. Other election administrators reflecting on these types of complexity praise Orr and

Gough for tackling an "impossible" job. In the face of these types of challenges, Chicago and Cook County understandably desire a free hand to administer elections in the way they think is best and are skeptical of proposals that favor centralization and bureaucracy.

Although they remain separate entities, Chicago and Cook County frequently must work together to run elections. For instance, because Chicago voters are eligible to vote for Cook County offices, vote totals for both jurisdictions must be combined before determining winners in those races. Furthermore, the two jurisdictions have gone beyond the degree of cooperation that is strictly necessary by entering into joint agreements with equipment vendors to supply uniform technology through all areas of Cook County. But some of the natural tension between the two offices was exacerbated by the implementation of this technology, which was initially flawed and caused delays in precinct reporting in the 2006 primary and general elections.[85] By some accounts, the relationship between the two jurisdictions has soured after these difficulties.

INCONSISTENT APPLICATION OF LAWS AND STANDARDS

Given the lack of central direction over Illinois election administration, some (but not all) Illinois election officials to whom we spoke thought that the state faced a problem of inconsistent procedures in different jurisdictions. Unfortunately, only anecdotal evidence exists upon which to base such conclusions, as the state has no systematic auditing program for evaluating the performance of election personnel.[86] The variance in opinions on this issue may say more about political attitudes than about actual reality, making things even less clear. Nonetheless, we are inclined to credit those who express concern about the existence of significant local variation in election administration practices, as they speak with a vividness and specificity that suggests a basis in fact, and the inherently decentralized structure of voting administration in the state of course invites just such local disparities.

Illinois's two largest elections offices, in Cook County and Chicago, were the least concerned about inconsistency across jurisdictions. Cook County officials admitted that some degree of inconsistency existed, but thought that it was not so severe as to justify large-scale reform, and tended to involve relatively minor matters. One official proposed that it would be enough for the SBE to start offering formal training for local election administrators themselves, as opposed to only offering training for poll workers.[87] A representative of the Chicago Board of Elections thought that inconsistency was even less of an issue and did not seem to think that Illinois' decentralized system raised any concerns about different jurisdictions taking different approaches.

Elsewhere, election administrators to whom we spoke did think that inconsistency was a real concern, albeit one that was not yet quantifiable. An elections official in DuPage County thought that important ambiguities and inconsistencies existed in a number of legal requirements and practices, including: (1) whether jurisdictions would accept a partially flawed voter registration application, (2) whether to count absentee ballots lacking postmarks,[88] (3) whether jurisdictions were performing the mandatory five-percent post-election audit of voting system accuracy (described above) (4) whether poll workers were requiring HAVA-mandated identification from first-time mail-in registrants voting at the polls, (5) procedures used to perform "logic and accuracy" tests on DRE voting machines before and after elections and recounts, (6) whether suspicious circumstances are reported to authorities for investigation and prosecution, (7) whether paper notice of cancellation is sent to a voter when a voter's registration is removed from the statewide database, and (8) the circumstances in which voter registrations are removed from the database. Because of ambiguity in the law governing recount proceedings, at least one local official thought that a statewide recount of ballots would likely devolve into a Florida-like debacle. One official at the state board of elections, whose job it is to field procedural questions from local administrators, said that he knew from firsthand experience that some jurisdictions were following inconsistent procedures in the areas of concern identified by DuPage County. The past director of the SBE agreed that the inconsistency concern is real.

Some of these officials felt that Illinois election administrators have pressured the legislature to make laws deliberately ambiguous. Illinois election jurisdictions are not integrated or accountable to a powerful central authority, they argued, but are accustomed to doing things their own way. They do not want strong, precise laws that force them to use the same practices as the neighboring jurisdiction. Therefore, when new legislation is being drafted, local election officials sometimes put pressure on legislators to leave enough "wiggle room" in the statute to allow them to do as they see fit. These officials also felt that inequality of resources and legal and technical expertise between jurisdictions and lack of meaningful monitoring and enforcement from the SBE contributed to the problem of inconsistency.

A good example of the "wiggle room" phenomenon is the Illinois provisional ballot statute, which provides that provisional ballots should be counted when it is at least equally likely as not that, based on information available to the administrator, the provisional ballot was cast by a voter properly registered in the precinct.[89] The decision is to be made based on the "totality of the circumstances."[90] As one administrator observed, this law leaves the administrator to make too many assumptions. However, another administrator felt that, in practice, the evidence will usually point obviously one way or the other, and that there would be few gray areas that would leave an administrator in doubt.

But even where wiggle room does not exist, some administrators felt that certain procedures would not be followed or taken seriously. One example is the mandatory five-percent audit of voting machine accuracy described above, which is required to occur after each election, before the results are announced. This procedure was initially adopted after the infamous 1982 election, and officials hoped that it would help deter fraud. It could also be used to catch malfunctioning voting machines that fail to record votes correctly. However, in practice, it appears that some election officials may not be completing the audit. The SBE, to which local officials are supposed to report the results of their audits, informed us that some jurisdictions have not reported all of their results all of the time. These omissions could be merely failures to report (the generous interpretation given by the SBE official to whom we spoke), but they could also represent failures to complete the audits themselves. But even a failure to report the results is a cause for concern, especially if the information in those results would have revealed or suggested irregularities.

Major inequalities in funding also exist across the state. These are not merely financial concerns, but have a real impact on voters' experiences. Today, the biggest financial problem appears to be the costs associated with maintaining new HAVA-compliant voting machines.[91] In East St. Louis, the city's election director worries that there will be no funding for performing required voting machine maintenance in his jurisdiction before the 2008 presidential primary and general elections – a concern echoed elsewhere in the state. This is a serious problem looming on the horizon. Our nation has previously seen proof of what should be obvious anyway, namely, that poorly maintained technology can lead to lost votes.[92] In contrast, the relatively wealthy DuPage County can often forgo expensive repairs because the county has a stock of extra voting machines on hand that can be swapped out for a malfunctioning machine when necessary.

RISK OF LITIGATION

The variations in local practices described above could serve as the basis for potentially contentious and costly litigation, thereby further eroding public trust in the state's voting system. A lawsuit with this premise might appear in the form of an election contest between candidates as in the *Bush v. Gore* litigation, but it might also appear as a general civil rights lawsuit alleging violation of voters' Equal Protection or other constitutional rights.[93] For the time being, Illinois may be insulated from such litigation because it is not perceived by most analysts to be a battleground state. However, insofar as Illinois becomes more prominent on the national scene – something it has attempted to do by moving up the date of its primary from mid-March to early February[94] – it risks having its election system critically scrutinized, and perhaps upended, in litigation. Similarly, if Illinois has a close statewide election for governor, as it did in 1982, or another important elected state office, litigation would be likely, and election attorneys could find an ample number of issues to raise. Such an election contest would almost certainly include claims that provisional ballots were not counted properly, and would also probably include a host of other claims related to chain of custody procedures, voting machine configuration, spoiled ballots and ballots with distinguishing marks, and other irregularities.

Precedent already exists for litigation attacking such inconsistencies: In 2002, a federal district court held that voter allegations that the voting machines in some Illinois jurisdictions generated more residual votes (ballots cast but not counted, either because no candidate is selected, or because ballot markings appear to select two candidates for a given office, resulting in no vote being counted) were sufficient to state a claim for violation of the U.S. Constitution's Equal Protection Clause and other rights.[95] It is not hard to analogize the problem of the disparate impact of different voting technologies to many of the other types of inequalities and inconsistencies in election administration discussed earlier, creating fertile ground for litigation. For example, if (as has been alleged by several election officials in the state) some jurisdictions adopt more lenient standards for the verification of provisional ballots than other jurisdictions, that inequality in vote-counting procedures would serve as an obvious basis for an Equal Protection challenge, whether filed in federal court or as part of a state-court election contest proceeding.[96]

If these issues do emerge in state-court litigation, it is not clear that Illinois courts will be able to put them to rest in a way that prevents the reputation of the state's entire election system from suffering. Illinois judges are elected, and in recent years special interest groups supporting and opposing tort reform have poured unprecedented amounts of money into judicial campaigns, especially in the southern part of the state,[97] as well as on the state's supreme court. One poll found that eighty-five percent of Illinois voters believe that judges are influenced by campaign contributions,[98] and the reputation of the judiciary suffered further erosion as a result of Operation Greylord, a 1984 investigation of corruption in the Cook County judicial system that resulted in the conviction of thirteen judges and fifty-one attorneys.[99] In this politicized environment, voters are likely to see the judicial resolution of any such litigation as political and therefore illegitimate, even if judges do their best to remain impartial.

The contest over the 1982 gubernatorial election[100] does not give one much reason for optimism in this regard. There, the Illinois Supreme Court split 4-3, largely on partisan lines (one Democrat joined three Republicans in dismissing the contest filed by the Democratic candidate). The reasoning of the majority opinion is legally dubious, striking down the state's contest law as unconstitutional because the special court assigned to hear the contest was not a conventional "court" within the meaning of the state constitution. A second and alternative ground offered by the majority opinion seems no more defensible, as contrary to precedent, it refused to let a claim go forward because there were insufficient allegations to cast doubt on the result of the election. Yet the complaint alleged facts that, if true, did just that. The dissenting opinion was livid in response. Right or wrong, the supreme court's resolution of that contest does not inspire confidence that, were another major statewide election contest to reach the supreme court again, the court would be able to render a decision that would be viewed as resting on law rather than politics.

Furthermore, if litigants begin bringing several of these types of Equal Protection claims, lower state courts could easily take differing approaches to the legal issues, creating a fractured jurisprudence that makes election administration even less uniform. This has been the trend in other areas of Illinois election litigation, where courts have not been content to follow precedent but have continually modified it and sometimes defied it. For instance, Illinois law includes twenty-two cases dealing with how to treat ballots that are ineligible to be counted when those ballots have become intermingled with eligible ballots and cannot be separated. Despite the high number of published opinions, no clear rule has emerged. Even the Illinois Fifth District Court of Appeals itself has issued a number of potentially conflicting rules: It once deducted a known number of ineligible ballots from a candidate's vote total after election judges testified that the absentee ballots at issue had been cast for that candidate;[101] in another case it reduced both candidates' vote totals in proportion to the per-

centage vote each candidate obtained in the precinct;[102] and in a third instance it used information about party affiliation contained in primary records to determine percentages to be used in reduction.[103]

Likewise, the state supreme court's legally dubious decision resolving the 1982 gubernatorial election has spawned considerable confusion concerning what is necessary for an election contest petition to survive a motion to dismiss for failure to state a claim.[104] This type of confusion may be exacerbated when political affiliations of courts change over time, creating an incentive for them to find reasons to deviate from precedent in order to achieve a desired political result. As any litigator will acknowledge, confusion in case law is an invitation for further litigation. Thus, the legal landscape in Illinois, combined with variations in local practices concerning vote-counting procedures, provides fertile ground for election litigation, if an election is considered sufficiently important and sufficiently close to be worth contesting. The prospect of major election litigation in Illinois, before a judiciary lacking in sufficient neutrality to appear "above the fray," is highly unsettling yet regrettably realistic.

Administrators, for their part, voiced a greater fear of litigation over voting technology than over inconsistencies in the voting process, although some of their own comments seem internally inconsistent. Some shared with us the view that the most likely basis for litigation in the 2008 presidential election would be technology failure, specifically attacks on the fundamental accuracy of voting machines. Most administrators, however, seem to think that in the event of a recount the technology would ultimately be vindicated.

They are less confident that the actions of those using technology would be similarly vindicated. Administrators we spoke to identified poor planning and poor training of poll workers and staff as key threats to well-run elections. These root causes can lead to almost any kind of problem, and particularly problems that administrators identified as likely: failure to follow Illinois' complex chain of custody rules for elections materials; failure to follow the rules governing whether to issue an ordinary or provisional ballot; errors in the counting of provisional votes; going too far to "help" voters cast their ballots; failure to properly configure DRE machines; failure to set aside defective ballots or ballots with identifying marks; failure to include grace period, absentee, or early voting returns in final results; failure to reset voting machines before the election; and allowing individuals to vote without first signing the poll book. Most of the items on this list are those that we, as election law scholars, would identify as exposing the state to risks of significant litigation in any important close election (and most items on this list do not concern technology at all).

Furthermore, the failure of local officials to follow rules in any of these respects could easily be converted into a plausible Equal Protection claim, simply by observing that local officials elsewhere did follow the rules.[105] Consequently, our conversations with some election officials in the state lead us to believe that they are insufficiently prepared for the threat – and consequences – of major election litigation in Illinois, in a way analogous to Florida's failure to prepare for the problems in its 2000 election.

REFERENCES

1. *See* ILL. CONST. art. III, § 5; Samuel K. Gove & James Nowlan, ILLINOIS POLITICS & GOVERNMENT 76 (1996).

2. Most famously, when Powell died of a heart attack shortly after the 1970 constitution was drafted (but before it had been ratified), $800,000 in cash was found in his office and Springfield hotel room. *See id.* at 224; George Tagge, *Find Paul Powell Hoard*, CHICAGO TRIB., Dec. 31, 1970, at 1.

3. *See* Samuel K. Gove & James Nowlan, *supra* note 1, at 223-26.

4. ILL. CONST. art. III, § 5; 10 ILL. COMP. STAT. 5/1A-1.

5. 10 ILL. COMP. STAT. 5/1A-3(7).

6. 10 ILL. COMP. STAT. 5/1A-4.

7. 10 ILL. COMP. STAT. 5/1A-2.

8. 10 ILL. COMP. STAT. 5/1A-3.1.

9. 10 ILL. COMP. STAT. 5/1A-7.

10. 55 ILL. COMP. STAT. 5/3-2001.

11. 10 ILL. COMP. STAT. 5/6-1 *et seq*; 10 ILL. COMP. STAT. 5/14-1 *et seq*.; 10 ILL. COMP. STAT. 5/18-1 *et seq*.

12. The other municipal jurisdictions are East St. Louis, Aurora, Galesburg, Bloomington, Peoria, Danville, and Rockford.

13. 10 ILL. COMP. STAT. 5/6-21.

14. 10 ILL. COMP. STAT. 5/6-22.

15. 10 ILL. COMP. STAT. 5/6-23.

16. 10 ILL. COMP. STAT. 5/6-25.

17. Email from James P. Allen, Communications Director, Chicago Board of Election Commissioners, Aug. 27, 2007; email from Peter McLennon, Policy Analyst, Cook County Clerk's Office, Aug. 3, 2007.

18. As of the Nov. 6, 2006, general election, Cook County, including Chicago, had 2,710,118 registered voters, out of 7,375,688 registered voters statewide. Email from Mark Mossman, Director of Election Information, Illinois State Board of Elections, Aug. 29, 2007.

19. 10 ILL. COMP. STAT. 5/6A-1 *et seq*. allow counties to opt to use a Board of Election Commissioners, rather than a county clerk, to run elections.

20. Cook County reports having a similar system.

21. Email from Mark Mossman, Director of Election Information, Illinois State Board of Elections, Aug. 29, 2007.

22. Figures in this paragraph were calculated from numbers provided by Mark Mossman, Director of Election Information, Illinois State Board of Elections, by email on Aug. 29, 2007.

23. County clerks are elected every four years. 10 ILL. COMP. STAT. 5/2A-16.

24. 55 ILL. COMP. STAT. 5/3-9005.

25. 1987 Ill. Atty. Gen. Op. 230 (Ill. A.G.).

26. Edwards County, a county of about 7,000 residents in southeast Illinois, had one computer but it was not used for election work. Email from Mark Mossman, Director of Election Information, Illinois State Board of Elections, Aug. 29, 2007. Tiny Calhoun County, with 3,983 registered voters, did not have a computer at all. *Id.*

27. 10 ILL. COMP. STAT. 5/1A-8, 5/24A-16.

28. The budget for Cook County's current fiscal year is about $21 million. Email from Peter McLennon, Policy Analyst, Office of Cook County Clerk David Orr, Aug. 3, 2007.

29. *See* 26 ILL. ADMIN. CODE 100.10-216.10.

30. *See* 26 ILL. ADMIN. CODE 204.10.

31. *See, e.g.*, Samuel K. Gove & James D. Nowlan, *supra* note 1, at 134-36, 161-63, 223-25.

32. *See* Mark Eissman, *U.S. to Probe Primary Vote Fraud, Federal Laws May Have Been Broken*, CHICAGO TRIB., Mar. 11, 1987, Chicagoland, at 1.

33. *See id.*

34. *See* Mickey Ciokajlo, *Clerk Halts 250 Trying to Vote as Absentee*, CHICAGO TRIB., Mar. 20, 2003, Metro, at 3.

35. 357 Ill.App.3d 594 (Ill.App. 1 Dist., 2004).

36. *See* Mike Fitzgerald, *Ex-committeeman Given 10 Months, $3,000 Fine Imposed in Vote-fraud Scheme*, BELLEVILLE NEWS DEMOCRAT, Mar. 11, 2006, at 1B.

37. *See* Roberta Baskin, Investigative Reporter, WLS-TV News, Testimony Before the United States Senate Committee of the Judiciary, Subcommittee on the Constitution, Chicago, Illinois, Sept. 19, 1983, S. Hrg. 98-672, at 52. Ms. Baskin described getting six voter registration cards under six different names and addresses in half an hour, without providing identification.

38. *See* Jay Mikesell, Canvasser, Testimony Before the United States Senate Committee of the Judiciary, Subcommittee on the Constitution, Chicago, Illinois, Sept. 19, 1983, S. Hrg. 98-672, at 113.

39. *See id.* at 112.

40. *See* J. Robert Barr, Chairman, Cook County Republican Central Committee, Testimony Before the United States

Senate Committee of the Judiciary, Subcommittee on the Constitution, Chicago, Illinois, Sept. 19, 1983, S. Hrg. 98-672, at 110.

41. *See id.*

42. 10 ILL. COMP. STAT. 5/4-10; 5/5-9; 5/6-37.

43. 10 ILL. COMP. STAT. 5/1A-16.

44. 10 ILL. COMP. STAT. 5/4-30; 5/5-25.

45. 10 ILL. COMP. STAT. 5/4-17; 5/5-24; 5/6-58.

46. *See* U.S. Election Assistance Commission, THE IMPACT OF THE NATIONAL VOTER REGISTRATION ACT, 2005-2006, at 27 (2006 Election Administration and Voting Survey).

47. 26 ILL. ADMIN. CODE 216.40.

48. *Id.*

49. *See* Chinta Strausberg, *Feds, PUSH to Monitor Vote Fraud Complaints*, CHICAGO DEFENDER, Mar. 19, 2002.

50. *See* Carlos Sadovi, *4 in Cook Face Vote-fraud Charges, Former Election Judge Cited in Hoax at Polls with her Husband*, CHICAGO TRIB., Feb. 23, 2007, Metro, at 5.

51. *See* Editorial, *Making Cicero Safe for Democracy*, CHICAGO TRIB., Nov. 2, 2000, at 22.

52. *See* Evan Osnos, *U.S. Watchdogs to Keep Eye on Cicero Elections*, CHICAGO TRIB., Oct. 26, 2000, News, at 1.

53. *See* John McCormick, *High-tech Vote Put to Test, New Machines Set for Their Big Debut*, CHICAGO TRIB., Mar. 21, 2006, News, at 1.

54. *See* George Pawlaczyk, *Challenger Ousts Greenwood as Democratic Committeeman*, BELLEVILLE NEWS DEMOCRAT, Mar. 18, 2004, at 4B.

55. *See Hileman v. Maze*, 367 F.3d 694, 694 (7th Cir., 2004).

56. 10 ILL. COMP. STAT. 5/22-1.

57. For a comparison of the old and new versions of this provision, see 2005 Ill. Legis. Serv. 3316, 3325.

58. 10 ILL. COMP. STAT. 5/22-1.

59. *Id.*

60. *See* MICH. COMP. LAWS ANN. §§ 168.30; 168.24.

61. *See* WIS. STAT. ANN. § 7.60.

62. *See* OHIO REV. CODE § 3505.32.

63. *See* Mike Fitzgerald, *Official May Have Voted Twice, Complaint Says*, BELLEVILLE NEWS DEMOCRAT, Apr. 26, 2006, at 1B.

64. *See* Michael Lavelle, then-Chairman of the Chicago Board of Elections Commissioners, Testimony Before the

United States Senate Committee of the Judiciary, Subcommittee on the Constitution, Chicago, Illinois, Sept. 19, 1983, S. Hrg. 98-672, at 24.

65. 10 ILL. COMP. STAT. 5/24C-15.

66. 10 ILL. COMP. STAT. 5/24B-15.

67. 10 ILL. COMP. STAT. 5/13-1; 5/13-2; 5/14-1.

68. *See* Jay Mikesell, Canvasser, *Testimony Before the United States Senate Committee of the Judiciary, Subcommittee on the Constitution*, Chicago, Illinois, Sept. 19, 1983, S. Hrg. 98-672, at 113.

69. *Id.*

70. 10 ILL. COMP. STAT. 5/13-1; 5/13-2; 5/14-1.

71. The in-person or absentee nature of the other occurrences could not be determined from the articles. One article described registration fraud, which could be the first step of an in-person or absentee scheme.

72. *See* Dan Webb, then-U.S. Attorney for the Northern District of Illinois, Testimony Before the United States Senate Committee of the Judiciary, Subcommittee on the Constitution, Chicago, Illinois, Sept. 19, 1983, S. Hrg. 98-672, at 17. Webb testified that to "accomplish this illicit process, the precinct captain needs a pool of registered voters whose names he can forge. Persons who have died or who have moved are prime candidates for this pool. It is therefore imperative to assure an honest election that these names be removed from the voting rolls prior to each election." *Id.* at 18.

73. 10 ILL. COMP. STAT. 5/19-1, 19-5.

74. 10 ILL. COMP. STAT. 5/19-6.

75. 10 ILL. COMP. STAT. 5/29-20.

76. 10 ILL. COMP. STAT. 5/19-4, 5/19-8.

77. A Cook County official described that on multiple occasions the county clerk had reported apparent instances of absentee ballot fraud to law enforcement authorities, and never heard back. Meanwhile, these signature verification requirements do not prevent problems of coerced or bought absentee votes.

78. Compare 10 ILL. COMP. STAT. 5/4-1 *et seq.*, which applies to counties with fewer than 500,000 residents, to 10 ILL. COMP. STAT. 5/5-1 *et seq.*, which applies to counties with populations of 500,000 or more. The codes are substantively similar, but feature different structures and language that could cause courts to interpret them differently.

79. *See Orr Seeks 5th Term as County Clerk in 2006*, CHICAGO TRIB., Dec. 9, 2005, Metro, at 3.

80. Email from Peter McLennon, Policy Analyst, Office of

Cook County Clerk David Orr, Aug. 3, 2007.

81. Email from James P. Allen, Communications Director, Chicago Board of Election Commissioners, September 25, 2007.

82. *See* R. Bruce Dold, *Election Board's Likely Choice for Director Carries Baggage*, CHICAGO TRIB., May 26, 1988, Chicagoland, at 4.

83. Two of the three board members are Democratic. Langdon Neal, its chair, is a Democrat, while Richard Cowen, its Secretary, is a Republican. *See* Mike Dumke, *The Men Behind the Curtain*, CHICAGO READER, Jan. 26, 2007, at 1. The final commissioner, Marisel Hernandez, is a Democrat. Email from James P. Allen, Communications Director, Chicago Board of Elections Commissioners, Aug. 23, 2007.

84. According to the 2000 census, Chicago had a population of 2,896,016 and Cook County, exclusive of Chicago, had a population of 2,480,725. *See* Illinois Census 2000, http://illinoisgis.ito.state.il.us/census2000/censusData/2000/il data.asp.

85. *See Equipment Blamed for Sluggish Local Returns*, CHICAGO TRIB., Nov. 9, 2006, at 8.

86. The State Board of Elections does have the power to "supervise elections," and sometimes will send a small team of individuals into an election jurisdiction as observers. 10 ILL. COMP. STAT. 5/1A-8. However, board staff explained to us that the SBE does not have enough staff or sufficiently defined standards to perform thorough audits.

87. The SBE does currently answer questions posed to it by local administrators, and also offers free seminars to help familiarize administrators with the SBE, its departments, and the types of help it has to offer. Email from Mark Mossman, Director of Election Information, Illinois State Board of Elections, Sept. 24, 2007.

88. However, the state legislature has just enacted a provision that resolves this ambiguity. *See* 10 ILL. COMP. STAT. 5/18A-15.

89. 10 ILL. COMP. STAT. 5/18A-15.

90. *Id.*

91. Because most jurisdictions purchased machines only recently using newly acquired HAVA funds, disrepair has not yet become a major issue. However, there will be no HAVA funds for repairs and, according to Illinois officials, the cost of repairing these machines once they start breaking down may be prohibitive for many jurisdictions.

92. *See Legal Skirmishes Go On; Bush Gore Lawyers Argue New Hand Recounts*, RICHMOND (VIRGINIA) TIMES-

DISPATCH, Dec. 3, 2000, at A1. The article describes testimony presented in one of the *Bush v. Gore* proceedings that failure to maintain Florida's Votomatic machines may have caused some votes to go unrecorded.

93. A paradigmatic example of this type of general civil rights suit is *League of Women Voters v. Blackwell*, described in more detail above in Chapter 3, in which plaintiffs alleged that then-Ohio Secretary of State Kenneth Blackwell and other defendants "promulgate and maintain a voting system in Ohio… that has wholly inadequate systems, procedures, and funding necessary to ensure the meaningful and equal exercise of the right to vote."

94. 10 ILL. COMP. STAT. 5/2A-1.1.

95. *See Black v. McGuffage*, 209 F.Supp.2d 889, 899 (N.D.Ill., 2002).

96. *See, e.g.*, Edward B. Foley, *The Future of Bush v. Gore?*, 68 OHIO ST. L. J. ____ (forthcoming 2007).

97. In 2004, political parties and special interest groups spent about $9 million to vie for a state supreme court race, labeled as the most expensive state supreme court race in American history at the time. See John Chase, *Politics a Means to End on Court, Justices Say Party Ties That Helped Them Get on Bench Don't Lead to Biased Rulings*, CHICAGO TRIB., Apr. 7, 2006, Metro, at 1. A 2006 appellate court race in the southern part of the state saw $3.3 million raised. *See* Michael Higgins, *State Judge Race Nets Record Funds*, CHICAGO TRIB., Nov. 10, 2006, Metro, at 4.

98. *See* Stephanie Potter, *Money Taints Judiciary, Panel Warns*, CHICAGO DAILY LAW BULLETIN, Feb. 13, 2006, at 1.

99. *See* John Patterson, *Is Illinois Really That Corrupt? Ryan Case Adds New Chapter*, DAILY HERALD, Apr. 23, 2006, News, at 1.

100. *See In re Contest of the Election for the Offices of Governor & Lieutenant Governor Held at the General Election on November 2, 1982*, 444 N.E.2d 170 (Ill., 1983).

101. *See Webb v. Benton Cons. High School Dist. No. 103*, 264 N.E.2d 415 (Ill. App. 5th Dist., 1970).

102. *See Jordan v. Officer*, 525 N.E.2d 1067 (Ill. App. 5th Dist., 1988).

103. *See Leach v. Johnson*, 313 N.E.2d 636 (Ill. App. 5th Dist., 1974).

104. *See Andrews v. Powell*, 848 N.E.2d 243 (Ill. App. 4th Dist., 2006).

105. *See* Edward B. Foley, *supra* note 96 (analyzing this kind of Equal Protection claim in the wake of *Bush v. Gore*).

Illinois:

NINE AREAS

INSTITUTIONAL ARRANGEMENTS

Illinois administers its elections in a highly decentralized fashion. Although Illinois has a State Board of Elections ("SBE"), consisting of eight members appointed by the governor, 10 ILCS (Illinois Compiled Statutes) 5/Art. 1A, this board plays a fairly limited role. Primarily, it shares information and offers assistance to local election officials, who have the real power. Illinois has 110 local election jurisdictions, consisting of the state's 102 counties, plus eight cities that have chosen to run their elections independently of their county. Each of these eight cities, including Chicago, governs elections through a three-member Board of Elections appointed by the county circuit court. DuPage County similarly uses a County Board of Elections to oversee its voting processes, while in the remaining 101 counties the elected county clerk is in charge of elections. The State Board of Elections has authority to promulgate statewide regulations and guidance for these local jurisdictions, but at present it does not use this authority.

VOTER REGISTRATION/STATEWIDE DATABASE

Illinois is one of the states that has not fully complied with HAVA's requirement that its statewide voter registration database match incoming voter registration applications with pre-existing databases. The SBE has entered into agreements to bring the database into compliance, however, and the current database is matched against state databases of deaths and of felony convictions. Registrations are automatically canceled when either form of match occurs. 10 ILCS 5/4-14.1; 5-9.1; 6-55; 10 ILCS 5/6-55; 26 IL ADC (Illinois Admnistrative Code)216.50 The database is managed primarily at the local level, and Illinois has no uniform procedures governing how localities should process and verify incoming registration applications, instead empowering local authorities to promulgate their own procedures. 10 ILCS 5/1A-16. The SBE does help different jurisdictions to coordinate the adding and purging of entries.

In addition to the typical in-person and mail-in forms of registration, see 10 ILCS 5/4-10; 5-9; 6-37; 10 ILCS 5/1A-16 Illinois also permits grace period registration, which allows voters to register until the fourteenth day before the upcoming election by appearing in person at a designated voter registration location. 10 ILCS 5/4-50; 5/5-50; 5/6-100. Otherwise, the regular registration deadline is twenty-eight days before the election. 10 ILCS 5/4-6; 5/5-5; 5/6-29. Voters who use grace period registration may not vote at the polls on Election Day, but may vote only using special procedures established at the discretion of the local election authority. 10 ILCS 5/4-50; 5/5-50; 5/6-100.

CHALLENGES TO VOTER ELIGIBILITY

Challenges to a voter's eligibility may be filed either before an election or at the polls. Pre-election challenges may be filed by any voter. 10 ILCS 5/4-12; 5-15; 6-44. Challenged voters defend their eligibility by appearing at a hearing scheduled by the county clerk. 10 ILCS 5/4-12; 5-15; 6-44. The clerk's decision may be appealed to the circuit court. 10 ILCS 5/4-13; 6-47; 6-52. At the polls, challenges may be brought by poll watchers, and are decided by the majority vote of judges of elections (poll workers). 10 ILCS 5/7-34; 17-23; *Gribble v. Willeford*, 190 Ill.App.3d 610, 617 (Ill.App. 5 Dist., 1989). Voters challenged on Election Day may defend themselves by answering questions to the satisfaction of the judges or, if that is unsuccessful, by signing an affidavit and providing either identification or an affidavit from another voter that the voter is qualified. 10 ILCS 5/7-45; 17-9; 17-10; 18-5. Voters who cannot overcome a challenge may cast a provisional ballot. 10 ILCS 5/18A-5.

PROVISIONAL VOTING

Illinois provides provisional ballots to challenged voters, voters whose names are not on the statewide database, and first-time voters who are not able to provide the identification required under HAVA, but only if the voters are in the correct precinct. 10 ILCS 5/18A-5. To determine whether to count a provisional ballot, county clerks and boards of election use a "totality of the circumstances" test to determine whether it is at least equally likely that the voter is eligible to vote in the precinct. 10 ILCS 5/18-15. In the November 2006 election, SBE figures that show thirty-seven percent of the 15,875 provisional ballots cast in Illinois were counted, compared to fifty-one percent of 43,464 provisional ballots cast in November 2004.

EARLY AND ABSENTEE VOTING

Illinois permits absentee voting only if the voter asserts he or she will be out of town, will be observing a religious holiday, or for other reasons will be unable to vote in person. 10 ILCS 5/19-1, 19-5. The state recently adopted an early voting program. The early voting program is not precinct-specific, but allows any voter to cast a ballot at any early voting location maintained by the relevant election authority. Early voting begins on the twenty-second day before each election, and continues until the fifth day before the election. 10 ILCS 5/19A-15. The 2008 election will be the first presidential election to feature early voting, and local election officials expect the number of individuals casting absentee ballots to decline as a result of early voting.

VOTING TECHNOLOGY

The overwhelming majority of Illinois' election jurisdictions use optical scan machines, except in providing disability access and early voting. Roughly forty jurisdictions use the ES&S M100 optical scan readers, and roughly sixty use Diebold Accu-vote optical scan readers. Chicago and Cook County, the two largest jurisdictions, use Sequoia Optech Insight optical scan machines. Only a few jurisdictions use DRE equipment, which must be capable of producing a paper audit trail. 10 ILCS 5/24C-11. While individual administrators appreciate the selection they have when shopping for voting machines, the variety of machines in use in Illinois makes it more difficult for the SBE, given its limited resources, to remain abreast of the technology and to provide the smaller jurisdictions with the support they need.

POLLING PLACE OPERATIONS

With certain exceptions, polling places are staffed by five poll workers, no more than three of whom may be from the same political party. 10 ILCS 5/13-1; 5/13-2; 5/14-1. Using lists submitted by the political parties, election administrators select poll workers, and these selections then must be confirmed by the county circuit court. 10 ILCS 5/13-1. County clerks or county or municipal Boards of Election Commissioners, rather than the SBE, are responsible for developing and implementing training courses for these poll workers. 10 ILCS 5/13-2.1; 5/14-4.1. However, the SBE does offer free training, which many smaller Illinois jurisdictions use to save time and money. The training must consist of at least four hours of instruction and an examination that tests reading skills, ability to work with poll lists, ability to add, and knowledge of election laws governing the operation of polling places. 10 ILCS 5/13-2.2. Failure to attend this course "shall subject such judge to *possible* removal from office at the option of the election authority" (emphasis added). 10 ILCS 5/13-3; 10 ILCS 5/14-5. Insufficient poll worker training was blamed for the most severe problem experienced in the 2006 elections, when 136 out of 223 precincts in Kane County, south of Chicago, failed to open on time. *See Human Error Gets Blame in Kane County Elections*, CHICAGO TRIBUNE, Nov. 17, 2006; *Voting Troubles Mar Clerk's Re-election*, CHICAGO TRIBUNE, Nov. 9, 2006.

BALLOT SECURITY

Illinois' chain-of-custody rules for ballots and voting materials are complicated, with separate provisions for jurisdictions that do and do not have Boards of Election Commissioners, 10 ILCS 17, 10 ILCS 18, jurisdictions that use "voting machines," 10 ILCS 24, jurisdictions that use "electronic, mechanical, or electric voting machines," 10 ILCS 24A, jurisdictions that use precinct-count optical scan voting machines, 10 ILCS 24B, and jurisdictions that use DRE machines, 10 ILCS 24C. The code provides inadequate definitions for many of these terms and, where the different sets of rules appear to overlap, it is often unclear which one of them controls. Because of this statutory complexity, and also because the code cannot keep up with changes in technology, some administrators worry that chain-of-custody rules are misunderstood and loosely followed. However, Illinois courts will not invalidate an election for failure to follow chain-of-custody statutes unless the failure affects the election's fairness. *See Andrews v. Powell*, 365 Ill.App.3d 513, 523 (Ill.App. 4 Dist., 2006).

POST-ELECTION PROCESSES

Illinois election law does not provide for automatic recounts. Instead, it provides for recounts only in connection with an election contest. Initially, a losing candidate who received at least ninety-five percent of the votes cast for the winner may petition for a "discovery" recount of up to a quarter of the precincts, but must pay the costs of this recount. The discovery recount has no impact on the official election results and serves only to determine whether evidence exists to support a formal election contest. If this evidence suggests a reasonable likelihood that a recount would change the result, a court can order a full recount. 10 ILCS 5/22-9.1; 10 ILCS 5/23-23.2. Some Illinois courts appear to have ignored the statute's "reasonable likelihood" language, dismissing contest petitions unless from the pleadings it appears that going forward would either *certainly or probably* change the result of the election. *See Andrews v. Powell*, 848 N.E.2d 243, 246 (Ill. App. 4 Dist., 2006). Because the statutes do not explicitly authorize them, the Illinois Supreme Court has concluded that no court has jurisdiction to hear federal election contests. S*ee Young v. Mikva*, 66 Ill.2d 579, 582-583 (Ill., 1977).

CHAPTER 5: MICHIGAN'S ELECTION ECOSYSTEM
STATEWIDE STABILITY, BUT LOCAL VULNERABILITIES

ALTHOUGH MICHIGAN has generally experienced fewer election administration problems than Ohio or Illinois, Detroit has been the scene of some serious voting problems in recent years. Detroit's problems include an inability to recount its absentee ballots in its 2005 municipal primary election, followed by misconduct in collecting absentee ballots in the 2005 municipal general election. Among other misconduct in that election, publicly financed "ambassadors" assisting certain absentee voters were observed advising absentee voters about which candidates the voters should pick, and the city clerk disobeyed a court order concerning the distribution of absentee ballot applications, for which she was held in criminal contempt.[1] Meanwhile, elsewhere in the state political parties have occasionally traded allegations of voter intimidation or other improper conduct as well.[2] Nevertheless, most parts of Michigan's election ecosystem have been functioning relatively smoothly of late. At the same time, aspects of the state's ecosystem remain vulnerable, and some potential problems could be compounded by the role that today's deeply divided state supreme court would play in election litigation.

In this chapter, we describe the following essential characteristics of Michigan's current election ecosystem: the predominant role that municipal officials (mostly elected), rather than county officials, play in administering Michigan elections; the healthy working relationship that exists between state and local election officials; the state's decade-old "Qualified Voter File," which now serves as Michigan's HAVA-compliant statewide voter database and which has been a model for other states; and a uniform system of optical-scan balloting now in use throughout the state. We also offer a summary of the state's most serious recent voting problems, primarily in Detroit. Notably, Detroit's mishandling of absentee ballots in that city's 2005 municipal election was only the culmination of years of concern about the city's election administration, and public attention to its problems that year precipitated the downfall of Detroit's three-term city clerk. Although Detroit appears to be in better shape today, with its elections under the administration of a new city clerk, it retains some of the preconditions that may have contributed to its earlier problems.

Accordingly, in this chapter we also look ahead to some changes and challenges on the horizon for Michigan elections. First, the Michigan Secretary of State has introduced her own election reform agenda, which merits a brief overview. In addition, Michigan is now implementing a nascent voter ID requirement that had been on hold for a decade until the state supreme court, divided on party lines, approved it earlier this year. Its implementation is providing a new opportunity for Michigan citizens to debate whether the main effect of an identification requirement is to protect the integrity of the vote, or instead is to discourage some citizens from voting. The partisan split in the state judiciary over this issue also highlights a concern over whether Michigan is prepared to handle potential election litigation in a manner that will inspire public confidence. Meanwhile, the state's decentralized approach to election administration may help elections to run smoothly on Election Day, but it also may continue to leave some localities vulnerable to corruption akin to the problems that recently plagued Detroit. And Michigan, like other states, must confront the increasing difficulty of grooming and training an adequate number of poll workers.

SOME BACKGROUND

While still more of a national bellwether than Illinois, Michigan today is less typical of the nation than is Ohio. Both before and after it became a state in 1837, Michigan developed with stronger ties to New England and the northeast United States, and weaker ties to the south. As part of its New England heritage, Michigan's political institutions developed with a tradition of local self-government built around a township structure (as did all the other states of the Northwest Territory, including Ohio, Illinois, and Wisconsin).[3] But in Michigan more than in many other states, townships remain the dominant political structure today,[4] which helps to explain why Michigan elections are administered primarily at the township (or municipal) level, rather than at the county level.

Detroit, with over 800,000 residents, is by far the state's largest municipality, dwarfing the second largest city, Grand Rapids, which has a population of under 200,000.[5] A number of smaller cities and towns then combine with many townships to encompass the state's ten million residents. However, Detroit is no longer the thriving industrial center that it once was. Instead, Detroit has been steadily losing population for several decades, and has recently become the country's poorest city,[6] as Michigan has found itself squarely among the rest of the economically struggling "rust belt" states.

Michigan's early growth was heavily influenced by its natural resources, particularly its forests, furs, and ores, as well as its position on the Great Lakes. Eventually its resources and geographic position gave rise to transportation routes that helped to spur the state's manufacturing economy, including most predominantly the Detroit auto industry.[7] In turn, this economic engine prompted waves of dramatic immigration to the state, including a substantial wave of African-Americans, as well as Southern whites, to the Detroit area in the early and mid twentieth century;[8] the development of interest groups and a thriving union movement;[9] and a number of accompanying voter mobilization efforts.[10] In recent presidential elections, voting turnout has hovered at around sixty percent of the state's voting age population (some five percentage points above the national average), although in 2004 the turnout was sixty-five percent (also more than five percent above that year's national average). Table 4 contains voter turnout data for the past four federal elections in all five of our studied states.

As an example of one type of voter mobilization effort, in 1975 Michigan was the first state to implement a "motor-voter" program. This program permitted residents to complete an application to register to vote at the same time that they were obtaining a state driver's license at any of the secretary of state's branch offices around the state. Then-Secretary of State Richard Austin became known as the father of the motor-voter concept for championing this approach as a means of facilitating the registration of the state's eligible voters. Many other states followed, and Congress then expanded upon this concept in the 1993 National Voter Registration Act, which requires all states to permit eligible voters to register to vote at any of a variety of public agencies and offices around each state.[11]

In a more recent Michigan reform, in 2003 state and local elections officials worked with state legislators to pass a package of bills that consolidated a variety of local and school district elections into only four potential election dates each year (not including certain special elections).[12] The consolidation measures, which became effective at the beginning of 2005, also standardized the location of a voter's polling place for all elections. Local election officials have welcomed this reform for bringing increased efficiency, predictability, and uniformity to all Michigan elections.

Also shaping Michigan's election ecosystem is that its political culture, in the rubric of politi-cal scientist Daniel Elazar, is usually described as primarily a "moralistic" one (along with Wisconsin and Minnesota), with secondary elements of an "individualistic" culture (the political culture that predominates in Ohio and Illinois).[13] In Elazar's typology, a moralistic political culture is one in which government is viewed as a commonwealth, bureaucracy is viewed favorably as capable of advancing the common good, and everyone is expected to participate in the community's political affairs. Political competition occurs over issues and principles, more than over parties or ideologies, and it is appropriate for the government to play a role in any area in which it can enhance community well-being. By contrast, in an individualist political culture, government is valued for its ability to promote efficient private transactions, politics is characteristically a dirty business for professionals, and strong political parties compete to advance the interests of their members.[14] Michigan's moralist political traditions, among other influences, may help account for the professionalism with which its many local officials efficiently conduct elections, while its individualist political

TABLE 4
VOTER TURNOUT PERCENTAGES BY ELECTION YEAR
(expressed as a percentage of a state's voting-eligible population)

	2006	2004	2002	2000
ILLINOIS	40.6	59.86	41.43	56.2
MICHIGAN	52.2	66.36	44.45	59.9
MINNESOTA	60.8	76.82	64.09	69.9
OHIO	47.5	66.44	38.8	56.7
WISCONSIN	53.3	76.24	45.43	67.6
TOTAL U.S.	**40.4**	**60.32**	**39.51**	**54.2**

Source: United States Election Project, http://elections.gmu.edu/Voter_Turnout.htm.

traditions may partially explain much of the lingering finger-pointing and suspicion that surrounds some aspects of the state's election ecosystem, and perhaps also the current partisanship in the state judiciary.

PREDOMINANT ROLE OF MUNICIPAL OFFICIALS

Michigan's system of election administration depends most heavily on municipal officials, assisted by both state and county officials. Both in geography and population, Michigan is the largest of the eight U.S. states that today place responsibility for conducting elections primarily at the municipal level.[15] Specifically, this means that some 274 city clerks and 1,242 township clerks, rather than officials in Michigan's eighty-three counties, are primarily responsible for the actual administration of Michigan elections, as well as for maintaining the voter registration records for voters registered in their individual jurisdictions. Their particular responsibilities include preparing and maintaining the voting equipment; recruiting and supervising a cadre of precinct "election inspectors," or poll workers, for each election; and processing voter registration applications, as well as purging outdated registrations from the roster of voters. Township clerks are all elected in partisan contests,[16] while city clerks may be either appointed or elected, typically in nonpartisan races, depending on the nature of the city's charter.[17]

In addition to the city and township clerks, each municipality also maintains a three-member city or township board of election commissioners. A city board of election commissioners consists of the city clerk, the city attorney, and the city assessor, while an un-

chartered township board consists of the township clerk, the township supervisor, and the township treasurer.[18] These election commissions are responsible for dividing their jurisdiction into precincts, assessing the need for election materials, including voting machines and ballots, and formally appointing precinct election inspectors. Communities with more than five voting precincts also are to have a city or township board of canvassers, composed of two Republicans and two Democrats, to canvass elections conducted by the local jurisdictions, although the current practice in most municipalities is to take advantage of a statutory provision that instead allows them to contract with their county board of canvassers, described more below, to canvass their election results.[19]

These municipal officials conduct their duties under the supervision – but not control – of the Michigan Secretary of State, who is elected on a partisan ticket for a four-year term. As the state's chief election officer, the secretary of state supervises all election-related issues in the state, but has no authority to terminate the local officials. As a matter of law, however, local officials are expected to comply with the secretary's directives concerning election administration. Indeed, more than four decades ago, the secretary of state sought an injunction to force a county board of election commissioners to follow the secretary's orders, and the state supreme court held that the county board had a legal duty to follow these orders.[20]

Also supervising elections at the state level is the Michigan Bureau of Elections, a division of the secretary of state's office. The bureau is headed by the state elections director, who is appointed by the secretary of state as a civil service appointee.[21] A four-member board of state canvassers, appointed equally from both major political parties by the governor, with the advice and consent of the state senate, is responsible for canvassing returns for statewide offices, as well as for preparing ballot language on initiative measures. Partisan conflict in how this board has handled several recent ballot initiatives has prompted the secretary of state to propose "professionalizing" the board by requiring that at least one board member of each party have prior election administration experience.

In between these state officials and the municipal officials, all eighty-three Michigan counties also have their own election administrators.[22] Specifically, each county has an evenly bipartisan four-member board of county canvassers, responsible for certifying elections held in the county; a board of county election commissioners, responsible for printing ballots and distributing voting materials to each municipality; and county clerks, responsible for receiving from the local precincts all of the canvass petitions for elected offices within the borders of their respective counties, and for running the formal training program for poll workers.[23] But it is the municipal officials, rather than these county officials, who conduct voting operations at the polling places and are responsible for precinct-level vote counting.

RELATIONSHIP OF MICHIGAN'S VARIOUS LEVELS OF ELECTION ADMINISTRATORS

Michigan's municipal clerks report a high level of satisfaction in their relationships with the state bureau of elections, and in particular with the current elections director, Christopher

Thomas. The bureau is seen as responsive and professional, and ready to provide advice in a timely manner. Local elections officials report with approval that Thomas himself sometimes answers many inquiries directly, typically within days and often even the same day that local officials seek his input.

This healthy relationship is partly the result of a conscious effort by the municipal clerks to develop a constructive dialogue, primarily through the Michigan Association of Municipal Clerks ("MAMC").[24] MAMC is an active organization of approximately 900 clerks and deputy clerks from cities and townships throughout Michigan. To help it address matters of election administration, MAMC and its counterpart the Michigan Association of County Clerks have a Council of Elections Officials, consisting of approximately a dozen members drawn equally from both counties and municipalities, which meets regularly (typically once a month). MAMC also has both a legislative committee and its own lobbyist, which together give the association a meaningful voice in the state capital. In the ten years since the MAMC's creation, its members have developed a number of credible relationships with state legislators and have worked together on a number of election administration reforms, including the election consolidation measures adopted in 2003, described above, and a measure adopted in 2006 advancing the deadline for filing as a write-in candidate from the Friday before an election to the second Friday before an election, to give local administrators more time to prepare for Election Day.[25] In addition, the MAMC has worked deliberately and successfully to build a strong partnership with the state bureau of elections, including Thomas, and to develop a unified response to current Secretary of State Terri Lynn Land's election reform agenda (discussed further below).

The healthy relationship among the various levels of Michigan election administrators is also a product of the relative stability of the leadership at the bureau of elections. Director Thomas has been the head of this bureau for over twenty-five years, providing professional service to three Michigan secretaries of state (of both major political parties) and ensuring continuity in the state's election processes. In doing so, he was able to build upon the continuity and local relationships established by his predecessor, Bernie Apol, who had served as the state's elections director for the previous fifteen years. Today, Thomas has a national reputation as an effective elections administrator and is frequently consulted by Congress and other states. He also serves on the U.S. Election Assistance Commission Board of Advisors, and has previously served as the President of the National Association of State Elections Directors. Meanwhile, the bureau of elections has a history of providing effective training materials and helpful interpretive memoranda to local officials, and since 2004 has issued a series of concise, informative newsletters concerning election administration issues in the run-up to each election.[26]

QUALIFIED VOTER FILE

One of Michigan's most notable election administration features is its Qualified Voter File ("QVF"). The QVF, which Michigan implemented in 1998, is a statewide database containing the name, address, date of birth, driver's license or state ID number, voting history, elec-

tronic signature, and voting district information for every registered voter in the state.[27] Given Michigan's leadership in establishing a "motor voter" program, it was perhaps natural for Michigan also to be at the forefront in establishing a statewide voter list, although in part it was the passage of the National Voter Registration Act of 1993 that spurred Michigan to create the QVF.

The QVF is accessible to election officials by secure Internet connection in every county office in the state, as well as in most cities and townships that have secure Internet capabilities. At the outset, the state supplied QVF hardware and software to all municipalities with a voting-age population of at least 5,000 people, while a number of smaller municipalities also initially acquired QVF access at their own expense. From the beginning, municipalities without adequate technological capabilities to access the QVF instead have been able to use their county's QVF hardware, and since 2006 the secretary of state's office has offered a streamlined system called "QVF Lite" that any municipality with a desktop computer and Internet connection can access.

When a municipal or county clerk receives a completed voter registration application, the clerk enters the application information into the QVF, where it is compared with information from the Michigan Driver's License database. If the information from both files matches, the voter is registered. If information about a voter's residence in a voter registration application conflicts with information from the department of motor vehicle's records, then the most recent information takes precedence.[28] If other information does not match, the record is sent to an error processing file and the voter may need to correct the inconsistencies in the information before being allowed to vote.

At least eighty percent of Michigan voters register and update their voter registration as part of a driver's license transaction. The QVF automatically updates according to changes made in such a transaction.[29] If the transaction provides information that the voter moved out of the particular jurisdiction where the voter was registered to another jurisdiction in the state, the voter's registration is transferred to the new jurisdiction.

Michigan's QVF system was a model for HAVA's statewide database requirement. The Carter-Ford Commission, in recommending in 2001 that all states implement a statewide voter database, described Michigan's QVF as one of two "outstanding" examples of such a system, and the one deserving careful consideration because "any state can copy it" and it was relatively inexpensive.[30] However, the Brennan Center has opined that despite the QVF's position as a HAVA model, its entirely mechanical algorithm for determining whether similar names in fact represent the same individual is less flexible than some alternatives, and therefore may produce more database errors.[31] In particular, typographical or other data entry errors in some fields, which could be caught through more flexible algorithms, may instead result in flagging a voter registration application as not matching the state's driver's license records. In response, Michigan officials report that after the mechanical algorithm identifies mismatches, election officials make every effort to resolve the discrepancies manually.

Other aspects of the organization of the QVF also merit brief description. The QVF system can correlate voter registrations with the zon-

ing laws, allowing it to know when someone tries to register with an address that is zoned for business. The QVF also is coordinated with Michigan's "Master Death File," a database keeping track of the deceased in the state. If someone's name is added to this database, the QVF will automatically remove them from the QVF database.[32] According to the Secretary of State's office, names of some 296,000 deceased voters have been removed from the QVF since 2004.[33]

At the same time, Michigan's list, like most statewide lists, remains burdened by a number of "deadwood" entries, most of them lingering from the time the QVF was created, representing voters who likely had died, moved, or changed their names without the state receiving any confirmation of it. The result is that as new registrants are added, the list swells and sometimes the number of registered voters in the database approaches or exceeds the number of voting-eligible residents. Indeed, the large-scale purge that Michigan accomplished in 2004 was partly the result of pressure from the U.S. Department of Justice over the fact that in certain portions of the state the number of voters in the state's database exceeded the voting age population. In response to this federal pressure to clean up the list, the state defrayed the costs for municipalities to mail new voter identification cards to all registered voters, and then used the cards that the Post Office returned as undeliverable to help identify some of this deadwood. Nonetheless, state officials estimate that the QVF may still contain roughly one million excess entries. (While this is an astounding number by some measures, for purposes of comparison it is worth noting that in 2006, Ohio and Illinois had over 800,000 and

900,000 "inactive" registrations, respectively, in their statewide databases.[34] Michigan does not separately report its "inactive" registrations, but if it did the vast majority of its estimated one million excess entries would likely be in this category.)

One reflection of the positive role that the QVF plays in Michigan elections is the fact that Michigan issued only 5,610 provisional ballots in the 2004 election (3,227 of which were counted), and only 2,426 provisional ballots in 2006 (952 of which were counted), as shown in Table 1 (in Chapter 3). The low number of provisional ballots is undoubtedly a combination of several factors, including not only the state's well-established and relatively accurate registered voter database, but also the fact that Michigan does not permit voters who have moved within the state to use a provisional ballot as a method of changing their registration status. Instead, in a practice not widely employed in other states,[35] a voter who has moved within a city or township and who appears at what would be the voter's correct polling place had the voter properly completed the change of address process, but who has failed to complete that process, will instead be told to return to the precinct of the voter's previous address to cast a ballot. There, the voter will also be asked to complete a change of address notice before voting. As for voters who have moved to a different city or township within Michigan, they also will be allowed to vote one last time in the precinct where they remain registered, provided they moved within sixty days of the election. Otherwise, they are ineligible to vote.

Another step that Michigan takes to reduce the amount of provisional voting is to help voters know their correct precinct. Since 2002, the secretary of state's office has maintained a "Voter Information Center," a publicly accessible website that permits voters to access their QVF records and determine their correct precincts and polling locations. Finally, Michigan issues "receipts" to voters at the time that they register to vote, and a voter who presents this receipt at the polls is entitled to vote a regular ballot even if the voter's name is not found on the rolls.[36] (The voter also completes a new registration form before voting.)

On a related note, the state permits a voter who claims to have registered but whose name is not found in the statewide database and who lacks the receipt just described also to vote a regular ballot, provided the voter signs an affidavit affirming that the voter did register before the registration deadline.[37] The voter must also complete a new registration application, and must provide photo identification that also confirms that the voter resides in that voting precinct. The voter then is allowed to cast a regular ballot, although in this case the ballot is marked as a "challenged ballot," meaning that the poll worker writes an identifying number on the back of the ballot (which is also recorded in the poll book), and then conceals the number with tape, before giving the voter the ballot.[38] Because these ballots could in theory be removed from vote totals in the event that a voter's ineligibility is established after the fact, the state formally classifies them as "provisional" ballots and includes them in its count of provisional ballots. In the 2004 and 2006 general elections, these ballots constituted approximately forty percent and twenty-five percent of Michigan's total provisional ballots, respectively.[39]

Michigan's QVF took some time to mature,

however. In its early years, it experienced its share of technical glitches and substantive errors, as well as resistance from some local election officials. For instance, when the state began to implement the QVF, most local jurisdictions already had their own registration lists and systems, many of which had been specially designed for local needs. One early challenge therefore was finding a way to preserve some of these localities' custom features, such as municipalities that already maintained electronic files of all of their voters' signatures, which they did not want to abandon. Local administrators report that the state worked with them to address these concerns. The state also had to deal with the fact that the local registration lists were in some 800 different formats, varying in their degree of accuracy, which could be merged only through a painstaking conversion process. Another challenge was to develop out of whole cloth a statewide street index that could map every residential address onto its assigned precinct.

Additionally, when the state first established the QVF by combining existing local lists into a state master, the state list initially contained hundreds of thousands of duplicate entries, resulting from the presence of identical voters' names on the lists of multiple jurisdictions. Although part of the purpose of a statewide list was to find and cull these duplicate entries, that process did not occur overnight or without difficulties. In the early stages of implementing the QVF, local clerks often took a variety of different approaches to such matters as the standards for determining what constituted duplicate entries, and it took some time and dedicated effort to develop uniform procedures. But by 1998, some 800,000 duplicate entries

had been removed. And by 2005, when a leader of the MAMC asked local officials for their views about the QVF, no one expressed an interest in doing away with it. Here again, one key to overcoming the early implementation issues likely was the healthy working relationship between the local officials operating many aspects of the system and the state administrators overseeing it.

PRECINCT-COUNT OPTICAL SCAN VOTING NOW UNIVERSAL THROUGHOUT MICHIGAN

In addition to its statewide database, Michigan also has now moved to a uniform statewide voting system. In 2002, somewhere in Michigan each of five types of voting systems were in use: optical scan ballots, direct recording electronic ("DRE") voting machines, punch card ballots, lever machines, and paper ballots.[40] That year, the Michigan legislature enacted a provision of the state election code mandating that the secretary of state select a uniform voting system to be used throughout the state, provided that federal funding became available to defray the substantial transition costs involved.[41] HAVA then provided the necessary funding.

The previous Michigan secretary of state had recommended moving to a uniform statewide voting system in the mid 1990s, but encountered resistance both because the state lacked the funding to do so and because at the time some feared that such a move would require all jurisdictions to use a particular vendor's equipment, not just a uniform type of voting system. The 2000 election, coupled with Congress' interest in providing federal funds for states to upgrade their voting equipment, caused Michigan to take up the challenge anew. Moving to a uniform statewide voting system was expected to ease administrative burdens on county and state election officials, reduce errors associated with the preparation and printing of a variety of ballot materials, eliminate a "technology gap" that existed in voting systems around the state, decrease the ongoing costs of running elections, and help voters and poll workers who moved within the state and otherwise might need to adjust to a different voting technology.[42]

Relying on the guidance of the state's Help America Vote Act advisory committee, in August of 2003 Secretary of State Terri Lynn Land chose as Michigan's uniform voting technology an optical scan voting system using precinct-based counting equipment.[43] One factor influencing the choice of this system was that sixty-five percent of the state's precincts were already using precinct-count optical scanning equipment. But also influencing Michigan's choice were a number of other perceived advantages, including the ease with which voting on optical scan ballots can be scaled up for elections with large turnouts simply by printing extra ballots (in contrast to DRE voting, which can accommodate larger turnout only through deploying additional DRE machines), and the fact that optical scan ballots are themselves a physical paper trail that both reassures voters that their selections will be properly counted and provides a reliable means of hand recounting disputed results. A primary disadvantage of optical scan ballots that Michigan recognized it would need to overcome was the system's comparative difficulty in accommodating the needs of some disabled voters. But other minor disadvantages, discussed below, also have subsequently materialized.

The state then certified three private vendors – ES&S, Diebold, and Sequoia – from whom each county could purchase precinct-count optical scan voting systems for the county's polling places.[44] Although jurisdictions that had already purchased new equipment within the past eight years were given ten years from the date when they acquired their previous system to comply with the uniform system, in fact by the August 2006 primary election all precincts in the state were using the uniform precinct-count optical scan system.[45] In May of 2006, the state also chose to accommodate disabled voters by using federal funds to acquire an AutoMARK™ machine for each of Michigan's roughly 4,000 polling places.[46] AutoMARK™ machines are ballot-marking devices that prepare a regular optical scan ballot by allowing a disabled voter to interact with the machine through a combination of touch screen, Braille keypad, headphones, or the voter's own sip/puff device or foot pump. Once the AutoMARK™ machine prints the completed ballot, the ballot then is cast by inserting it into the regular scanning device for the voter's precinct. The state had mixed success with the AutoMARK™ machines in their inaugural election, as some of the equipment did not perform as smoothly as expected.[47] The state believes that the vendor has now addressed the problems that arose in 2006, although the upgraded devices themselves must still be retested when fully configured to operate with each polling place's entire optical scan system. Meanwhile, some legal issues remain (and are being litigated in California[48]) about whether AutoMARK™ equipment provides a sufficient accommodation for all disabled voters, given that even using the AutoMARK™ machine, some disabled voters may continue to require assistance to vote.

Today, state election officials appreciate having a statewide voting technology, which stream-lines their ability to oversee and assist local election administrators. Meanwhile, Michigan's local election administrators also seem generally satisfied with the state's move to uniform equipment, although they note that the state's choice of optical scan ballots means that last-minute changes to the ballot are now much harder to accommodate than under either punch card or DRE systems (in which case only the voting machines need adjustments, rather than the ballots themselves, which must all be reprinted prior to the election). Local officials also murmur about the burdens associated with optical scan ballots, noting that they are expensive to print, heavy to transport, expensive to mail to absentee voters, and sensitive to humidity and moisture.[49] Finally, they note that the precinct-count feature of optical scan ballots does nothing to reduce the residual voting rates for absentee voters (although DRE technology similarly provides no residual voting rate improvements for absentee voters). Augmenting the absentee voting process with an early voting option at clerks' offices might partially ameliorate this disadvantage, although local Michigan election officials express greater interest in adopting some form of no-reason absentee voting. While no-reason absentee voting, simply by increasing the amount of absentee balloting, would reduce Election Day crowds at the polls, it also would increase the potential for undetected residual voting.

But at least for the short term, Michigan appears to have achieved a relative degree of stability in its voting technology. In contrast to states using DRE technology (for which lingering concerns about software tampering, or the viability of voter verifiable paper audit trails, render it currently vulnerable to legislative or administrative demands for replacement or upgrades), Michigan faces a comparatively low risk that it will need to scrap its entire system, provided that its AutoMARK™ equipment is able to accommodate disabled voters effectively.

MICHIGAN'S RECENT ELECTION ADMINISTRATION PROBLEMS

In the 2004 election, a record high turnout resulted in long lines at some polls, although nothing like the lines in Ohio.[50] Meanwhile, in Detroit, political parties skirmished over the activities of poll watchers, and in a prelude to the 2005 election described more fully below, the city clerk's office fended off allegations of manipulating and improperly handling absentee ballots.[51] Problems of voter intimidation and disruption, primarily associated with the activities of polling place challengers and monitors, occurred in many precincts. Scattered reports of deceptive practices came in from other locations as well, including allegations that some absentee voters received phone calls giving them a false address for the return of their absentee ballots.[52] And litigation, akin to that in Ohio, arose over whether HAVA required provisional ballots cast in the wrong precinct nonetheless to be counted.[53] (In an appeal of a case from Ohio, the U.S. Court of Appeals for the Sixth Circuit ultimately answered "no" to this question, in a ruling that also applies to Michigan.[54]) But overall the election was relatively smooth.

In the 2006 election, with the entire state now uniformly employing precinct count optical scan ballots, Michigan again experienced a few isolated problems. For instance, notwithstanding the hypothetical ease with which optical scan voting can be scaled up to accommodate heavy turnout, some precincts in Thomas Township (in Saginaw County) still ran short on ballots, and had to supplement them with photocopied ballots that then had to be hand-counted (which is still a more practical solution to unusually high turnout than trying to deploy additional DRE equipment, in a state using touch-screen voting).[55] In neighboring Saginaw Charter Township (also in Saginaw County), moisture caused some ballots to expand, leading some of the scanning machines to jam.[56] In other places, poll workers also committed occasional errors, such as distributing a school district ballot to voters who did not live in the school district.[57] And in response to allegations that Democratic poll challengers wearing vests that said "Don't Leave Without Voting. I Can Help You," were misleading voters into thinking that the challengers were election officials, one court issued an injunction prohibiting poll challengers from initiating contact with voters.[58] Meanwhile, election administrators described generally heavy burdens involved in complying with key HAVA requirements on a relatively short time line, particularly in preparing new voting equipment for use and subjecting it to thorough pre-election calibration and testing. But with the exception of one precinct that reportedly opened a few minutes late,[59] none of the 2006 problems prevented voters from voting, or called into question the outcomes of any races.[60]

Instead, Michigan's most serious election administration problem in recent history occurred in the 2005 Detroit municipal election. There, although some allegations surfaced that election workers made clerical mistakes at the

polls on Election Day, as well as in recording voter information to the QVF,[61] by far the most serious problems concerned the city's handling of its absentee voting. Detroit, which has a record of absentee voting in local elections at a rate of over thirty percent, or more than twice the national average (and also well above Michigan's statewide average of about twenty percent),[62] had been dogged by claims of improprieties in its absentee voting for a number of elections before 2005. That year, a variety of irregularities in how the city clerk's office handled absentee balloting came to light after two city council candidates sought a recount of the August 2005 primary election's absentee ballots.

As a prelude to problems with the recount, Detroit had some difficulty completing the canvass of its primary election.[63] The official-results then contained irregularities in many poll districts, primarily in the form of discrepancies between the number of ballots cast and the number of voters who applied to vote. In addition, many absentee ballot boxes no longer had intact seals, as required to comply with the critical chain-of-custody procedures necessary to protect the integrity of the voting process. When the Detroit city clerk, Jackie Currie, was unable to explain these discrepancies, county canvassers concluded that almost forty percent of the precincts subject to the recount could not be recounted.[64] One city council candidate then commenced a lawsuit in state court, and an FBI investigation also ensued.[65]

As the November 2005 general election approached, the state court hearing the lawsuit cited Currie for criminal contempt of court when she defied the court's order that she not send out absentee ballot applications for the general election except to voters who had requested them. Despite the order (which the Michigan Court of Appeals affirmed in late 2007[66]), she continued her practice of using an internally generated "permanent absentee voter" list to send out 150,000 such applications. She also continued to conduct an "ambassador" program, in which she sent paid assistants to nursing homes to help residents cast their absentee ballots.

Currie, who had been charged with absentee ballot fraud in 1964 along with her husband (who ultimately pleaded guilty to a reduced charge),[67] sought to defend both the sending of applications to the permanent absentee voter list, and the dispatching of ambassadors to help certain voters, as efforts to increase voter turnout and to provide assistance where it was needed. But in response to allegations that Currie's ambassadors sometimes returned absentee ballots by hand or advised voters for whom to vote, and allegations that absentee ballots sometimes were addressed to vacant or abandoned buildings, were cast in the name of dead voters, or were filled out by poll workers after polls closed, the court appointed monitors from Wayne County and the secretary of state's office to oversee Detroit's absentee balloting at the general election. Several days before the election, the monitors testified that they had witnessed ambassadors encouraging absentee voters to vote for Currie, who was in her own bid for a fourth term as city clerk. The court then ordered Currie removed from the absentee voting process and tasked the Wayne County Election Commission with overseeing it instead.[68] In a dramatic repudiation of her conduct by the electorate itself, Currie thereafter was defeated at the polls by Janice Winfrey, by a margin of fifty-three percent to forty-seven percent.[69]

State election officials generally regard the Winfrey administration as the dawning of a whole new day. At the same time, many other circumstances that surround Detroit's elections have not changed. The city continues to serve a large population of absentee voters, many in group homes, a circumstance ripe for both nefarious and inadvertent vote manipulation. The fact that the city's population is the poorest in the country may only compound these risks, to the extent that absentee voters, as well as volunteer election workers, can be induced to commit election fraud in exchange for some personal financial benefit. Meanwhile, Detroit's portion of the Qualified Voter File remains in need of correction, although the clerk's office is now making this more of a priority than did the previous administration, and has implemented an active file maintenance program.

UPCOMING CHANGES AND CHALLENGES

While some aspects of Michigan's election ecosystem, including its "motor voter" approach to voter registration and its early implementation of a statewide database, are functioning smoothly enough to have served as models for other states, the state's ecosystem continues to evolve. To her credit, Secretary of State Terri Lynn Land has noted that "keeping Michigan elections contemporary requires constant attention and vigilance," and to that end she put forward a twenty-point election reform agenda as part of her 2006 re-election campaign.[70] In addition, the state is now working to implement a controversial voter identification statute that had been dormant since it was passed in 1996, at the same time that the U.S. Supreme Court is considering the constitutionality of Indiana's analogous but more stringent voter identification requirement. Meanwhile, other challenges to Michigan's election ecosystem are on the horizon.

Secretary Land's Reform Agenda. Secretary Land's twenty-point plan includes several measures related to absentee voting, several measures related to the state's roster of registered voters, several measures involving polling place operations, several measures addressing post-election canvassing and recounts, and several miscellaneous measures. With respect to absentee voting, Secretary Land proposes: allowing first-time voters who register by mail to vote by absentee ballot, rather than being required to vote in person, provided they make some personal appearance elsewhere to verify their identity; instituting early in-person voting; clarifying the kinds of help that election assistants can provide to absentee voters; eliminating the notarization requirement for overseas absentee ballot applications (recently enacted); and establishing permanent absentee voter lists, limited to only those voters who request to be included on the list. Her proposals related to the state's registration list include: regulating third-party registration drives; saving administrative expense by creating a roster of "inactive" voters, consisting of voters whose confirmation notices are returned as undeliverable but who cannot yet legally be purged from the registration list under the National Voter Registration Act (which requires two federal elections to pass without voter activity before a voter can be purged); and pre-registering voters at age 16, as part of the state's program for young drivers, and then automatically adding them to the QVF on their 18th birthday.[71]

Secretary Land's proposals concerning polling place operations include: creating an electronic poll book to expedite voter check-in; experimenting with "voting centers" or "super precincts" that would reduce the number of polling places and allow voters to vote more conveniently; clarifying permissible Election Day activities near polling locations; and implementing a photo identification requirement, discussed further below. Her post-election reform proposals include: revising the qualifications for serving on the Board of State Canvassers; giving increased authority to the county boards of canvassers; conducting random audits of individual precincts; and creating uniform statewide rules for conducting local recounts.[72] A number of Secretary Land's proposals have found sponsors in the state legislature, but in most cases their future prospects are unclear, with the most important exception being the implementation of a voter identification requirement.

Michigan's "New" Voter Identification Requirement. Secretary Land's interest in implementing a voter identification requirement received a dramatic boost in July 2007, when the Michigan Supreme Court upheld the constitutionality of the state's decade-old voter ID law. The law, enacted by the Republican-controlled legislature in 1996, had never been implemented because the state's Democratic Attorney General at that time deemed it unconstitutional and suspended the law before it became effective. In 2005, the Michigan legislature re-enacted a revised version of the photo identification requirement, slightly altered to permit the use of digitized signatures in the state's Qualified Voter File, and in February 2006 the Michigan House of Representatives requested an advisory opinion from the state court concerning the constitutionality of the new law. The court directed the state Attorney General to file briefs both in favor and against the law. The Michigan Association of County Clerks filed a brief opposing the law.

In July 2007, the state supreme court issued a divided opinion upholding the law.[73] The five Republican justices found that the law did not constitute an impermissible poll tax or otherwise unduly impair the right to vote, because the law permits people without acceptable forms of identification to vote after signing an affidavit that they lack identification, and because the $10 fee to obtain a state identification card can be waived for the elderly, disabled, and poor. The two Democratic justices on the court dissented, arguing that the law imposes a severe and unjustifiable burden on Michigan voters, a burden that disproportionately impacts the state's racial and ethnic populations, as well as the poor, elderly, and disabled.[74] They argued that voters who do not have identification and instead sign an affidavit of identity may be subject to a polling place "challenge" concerning their identity, a potential that may intimidate some voters from appearing at the polls.[75] One dissenter also argued that even those who were entitled to have the fee waived would face additional financial (and logistical) costs in obtaining the identification card, particularly in the form of procuring the underlying documents necessary to apply for the card, and that these burdens would disproportionately impact the poor, the elderly, and immigrants.[76]

In response to the advisory opinion, Secretary Land issued instructions to implement the voter identification law. As required by the federal Voting Rights Act (because two townships in Michigan are subject to the preclearance requirement of section 5 of the Act),

Secretary Land sought preclearance from the U.S. Department of Justice of her implementing instructions. Her instructions concisely explain the identification requirement and the option of signing an affidavit in lieu of presenting photo identification. They also make clear that voters are not more vulnerable to challenge by signing an affidavit to meet the identification requirement than by presenting a photo identification. Instead, any challenge must be based on a specific reason to believe that a particular voter is not eligible to vote.[77]

Although the association of county clerks had opposed the voter identification requirement, some local administrators have been eager to be able to ask voters for identification, in order to confirm that voters are who they say they are. Unlike in some other states, Michigan poll workers do not match voters' signatures when they appear at the polling place with signatures on file in the poll books obtained from the voters' applications to vote. Instead, prior to the identification requirement, most Michigan poll workers compared the address and birth date that the voters provided on their application to vote (which voters complete at the polls) with data found on the registration list. Accordingly, the new photo identification requirement will for the first time give poll workers this additional means of verifying each voter's personal identity. Other local election officials, however, are worried about the identification requirement adding to the time that it takes to process each voter, creating lines and potential delays at the polls. Only experience will tell whether the requirement complicates or eases the voting process, although Michigan is now developing an electronic poll book that would allow poll workers to swipe a voter's driver's license, potentially speeding the process. Also unclear until the requirement is implemented is its impact on the number of provisional ballots that are cast, as well as counted, in a major election.

Meanwhile, the U.S. Supreme Court's consideration of the challenge to Indiana's much more stringent photo identification law is a wild card in predicting the impact of Michigan's identification requirement. The Indiana law is more stringent in that it lacks both Michigan's mechanism for helping indigent individuals to acquire an acceptable form of identification, and Michigan's option that allows individuals without identification to vote after signing an affidavit. Thus, if the Supreme Court upholds the Indiana law, the Michigan law presumably would have an easier time surviving a legal challenge. But if the Supreme Court invalidates the Indiana law, it will invite litigation over whether the less stringent Michigan requirement is also unconstitutional.[78]

Foreseeable Challenges. In addition to the challenge of implementing the new voter identification requirement smoothly and sensibly, Michigan may need to address several other election administration issues in the near future. Two key issues are preventing a recurrence of the kinds of misconduct that have occurred in Detroit, and finding and training an adequate number of poll workers. Meanwhile, the state's currently politicized judiciary leaves the entire election ecosystem vulnerable in the event that any critical matter of election administration, including an election contest, were to end up in court.

Reliably preventing a recurrence of Detroit's recent problems is a complicated task. The problems likely reflect a combination of fac-

tors, at least including insufficient training of election workers, inaccurate voter registration lists, and sloppy practices. They may also be a reflection of a culture of corruption, and of the power that an elected city clerk can have, especially in an impoverished community heavily dependent on government services and government jobs, where otherwise law-abiding citizens may more easily succumb to temptations to engage in bribery and graft. Under the new city clerk, Detroit has abolished its "ambassador" program for absentee voters; is improving the accuracy of its voter lists; and is working to develop better practices to protect the chain of custody (and therefore the recountability) of its ballots. It also has enhanced its election inspector training programs, to insure that its election workers understand what they can and cannot do, particularly in handling absentee ballots. But none of these cultural shifts can be accomplished overnight. Nor is Detroit the only municipality with similar potential weaknesses. Coupled with the fact that a number of Michigan cities elect their clerks, and that these election administrators are not subject to dismissal for poor election administration, some risk remains that a municipal clerk will take advantage of the circumstances often present in a large urban voting area to administer elections in a way that reinforces the clerk's own political base, or advances the clerk's own political ambitions, rather than serving the voters. Aggressive state and county oversight may help reduce this risk.

A related issue involves providing adequate staff to run the polls. In this regard, not just Detroit but Michigan as a whole finds itself confronting the same difficulty today that many other states do. Each of Michigan's over 5,000 precincts must have at least three "election inspectors," or poll workers,[79] although most precincts in fact need five or six workers. They must be drawn as evenly as possible from both major political parties, including at least one representative from each party. But the ranks of Michigan's election inspectors are aging, and each year fewer experienced workers return, whether through death, disability, or disinterest (particularly as poll operations become increasingly complex, technical, and stressful, turning off some long-time election inspectors). Meanwhile, younger replacements are not always volunteering in sufficient numbers to replace the shortfall.

Furthermore, even when sufficient new workers volunteer, they are often not well-trained. New Michigan poll workers are required to attend a training course in the weeks before the election (and then to repeat the training at least once every two years). But even the best training programs may leave poll workers only crudely familiar with the increasing number of details of administering an election – even if they can remember everything taught in the training course. Yet it would be difficult to compel them to attend more training, given that they are volunteers, paid only a pittance for devoting an entire day to the electoral process. Election inspectors work from before the polls open at 7:00 a.m. until after they close at 8:00 p.m., and for their service they typically receive only a modest stipend, set by each local municipality, usually less than $10 per hour (sometimes as little as $7 per hour, although in a few localities it may be as much as $15 per hour).[80]

To deal with this, local officials describe the need to spend more time and become more innovative in recruiting poll workers. As a partial solution, since 1997 Michigan law has allowed 16- and 17-year-olds, though not yet voters, to serve as election inspectors, provided that the primary election inspectors in each precinct are at least eighteen.[81] The response to this initiative has been nothing but positive, and with creativity local officials may be able to take greater advantage of it. Meanwhile, the secretary of state continues to look for new ways to improve poll worker training, including developing on-line training and refining the two-day "school" that the bureau of elections runs to train the trainers, who themselves must be certified in order to conduct training programs for election inspectors.[82] And Detroit reported "overwhelming" response to its media appeals for volunteers to work the November 2007 election,[83] even as some other Michigan localities continued to struggle to find enough poll workers.

Finally, Michigan's election ecosystem may be at risk given the obvious partisan tension in the state supreme court. As described above, this divide was evident in the court's recent decision regarding the state's voter identification statute. But it has not been limited to just this case. Indeed, the ideological feud within the court has boiled over into public view in a number of cases and an embarrassing series of recent events. In an article in *The New York Times* in early 2007, the feuding was described as a "soap opera," the court's justices were admonished to "start acting like grown ups," and the justices themselves accused each other of pitching "tantrums."[84]

Fortunately, election contests have been rare in Michigan. In part this is because the state has an effective administrative recount process that can handle most issues, including claims of fraud. A seldom invoked provision of state law also permits a judicial contest of an election in which the outcome depends on whether to count specific ballots that were formally challenged on Election Day.[85] Such a challenge may occur when either an election inspector or an elector present at the polling place has good reason to suspect that an applicant to vote is not a qualified voter. When a challenge occurs, the ballot is coded so that it can be specifically identified in a subsequent contest action, allowing the court hearing such an action to make a specific adjustment to the official results based on the outcome of the contest.[86]

Michigan law also leaves room for other types of litigation over the validity of an election outcome, primarily through a *"quo warranto"* proceeding. These proceedings provide a mechanism for courts to consider claims that material fraud or error has affected the outcome of an election, resulting in a "usurpation of office" by the wrong individual.[87] The few applications of this statutory provision suggest that a Michigan court would be willing to vacate or even reverse an election outcome if a candidate could show that such fraud or error had occurred.[88]

Although Michigan has no recent history of litigating the outcome of an election, it is not hard to imagine any number of election problems or allegations of election misconduct ending up in court. Furthermore, the increasing complexity of administering today's elections only provides more potential ways for problems to arise that candidates could claim have tainted an election outcome. It therefore is important to consider the place in Michigan's election ecosystem of its state courts.

To give an extreme example, the Chief Justice of the Michigan Supreme Court is up for re-election in 2008 and is likely to face an aggressive challenge. If an election contest or *quo warranto* action arose concerning his re-election, it obviously would put the rest of the Michigan judiciary in an awkward position (assuming that he and his colleagues recused themselves and let lower court judges resolve it). Even discounting the likelihood of this remote (though plausible) example, it is not difficult to imagine the public cynicism that could attend the current supreme court's resolution of any post-election contest, or other disputed matter of election administration that might determine a specific election outcome.

Once again, this demonstrates the critical importance of resolving as many matters of election administration as possible in advance of any particular election. But preparation also should include planning for the possibility of a difficult issue that must be resolved after an election. Until Michigan either develops an alternative process for adjudicating those election disputes that some day will arise over a specific election, or its state supreme court re-establishes to the public its professionalism and neutrality, Michigan will have a weaker system for resolving a statewide or high-profile election contest than it should.

REFERENCES

1. *See Taylor's Triumph*, (DETROIT) METRO TIMES, Nov. 23, 2005, http://www.metrotimes.com/editorial/story.asp?id=8532.

2. *See* Sven Gustafson, *Dems to Send Lawyers, Volunteers Swarming to State's Polling Places*, LANSING STATE JOURNAL, Nov. 2, 2006, at 4B.

3. *See* William P. Browne & Kenneth VerBurg, MICHIGAN POLITICS AND GOVERNMENT 300-301 (1995); Secretary Terri Lynn Land, *Michigan's Election System Structure Overview*, http://www.michigan.gov/sos/0,1607,7-127-1633_8716-27476--,00.html.

4. *See id.* at 300-301.

5. U.S. Census Bureau 2005 estimates. *See* http://www.census.gov/popest/cities/tables/SUB-EST2005-04-26.xls.

6. *See* Debbie Gebolys & Tim Doulin, *Poor Picture of Ohio*, COLUMBUS DISPATCH, Aug. 29, 2007, at 1A.

7. *See* William P. Browne & Kenneth VerBurg, *supra* note 3, at xxi, xxxi-xxxii, 3; THE HISTORY OF MICHIGAN LAW 1-2 (Paul Finkelman & Martin J. Hershock, eds., 2006).

8. *See id.* at xiv.

9. *See* William P. Browne & Kenneth VerBurg, *supra* note 3, at 14.

10. *See* id. at 22.

11. *See* 42 U.S.C. § 1973gg.

12. *See* MICH. COMP. L. ANN. § 168.641; Chong W. Pyen, *Bills May Simplify Elections: All State Voting Would Be Consolidated Into 4 Designated Days*, THE ANN ARBOR NEWS, Jan. 2, 2004. at B1.

13. *See* William P. Browne & Kenneth VerBurg, *supra* note 3, at 11.

14. *See id.* at xxiv-xxviii; Daniel J. Elazar, *American Federalism* 115-121 (1984).

15. *See* HELP AMERICA VOTE ACT: MICHIGAN'S STATE PLAN, Sept. 27, 2005, at 3, *available at* http://www.michigan.gov/sos/0,1607,7-127-1633-77937--,00.html.

16. MICH. COMP. L. ANN. § 168.341.

17. MICH. COMP. L. ANN. § 168.321.

18. MICH. COMP. L. ANN. §§ 168.25, 168.26. In charter townships, the commission consists of the clerk and two appointees of the township board. MICH. COMP. L. ANN. § 42.4.

19. MICH. COMP. L. ANN. § 168.30a; http://www.michigan.gov/sos/0,1607,7-127-1633_8716-27476--,00.html.

20. *Hare v. Berrien County Bd. of Election Com'rs*, 129 N.W.2d 864, 866 (Mich., 1964).

21. MICH. COMP. L. ANN. § 168.32.

22. *Id.*

23. *Id.*

24. For the MAMC website, see http://www.michiganclerks.org.

25. *See* MICH. COMP. L. ANN. § 168.737a.

26. These can be found at http://www.michigan.gov/sos/0,1607,7-127-1633_11976_33971---,00.html, or through links on the Michigan Secretary of State's website at http://www.michigan.gov/sos.

27. MICH. COMP. L. ANN. § 168.509q.

28. MICH. COMP. L. ANN. § 257.307.

29. MICH. COMP. L. ANN. § 257.204a.

30. *See* National Commission on Federal Election Reform, TO ASSURE PRIDE AND CONFIDENCE IN THE ELECTORAL PROCESS 32 (2001), *available at* http://www.reformelections.org/ncfer.asp#finalreport.

31. *See* Justin Levitt, Wendy R. Weiser, & Ana Munoz, MAKING THE LIST: DATABASE MATCHING AND VERIFICATION PROCESSES FOR VOTER REGISTRATION (Brennan Center for Justice, March 24, 2006).

32. MICH. COMP. L. ANN. § 168.510.

33. Lisa M. Collins, *Feds Demand Michigan Voter Roll Cleanup*, DETROIT NEWS, Feb. 28, 2006, at 1A.

34. *See* U.S. Election Assistance Commission, THE IMPACT OF THE NATIONAL VOTER REGISTRATION ACT, 2005-2006, at 27 (2006 Election Administration and Voting Survey).

35. Indeed, we are unsure how a court would respond to a claim that permitting a voter to vote in a jurisdiction in which the voter no longer resides violates the judicially enforceable principle of "one person-one vote," made applicable to state and local elections some forty years ago in *Reynolds v. Sims*, 377 U.S. 533 (1964), and *Avery v. Midland County*, 390 U.S. 474 (1968).

36. MICH. COMP. L. ANN. §§ 168.500d, 168.523a.

37. MICH. COMP. L. ANN. § 168.523a.

38. *See id.*; MICH. COMP. L. ANN. §§ 168.745, 168.746.

39. *See* Secretary Terri Lynn Land, *County Provisional Ballot Report*, Nov. 7, 2006 General Election.

40. *See* HELP AMERICA VOTE ACT: MICHIGAN'S STATE PLAN, supra note 15, at 7-8; Secretary Terri Lynn Land, A UNIFORM VOTING SYSTEM FOR MICHIGAN 9 (Aug. 4, 2003), *available at* http://www.michigan.gov/ documents/Uniform_Voting_System_2_71047_7.pdf.

41. MICH. COMP. L. ANN. § 168.37.

42. *See* Secretary Terri Lynn Land, A UNIFORM VOTING SYSTEM FOR MICHIGAN , *supra* note 40, at 5-6.

43. *See id.* at 1.

44. *See* Michigan Secretary of State, *Press Release: Halfway There!*, Apr. 19, 2005, *available at* http://www.michigan.gov/sos/0,1607,7-127--115817--,00.html.

45. *See* Stacey Range, *Poll Workers Mastering Tech Challenges to Voting*, LANSING STATE JOURNAL, Nov. 6, 2006, at 1A.

46. *See Secretary of State Land Introduces Accessible Equipment for Voters with Disabilities*, U.S. STATE NEWS, 2006 WLNR 7541030, May 2, 2006.

47. *See* Stephen Frye, *Clerks Criticize Voting Machines*, OAKLAND PRESS (Michigan), Dec. 30, 2006, at A1.

48. *See Complaint, Paralyzed Veterans of America v. McPherson*, No. 3:06-cv-4670 (N.D. Cal. filed Aug. 1, 2006), *available at* http://moritzlaw.osu.edu/blogs/tokaji/PVA-Complaint.pdf.

49. *See* Barrie Barber, *Williams Could Demand Recount*, SAGINAW NEWS, Nov. 10, 2006.

50. *See State Certifies Nov.2 Election*, GRAND RAPIDS PRESS, Nov. 23, 2004, at B6.

51. *See* David Josar, Lisa M. Collins & Brad Heath, *Absentee Ballots Tainted?*, DETROIT NEWS, Oct. 30, 2005, at 1A.

52. *See* Kate Zernike & William Yardley, *THE 2004 CAMPAIGN: Complaints; Charges of Dirty Tricks, Fraud and Voter Suppression Already Flying in Several States*, N.Y. TIMES, Nov. 1, 2004, sec. A, p. 16.

53. *See Bay County Democratic Party v. Land*, 347 F. Supp. 2d 404 (E.D. Mich. 2004).

54. *See Sandusky County Democratic Party v. Blackwell*, 387 F.3d 565 (6th Cir. 2004).

55. *See* Barrie Barber, *supra* note 49.

56. *See id.*

57. *See* Theresa Roach, Justin Engel, & Erin Alberty, *Turnout Forces Count by Hand*, SAGINAW NEWS, Nov. 8, 2007.

58. *See Mich. Republican Party: Wayne County Judge Rules Michigan Democratic Party and their Challengers Violated Michigan Election Law*, U.S. FEDERAL NEWS, Nov. 7, 2007; *see also* Nathan Cemenska, *Overview of Michigan Voting Process in November, 2006*, Election Law @ Moritz, http://moritzlaw.osu.edu/electionlaw/ election06/MichiganElectionOverviewNovember2006.php.

59. *See* Lisa Almendinger, John Mulcahy, Tom Gantert, & Art Aisner, *Local Voter Turnout Steady*, ANN ARBOR NEWS, Nov. 8, 2006.

60. *See* Nathan Cemenska, *supra* note 58.

61. *In Michigan, Even Dead Vote*, DETROIT NEWS, Feb. 26, 2006, at 1A.

62. *See* David Josar, Lisa M. Collins & Brad Heath, *Absentee Ballots Tainted?*, *supra* note 51. Of course, excluding Detroit's contribution the statewide figure would be in the high teens.

63. *See id.*

64. *See id.*

65. *See* Taylor's Triumph, *supra* note 1; *FBI Goes to Court Over Detroit Ballots*, CLICKONDETROIT.COM, Nov. 8, 2005, at http://www.clickondetroit.com/print/ 5281743/detail.html.

66. *See Taylor v. Currie*, ___ N.W.2d ___ (Mich. Ct. App., Oct. 25, 2007), *available at* http://courtofappeals.mijud.net/ documents/OPINIONS/FINAL/COA/20071025_C269684_1 15_269684.OPN.PDF.

67. *See* David Josar, Lisa M. Collins & Brad Heath, *Absentee Ballots Tainted?*, *supra* note 51, at 1A.

68. *See Monitor Finds Evidence of Detroit Absentee Voter Fraud*, CLICKONDETROIT.COM, Nov. 4, 2005, at http://www.clickondetroit.com/print/5254036/detail.html; *Taylor v. Currie*, *supra* note 59.

69. *See* Taylor's Triumph, *supra* note 1.

70. *See* MICHIGAN ELECTIONS: A PLAN FOR THE 21st CENTURY, available at http://www.michigan.gov/documents/ Election_Reform_20061_148801_7.pdf.

71. *See id.*

72. *See id.*

73. *In re Request for Advisory Opinion Regarding Constitutionality of 2005 PA 71*, ___ N.W. 2d ___, 479 Mich. 1, 2007 WL 2410868 °12 (Mich. 2007).

74. *See id.* at °23, °35-°36.

75. *See id.* at °27, ° 31. The majority countered that a voter could still only be challenged on the basis of a specific reason to believe the voter was not qualified. *See id.* at °14.

76. *See id.*, 2007 WL 2410868 °25-°26.

77. *See Secretary Terri Lynn Land, Implementing Michigan's Voter Identification Requirements*, Oct. 19, 2007, *available at* http://www.michigan.gov/documents/sos/Photo_ID_Proc_for _Elec_Inspector_212804_7.pdf.

78. The Detroit branch of the NAACP has already signaled an interest in challenging the Michigan voter identification requirement. *See* Santiago Esparza, *NAACP to Challenge Voter Law*, DETROIT NEWS, Oct. 26, 2007, at 1B.

79. *See* MICH. COMP. L. ANN. § 168.674.

80. *See* http://www.michiganclerks.org/resources/ documents/WageCompar-ElectWorkDec06.xls.

81. *See* MICH. COMP. L. ANN. § 168.677(4).

82. *See* MICH. COMP. L. ANN. § 168.33.

83. *See* John Wisely, *Metro Detroit: Elections Workers Needed*, DETROIT FREE PRESS, Oct. 2, 2007, at 3.

84. Adam Liptak, *Unfettered Debate Takes Unflattering Turn In Michigan Supreme Court*, N.Y. TIMES, Jan. 19, 2007, at 21.

85. MICH. COMP. L. ANN. § 168.748.

86. MICH. COMP. L. ANN. §§ 168.727, 168.745.

87. MICH. COMP. L. ANN. § 600.4505.

88. *See, e.g., St. Joseph v. City of St. Joseph,* 127 N.W.2d 858 (Mich. 1964); *Attorney General ex rel. Miller v. Miller,* 253 N.W. 241 (Mich. 1934); *Smith v. Scio Twp.,* 433 N.W.2d 855 (Mich. App. 1988); *Gracey v. Grosse Point Farms Clerk,* 452 N.W.2d 471 (Mich. App. 1989).

Michigan:
NINE AREAS

INSTITUTIONAL ARRANGEMENTS

The Michigan Secretary of State is the state's chief election officer, assisted by the state elections director, who is appointed by the secretary of state and who heads the state bureau of elections. M.C.L.A. (Michigan Compiled Laws Annotated) §§ 168.21; 168.32. The bureau of elections oversees Michigan's statewide voter database, publishes newsletters, and assists local officials with the administration of elections. At the local level, primary authority for conducting elections is assigned to municipal clerks, most of them elected, although county officials also play a role. M.C.L.A. §§ 168.30a, 168.23, 168.24a. City, village, and township clerks maintain registration records for their individual jurisdictions and oversee Election Day operations at the polls. M.C.L.A. §§ 168.502, 168.678. Each municipality also maintains a three-member city or township election commission, responsible for dividing their jurisdiction into precincts, assessing the need for voting machines, ballots, and other materials, and appointing precinct "election inspectors," or poll workers. M.C.L.A. §§ 168.30 et seq. County clerks are responsible for training poll workers, M.C.L.A. § 168.33, and also receive and compile unofficial returns from all precincts in their county immediately following an election, M.C.L.A. § 168.809. Boards of county canvassers determine the results of races for offices within the borders of their respective counties, M.C.L.A. § 168.826, and transmit tallies in multi-county and statewide races to the Board of State Canvassers. M.C.L.A. §§ 168.828, 168.841.

VOTER REGISTRATION/STATEWIDE DATABASE

Michigan's Qualified Voter File ("QVF"), its statewide voter registration database, is now a decade old. It receives information and updates directly from the state's Driver's License database, and also is coordinated with Michigan's "Master Death File," a database tracking the state's deceased. M.C.L.A. §§ 168.509q; 168.510. Voters are removed from the QVF if the United States Postal Service sends a letter to the election board notifying them that the voter has moved outside of the jurisdiction. M.C.L.A. § 168.509aa.

Voters can register to vote by mail or in person, either by appearing at the clerk's office or while obtaining a driver's license. M.C.L.A. §§ 168.500a; 168.509v. Registration applications must be received on or prior to the thirtieth day before an election. M.C.L.A. § 168.497. The application will be rejected if the voter fails to sign the application, M.C.L.A. §§ 168.500a, 168.509r(3), 168.509o(3), and also may be rejected if the voter provides an addresss that is zoned for business. Voters will receive notification if their application is rejected, and will have an opportunity to correct the deficiency as long as it is prior to the thirtieth day before an election. M.C.L.A. § 168.500d.

CHALLENGES TO VOTER ELIGIBILITY

Before Election Day, a voter's eligibility can be challenged either by a municipal clerk or by another voter. M.C.L.A. § 168.512. Voters who fail to respond to a clerk challenge will be removed from the QVF after two November general elections. M.C.L.A. § 168.509cc. Voters challenged by another voter must appear before the clerk within thirty days of the challenge to defend themselves or they will be removed from the QVF. M.C.L.A. § 168.512. A voter who challenges another voter without good cause can be charged with a misdemeanor. M.C.L.A. § 168.512. On Election Day, election inspectors and any registered voter of the precinct may challenge another person's eligibility to vote, but only on the basis of a reasonable belief that the voter is ineligible. M.C.L.A. §168.727 subd.(1). Polling place challengers also may be appointed by candidates, political committees, and citizen groups. M.C.L.A. § 168.730(1). Challenged voters are asked questions about their eligibility under oath, and those who affirm their eligibility are allowed to vote using ballots marked as "challenged" with an identifying number so that they may subsequently be excluded from the official tallies if a challenged voter is determined to have been ineligible. M.C.L.A. §§ 168.729, 168.745-749.

PROVISIONAL VOTING

Only 5,000 provisional ballots were cast statewide in Michigan in 2004, and only 3,000 in 2006. The state has a very low rate of provisional voting in part because it does not allow voters who have moved within the state to use a provisional ballot as a means of changing their voter registration address. M.C.L.A. § 168.523a. Instead, if they have moved either within sixty days before the election, or only within the same municipality, such voters may return to the precinct of their former address to vote one last time. M.C.L.A. § 168.507a(2).

Michigan uses two different types of provisional ballots. Voters who sign an affidavit attesting to having registered but whose names are not found in the QVF may vote a standard ballot, provided they can show proper identification. M.C.L.A. § 168.523a. The ballot is marked as a "challenged" ballot, and counted as an ordinary ballot. M.C.L.A. § 168.523a(4). Voters who cannot produce proper identification or proof of residence at the polls may vote the second type of provisional ballot, termed an "envelope" ballot. M.C.L.A. § 168.523a. This type of ballot is only counted if election officials can verify the voter's eligibility after the election. M.C.L.A. § 168.523a(5). Voters using an envelope ballot have six days after the election to provide proper identification. M.C.L.A. § 168.523a(7).

EARLY AND ABSENTEE VOTING

Michigan does not presently provide for either early voting or no-excuse absentee voting. Absentee ballots are available for voters who are: physically unable to come to the polls; unable to come to the polls for religious reasons; working as a poll worker in another precinct; at least 60 years old; expecting to be absent during the poll operation hours; or confined waiting trial on felony charges. M.C.L.A. § 168.758. A request to vote absentee must arrive between the seventy-fifth day prior to the election and the Saturday prior to the election. M.C.L.A. § 168.759. A completed absentee ballot must arrive by 8:00 p.m. on Election Day, whether by mail or in person, except on extenuating circumstances. M.C.L.A. §§ 168.764a, 168.759b.

VOTING TECHNOLOGY

Optical scan ballots with in-precinct electronic tabulating equipment are now used throughout the state. For November elections and their primaries, precincts with more than 1,000 registered voters must have at least one tabulating machine for every 500 voters. Precincts with 1,000-3,000 registered voters must have one machine for every 600 voters. In other elections, the local election commission determines the number of machines. M.C.L.A. § 168.661. If the voting machines fail during the election, officials can use special paper ballots. M.C.L.A. § 168.782b. Each precinct must also have available at least 125% of the number of provisional ballots that were cast in the election held four years earlier. M.C.L.A. § 168.689.

POLLING PLACE OPERATIONS

On Election Day, at least three "election inspectors" (poll workers) must be present at each precinct (although more are typically required in most precincts), including at least one from each major political party. M.C.L.A. §§ 168.672, 168.674. Municipal clerks must train election inspectors within twenty days prior to each election. M.C.L.A. § 168.683. Each inspector must either have attended at least one training session or passed an examination in the past two years. M.C.L.A. § 168.683. In turn, municipal clerks must complete a State Board of Elections training program on how to train precinct election inspectors. M.C.L.A. § 168.33. Visually impaired voters can receive assistance from a person of their choosing, and disabled voters who cannot physically mark the ballot can receive assistance from election inspectors. M.C.L.A § 168.751. If election inspectors deem it necessary, a language interpreter also may accompany a voter into the voting booth. M.C.L.A. § 168.736.

BALLOT SECURITY

Michigan statutes have detailed chain-of-custody provisions for both physical ballots and voting equipment. M.C.L.A. §§ 168.714-716, 168.724, 168.726, 168.735, 168.765-767, 168.805. If the chain of custody is not followed, the votes affected may be "unrecountable" should a dispute arise (in which case the original tallies must stand). M.C.L.A. § 168.871(1)(c). Prior to the election the municipal clerk will arrange, test, and lock the voting machines at the polling places. The machines then must be under the supervision of an election inspector at all times. M.C.L.A. § 168.778. On Election Day, the elections inspectors must periodically examine machines to make sure no tampering has occurred. M.C.L.A. § 168.790. When the polls close, the inspectors seal the machines and display the counters and any person in the polling place may compare the returns with the counters on the machines. M.C.L.A. § 168.791. After counting the ballots at the precinct, poll workers tie the ballots together, place both the ballots and the memory cartridges from the optical scan tabulators in ballot bags, and seal the bags. M.C.L.A. § 168.735. The sealed bags are then placed in ballot containers with metal seals. M.C.L.A. § 168.805. The poll workers record the identification number for each seal, sign the poll books, and deliver the containers to the municipal clerk. M.C.L.A. § 168.805.

Michigan has just implemented a photo identification requirement for all voters who vote at the polls. Voters without acceptable identification may vote a regular ballot if they sign an affidavit concerning their lack of identification. M.C.L.A. § 168.523.

POST-ELECTION PROCESSES

At the end of Election Day, election inspectors read the results from the tabulating machines and enter them into the statement of returns. M.C.L.A. § § 168.801 et seq. If the totals exceed the number of voters who submitted ballot applications in that precinct, election inspectors will randomly select ballots and deduct them until the numbers match. M.C.L.A. § 168.802.

A recount is automatic if a statewide election has a margin of 2,000 votes or fewer. M.C.L.A. § 168.880a. In addition, any candidate or voter who believes fraud or mistake has occurred in the vote counting can petition for a recount. A petitioner must pay $10 per precinct to be recounted, which will be refunded if the recount changes the outcome of the election. For national or statewide offices, the petition must be filed within 48 hours of the completion of the official canvass. For other elections, the deadline is within six days. M.C.L.A. §§ 168.865-868, 168.879-882. In recounts for federal offices, statewide offices or ballot issues, Michigan circuit judges, and state legislative seats, the board of state canvassers conducts the recount; in all other cases, the appropriate board of county canvassers conducts the recount. M.C.L.A. §§ 168.879, 168.841.

Recounts should be completed within thirty days following the last day on which the recount petition could have been filed, except in primary elections, when the time is twenty days. M.C.L.A. § 168.875. At the discretion of the board of canvassers, recounts of machine tabulations may themselves involve machine retabulations, rather than manual tallying. M.C.L.A § 168.871(6).

Michigan's post-election judicial contest statute applies to elections in which the eligibility of "challenged" ballots is in question. M.C.L.A. § 168.747-749. For many other issues, such as absentee ballot fraud or voting machine malfunctions, the state's *quo warranto* statute also can be used to litigate the legitimacy of an election outcome. M.C.L.A. § 168.861.

CHAPTER 6: WISCONSIN'S ELECTION ECOSYSTEM
PROGRESSIVE REFORM AND DECENTRALIZED ADMINISTRATION

LIKE ANY OTHER STATE, Wisconsin's election ecosystem can only be fully understood in light of its history and political culture. Although Wisconsin today is associated with a progressive vision of democracy, that was not always the case.

In the 1800s, "machine" politics was a prominent feature of Wisconsin government. Perhaps the most famous incident occurred in the 1855 gubernatorial election, at a time when Democrats controlled state politics. The party-boss candidate, incumbent Democrat William Barstow, won by 157 votes, amid allegations of ballot tampering. This led the Republican challenger Coles Bashford to hold his own competing inauguration. For three months, the Wisconsin Supreme Court investigated while both candidates claimed victory. Eventually, the court found ballot tampering in fact had occurred, causing Barstow to resign and Bashford to be sworn in as the state's first Republican governor. This was hardly the end of political corruption in Wisconsin, however, as Governor Bashford ultimately left Wisconsin in disgrace after it was discovered that he had received some $50,000 from railroad companies.[1]

A signal event in cleaning up Wisconsin's politics was the election of 1900, which ushered in an era of reform led by Robert LaFollette. LaFollette and his Progressive Republican allies sought to curtail corruption, limit the influence of political parties, and enhance participatory democracy.[2]

To a considerable extent, Wisconsin's current election system retains features of the political culture associated with the LaFollette era of progressive reform. Citizens of Wisconsin vote in exceptionally large numbers,[3] and since 1976, the state has permitted voters to register at the polls on Election Day.[4] At the state level, an administrator appointed by and responsible to a bipartisan board oversees matters of election administration.[5] Wisconsin has mostly been free of the accusations that have dogged chief election officials in other states, particularly secretaries of state elected on a partisan basis. At the local level, election administration is primarily entrusted to municipal, rather than county, officials. Despite the fact that many of these officials are elected, they are generally respected for the professional and nonpartisan manner in which they administer elections.

At the same time, Wisconsin's decentralized system of running elections has a significant downside. In other states where elections are administered at the county level, the local entities responsible for administering elections may number only in the dozens. In Wisconsin, by contrast, elections are run at the municipal level, with state law vesting primary authority over election administration in city, town, and village clerks. There are 1,851 municipalities in the state, ranging in size from small towns with a single polling place to the City of Milwaukee, with 343,867 registered voters.[6] Foremost among the challenges that this fragmented system presents is the difficulty of achieving uniformity in the administration of elections across the state.

The most glaring example of this is the state's problem-filled transition to a statewide registration system mandated by HAVA, made especially difficult because most Wisconsin municipalities did not even have voter registration before 2006. Another issue, certainly not unique to Wisconsin, is the difficulty that the state might experience in the event of a contested statewide election. Wisconsin voters opted for Senator Kerry over President Bush by only a few thousand votes in 2004, and the state would likely have become a focal point for post-election jousting over the outcome had Ohio swung the other way. As discussed below, Wisconsin would then have faced the prospect of a fragmented recount and contest procedure that would have been difficult to resolve under the existing federal calendar.

Despite the state's progressive tradition, the nation's increasing partisanship attending issues of election administration since 2000 has not left Wisconsin unaffected. The most significant election administration dispute has been over voter identification. Wisconsin Republicans argue that such measures are needed to combat fraud, arguing that a photo identification requirement is needed to confirm that the person voting is really who he or she claims to be, especially given the state's liberal registration rules. Democrats on the other hand oppose photo identification requirements, arguing that there is little evidence of actual polling place fraud and that a photo identification requirement would disproportionately affect racial minorities and other groups who are already underrepresented in the electorate. Wisconsin's debate thus echoes the one raging throughout the country over the extent to which different electoral practices promote or hinder the values of access and integrity.

We divide our discussion of Wisconsin's election ecosystem into five parts. First, we provide a structural overview of the state's election system, focusing on the delegation of authority to municipal election officials, as well as recent changes in state-level authority over election administration. Second, we examine Wisconsin's Election Day registration system. Third, we discuss the debate over voter fraud and voter identification. Fourth, we examine the problems that have attended the implementation of Wisconsin's statewide registration database. Fifth, we examine the state's system for resolving post-election disputes, including problems that might occur in the event of a contested presidential or other statewide election.

STRUCTURAL OVERVIEW

In one sense, Wisconsin has one of the most decentralized – one might even say fragmented – election systems in the country. As a matter of state law, primary authority for running elections rests with officials at the municipal rather than the county level.[7] In Wisconsin, municipalities may be towns, villages, or cities. Each municipality has a clerk, who is in charge of overseeing the administration of elections in his or her jurisdiction. The statutory duties of municipal clerks include: the purchase and maintenance of voting equipment; the distribution of ballots to polling places; the delivery of absentee ballots; voter education; the accommodation of people with disabilities; reporting suspected election fraud to district attorneys; and otherwise ensuring compliance with state election laws.[8] Municipal clerks also have responsibility for the training of poll workers, making sure that they are familiar with both state law and the voting equipment used.[9]

To say that municipalities in Wisconsin vary greatly would be an extreme understatement. In size, they range from tiny villages with only a handful of registered voters to the cities of Milwaukee and Madison. For example, in the November 2006 general election, the Village of Livingston (located about 65 miles west of Madison) reported only three voters, none of whom voted absentee.[10] By contrast, the City of Milwaukee reported a turnout of 172,676, with over 11,000 voters casting absentee ballots, and a total citywide voter registration of over 300,000.[11] A lengthy report following Milwaukee's 2004 election found serious administrative problems in voter registration, absentee ballots, polling place accessibility, poll worker recruitment and training, and other areas. Especially troubling was the handling of registration forms, though it was believed that the implementation of the statewide registration database would mitigate some of these errors.[12] Although the city has worked hard to make improvements, this experience exemplifies the difficulties in running elections in large urban municipalities.

It is sometimes said that there are really two Wisconsins: Milwaukee, and the rest of the state. Milwaukee is not only larger but also much more racially and ethnically diverse than the rest of the state, with a higher percentage of people living below the poverty line.

Scratching the surface, however, reveals a much more complex reality. While Milwaukee is indeed the biggest city in the state, there are thirteen Wisconsin cities with populations over

50,000.[13] Yet most Wisconsin municipalities have fewer than 5,000 registered voters and, for this reason, under state law were not even required to have voter registration before 2006. Until then, fewer than 350 of the state's 1,851 municipalities actually had voter registration, although approximately three-quarters of the voting population lived in larger municipalities with voter registration.

The issues that Wisconsin's diverse municipalities face in running elections vary with their size. The City of Milwaukee faces huge challenges each election cycle in making sure its registration lists are accurate, recruiting and training enough qualified poll workers, and ensuring that absentee ballots are distributed sufficiently in advance of Election Day. Smaller jurisdictions face a different set of problems. A typical town clerk in a smaller jurisdiction may have a skeleton staff (if any at all), a small budget, and a number of other responsibilities in addition to elections. As of 2007, approximately 400 of Wisconsin's 1,851 municipal clerks did not have email access, a reality that complicates efforts to make sure that election officials are kept updated and that election administration is consistent across the state.

The mechanism for selecting municipal election officials is not uniform in Wisconsin. Some are elected on a nonpartisan basis and others appointed by the municipality's governing body. Any city or county with a population greater than 500,000 (currently only Milwaukee) must have a board of election commissioners, consisting of three members.[14] Those members are selected from lists provided by the two largest political parties in the jurisdiction – two commissioners from the majority party and one from the minority party.[15] Thus, in Milwaukee, the

City Board of Elections Commissioners is responsible for administering elections, with the board's members and executive director appointed by the mayor.

Whether elections are administered by an elected clerk, an appointed clerk, or an appointed board, it is possible to imagine allegations of bias emerging. Even when election officials are not selected on a partisan basis, they might discharge their duties in a partisan manner. Yet there is little evidence that this has actually happened in Wisconsin's recent history. This may be attributable to the state's moralistic political culture, which places a high value on nonpartisanship and professionalism.[16]

In most states, county officials have primary responsibility for running elections. By contrast, in Wisconsin the duties of county officials are more limited, though they are certainly important. Wisconsin's seventy-two county clerks are responsible for making sure that municipalities have adequate supplies, most notably ballots.[17] In addition, county clerks are responsible for convening three-member canvassing boards that handle post-election recounts in federal, state, or county elections.[18] Typically, the county board of canvassers consists of the county clerk and two other members, one a Democrat and one a Republican, as a way of promoting neutrality. Wisconsin elects its county clerks, with candidates running as nominees for their party.[19]

County clerks can play a critical role in getting municipal clerks within their jurisdiction on the same page, especially where changes must be made. An example is the transition to new voting technology, pursuant to HAVA's requirements, that took place prior to the 2006

elections. Although each municipality was responsible for choosing its own election system, the Clerk of Dane County (which includes the City of Madison and surrounding areas) worked to promote uniformity across the county. With the encouragement of the county clerk, the sixty-one municipalities in the county ended up moving to the same optical-scan voting technology. Later, the county clerk's office encouraged municipalities to adopt a consistent coding system and invited clerks to attend equipment demonstrations. The county clerk also became the purchasing agent for the machines that the municipalities selected to meet HAVA's disability access requirements.

In addition to providing ballots for all elections, Dane County assists its local officials by offering training for inspectors and clerks in the county. The county also serves as a registration "provider" for twenty-nine municipalities, assuming responsibility on their behalf for entering and maintaining information in the statewide voter registration system required by HAVA. As in other counties, the job of the county's elected clerk is not limited to elections. Yet the Dane County Clerk, himself a former municipal clerk,[20] reports that he spends more than half of his time on elections, much of it communicating with municipal clerks.

The high degree of municipal authority in Wisconsin undoubtedly has both benefits and costs. On the positive side, running elections at the local level means that each clerk is responsible for a smaller number of voters. This can make it easier to ensure that registration lists are accurate. It may also make it easier to recruit poll workers and may contribute to smoother election-day operations. Among the negatives are that the resources, both time and money, of municipal clerks are very limited. It can also be difficult to ensure consistency across the state, or even within a single county, given both the number of municipalities contained in each and the differences between them.

At the state level, Wisconsin law until 2007 vested ultimate authority over election administration with the State Elections Board (SEB). The board consisted of eight members, one designated by each of the following: (1) the chief justice of the Wisconsin Supreme Court, (2) the governor, (3) the majority leader of the state senate, (4) the minority leader of the state senate, (5) the speaker of the state assembly, (6) the minority leader of the state assembly, (7) the chair of the Democratic Party, and (8) the chair of the Republican Party.[21] The State Elections Board was also responsible for the enforcement of campaign finance laws, as well as the administration of elections.[22] In practice, much of the state-level responsibility for election administration lay with the executive director of the State Elections Board, who, by statute, served as the chief election officer for the state and discharged the board's responsibilities on a day-to-day basis.[23] Like all employees of the board, the executive director was required to be nonpartisan.[24]

From 1983 until 2007, Kevin Kennedy served as the executive director of the Wisconsin State Elections Board. Mr. Kennedy's long tenure and reputation for professionalism and nonpartisanship allowed him to exercise his election administration responsibilities with relatively little interference from the board, the partisan composition of which has varied

during his tenure. On the whole, the office appears to have been reasonably successful in ensuring some consistency in the administration of elections across the state, notwithstanding the inherent difficulty of doing so given the number and diversity of local jurisdictions.

In 2007, the Wisconsin legislature enacted a law that significantly restructured the administration of elections at the state level. Under 2007 Wisconsin Act 1 ("Act 1"), responsibility over election administration is now vested in a six-person Government Accountability Board ("GAB").[25] This board consists entirely of retired judges. A committee consisting of appellate judges is responsible for submitting a list of possible GAB members to the governor, who is to select nominees from this list. GAB members must then be confirmed by the legislature. After the initial group of nominees, confirmation must be by a two-thirds vote of the state senate.[26] Any measure passed by the board must be taken by four of the GAB's six members. The structure is designed to ensure that every member of the board enjoys bipartisan support and that the board, as a whole, will act in an evenhanded manner. At the same time, it is conceivable that the four-vote requirement could lead to gridlock, if the board is evenly divided along ideological or partisan lines.

The creation of the GAB was prompted not by defects in the system for administering elections, but rather by dissatisfaction with how the state's campaign finance and lobbying rules were being enforced. In particular, good government groups believed that the state elections and ethics boards had been too lax in their enforcement of campaign finance, ethics, and lobbying laws. In addition, reform-

ORGANIZATIONAL CHARTS OF THE OLD AND NEW STRUCTURES OF WISCONSIN'S ELECTION SYSTEM

CHART 1
Administrative Structure before 9/1/2007

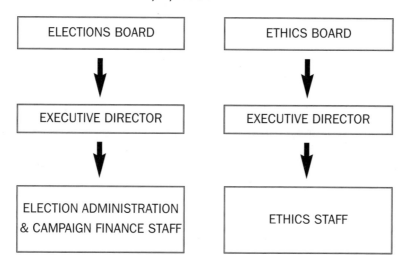

CHART 2
Administrative Structure after 9/1/2007

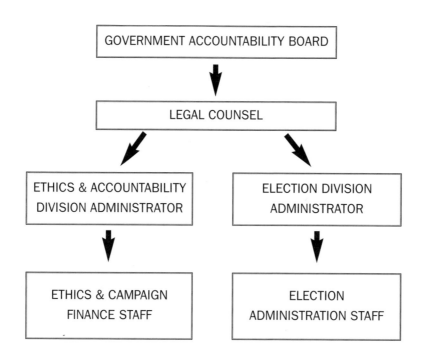

ers sought to consolidate responsibility for overseeing state lobbying regulations, which previously had been vested in the State Ethics Board, with responsibility for enforcing campaign finance laws, which had been under the purview of the State Elections Board. Under Act 1, the position of the executive director of the State Elections Board – along with the elections board itself – has been eliminated.

Although reforming the administration of elections was not the main purpose behind Act 1, the new structure will have an impact – perhaps a substantial one – on election administration. The newly created GAB is required to employ legal counsel, as well as separate chief administrators, for the newly created "Elections Division" and "Ethics and Accountability Division." These divisions take on responsibilities previously performed by the executive directors of the State Elections Board and State Ethics Board. The other employees of the former elections and ethics boards will, by statute, automatically be transferred to the two divisions of the new GAB.[28] The GAB was scheduled to begin its work on September 1, 2007, or the 31st day after the legal counsel and division administrators were chosen. The first members of the GAB were chosen in July 2007, and the board's first meeting took place on August 23, 2007.[29] The six members of the board are Judges Michael W. Brennan, Tom Cane, David G. Deininger, William Eich, James B. Mohr, and Gerald C. Nichol. The GAB is presently looking to hire its legal counsel and has postponed major organizational decisions until that has been accomplished.[30]

It is too early to evaluate the new state structure for overseeing election administration in Wisconsin. This structure appears to be novel, insofar as no other state unifies ethics and elections administration under the authority of a single board.[31] The manner in which GAB members are chosen may ultimately improve public confidence in elections. The utilization of former judges, who are selected by a supermajority of the state senate, provides reason to hope that they will discharge their responsibilities without regard to partisan effects. At the same time, the fact that the GAB is composed of an even number of members and must act by majority vote creates the risk of deadlock. In addition, there is a possibility that election administration will get lost in the shuffle, given the enhanced focus on ethics and campaign finance regulation that motivated the enactment of Act 1. Alternatively, with the GAB's elections division now responsible *only* for election administration (and not for campaign finance), its ability to focus on this area may improve. It is also possible that the GAB will play a more aggressive role in election administration, rather than delegating to staff as has mostly been done until now, something that could have either positive or negative consequences. What is clear is that there is a pressing need to monitor how effectively the GAB handles matters of election administration that are within its charge, particularly with the attention that is likely to fall on Wisconsin's system during the 2008 election cycle.

ELECTION DAY REGISTRATION

It is common to refer to states as "laboratories of democracy." Wisconsin in particular has often been so labeled historically, due to its experiments with progressive reforms that began in the early twentieth century.[32] While the "laboratory" metaphor is a common one, it is all too rare for policymakers and observers to take a careful look at the distinctive features of a state's election system and assess how well they actually function. To the contrary, policy debates surrounding election administration often occur in a factual void, with much opinion but little evidence offered.

Wisconsin provides an ideal site for making good on the laboratory metaphor, by examining the evidence on how well the novel features of its system work. One of the most important aspects of Wisconsin's election system is Election Day Registration ("EDR"). Since 1976, state law has allowed eligible citizens to register to vote on the day of an election. Wisconsin is one of only nine states with EDR,[33] and its relatively long track record makes it an especially valuable state in which to consider how well it has worked.

In 2006, approximately 358,000 Wisconsin voters registered on Election Day, out of over 2.1 million people voting. Under state law, a citizen who is eligible to vote may appear at his or her polling place and register at that location. This procedure may also be used by voters who were previously registered elsewhere, either in or out of state, and moved without re-registering at their new address. In order to register on Election Day, voters must certify that they are qualified and have not voted elsewhere.[34] The voter must also provide acceptable proof of residence, such as a driver's license or other official ID card, university ID card, bank statement, utility bill, or paycheck.[35] A voter who cannot provide documentary proof of residence may still register, if another voter in the same municipality corroborates (or "vouches" for) the address of the voter seeking to register.[36] Thus, a voter may make use of Wisconsin's EDR process either by providing acceptable proof of residence

or by having his or her residence corroborated by another voter.

Election officials with whom we spoke believed that EDR facilitates participation by eligible voters, and there is considerable empirical research to back up the claim that EDR does in fact increase turnout. Before instituting EDR in 1976, Wisconsin's voter turnout was in the middle of the pack in comparison to other states. After the institution of EDR, Wisconsin moved to the front of the pack. This is consistent with the experience of Minnesota and Maine, the other two states that adopted EDR about the same time, both of which also subsequently saw a jump in their turnout. These three states sustained their high turnout rates in the years that followed, even as other states saw their turnout drop.[37] This trend continued in the 2006 elections, with the seven[38] EDR states averaging 48.7% turnout, compared with 38.2% in non-EDR states.[39]

Of course, this statistic alone would be insufficient to demonstrate a causal relationship between EDR and turnout; the high turnout might instead result from other factors, such as the political culture of states that have adopted EDR. When viewed in light of the substantial empirical research that has been done over the years, however, there can be little doubt that EDR has a significant positive effect on participation. This research shows that EDR has not only increased the size but also changed the composition of the electorate, making it more representative of the citizenry as a whole.[40] One study found a significant reduction in the turnout gap among voters with different levels of educational attainment.[41] There is also evidence that EDR increases turnout rates for young voters and new state residents.[42] This is consistent with survey research showing that fewer voters perceive the registration process to be difficult in EDR states.[43]

In addition to increasing turnout, EDR carries some benefits for election administrators. For one thing, EDR states are exempt from the National Voter Registration Act's requirements that "fail-safe voting" be provided for those who move prior to an election.[44] Wisconsin election officials noted that other states' election officials sometimes complain about the burden of complying with the NVRA's requirements regarding registration list maintenance.[45] EDR also is useful for people who pre-registered only to have been erroneously left off the list or dropped by an administrative error.

Perhaps the most significant positive consequence of EDR is that it essentially eliminates the need for provisional ballots. States without EDR must use provisional ballots for voters who believe that they registered but whose names do not appear on the registration list when they arrive at the polls. But EDR eliminates the need for provisional ballots in these circumstances because voters may register at their polling place on Election Day, regardless of whether they previously registered. In general, the only circumstances in which a Wisconsin voter would cast a provisional ballot are: (1) if the voter registered by mail before an election without providing the documentation required by HAVA at the time of registration, and also does not do so at the time of voting, or (2) if the voter has a driver's license but cannot provide the driver's license number when registering, as required by HAVA.[46]

Accordingly, provisional ballots are extremely uncommon in the State of Wisconsin.[47] The city clerk of Franklin, which has over 24,000 registered voters, stated that the city had only had three instances in which a provisional ballot could have been issued in 2006 and 2007. In each of those instances, the voters in question chose to go home and come back with appropriate documentation, rather than casting a provisional ballot. The clerk of the City of New London (approximately 3,700 registered voters) reported only having had one provisional ballot, while the Clerk of the Town of Dale (approximately 1,400 registered voters) reported having none. Even in the City of Milwaukee, the state's largest municipality, provisional ballots are exceedingly unusual. Only forty-one provisional ballots were issued in the November 2006 general election and, according to the Assistant Director of the Milwaukee Election Commission, approximately thirty of those were issued for improper reasons.

EDR's detractors cite two main problems. The first is that it may complicate operations at polling places, by requiring poll workers to do something that is not required in non-EDR states. Although we are aware of no empirical research examining whether EDR worsens lines at the polls, it does seem reasonable that registering voters at the polls would consume some of the poll workers' time and attention and might necessitate additional staffing. On the other hand, this "cost" must be weighed against the benefit to poll workers – and thus to voters – of not having to deal with provisional ballots. The second argument is that EDR increases fraud. Wisconsin has been the site of headline-grabbing allegations of fraud and a vigorous campaign on the part of some legislators to require photo identification in order to vote.[48] This debate, as well as the substantial amount of evidence available in Wisconsin, makes the state an especially valuable one in which to investigate this claim.

FRAUD AND THE VOTER ID DEBATE

Examination of Wisconsin's system also is especially useful given the fierce debate over voter fraud and the related debate over voter identification. The focal point for concerns about fraud has been the City of Milwaukee, in which there have been media reports of ineligible voting in recent election cycles.[49] As required by state law,[50] these matters have been referred to prosecutors, who have engaged in extensive investigations of voter fraud. Concerns about voter fraud have also led some Wisconsin legislators to propose that voters be required to show photo identification in order to have their votes counted.

At the outset, it is helpful to recognize two distinctions. The first distinction is between fraud and mistake. An example of fraud is someone knowingly attempting to vote twice, or a noncitizen intentionally attempting to cast a vote despite knowing that she is not eligible. An example of mistake is an ineligible felon voting in an election, without knowing that state law prohibits him or her from doing so. Under Wisconsin law, such a voter would not be guilty of fraud.[51] The second distinction is between fraud on the part of voters and fraud on the part of insiders such as election officials. An example of voter fraud is people double voting or pretending to be someone else they are not. Insider fraud, by contrast, involves an election official (or someone else with special access) tampering with the voting process. Examples include stuffing ballot boxes or tampering with electronic voting machine's software to alter vote tallies.

There are few states in which allegations of voter fraud have received greater scrutiny than Wisconsin – and few municipalities in which they have received greater attention than the City of Milwaukee. In the course of preparing this report, we spoke to attorneys in the Milwaukee district attorney's office, as well as local and state election officials, in an effort to understand the allegations that EDR leads to increased voter fraud. On the whole, voting fraud is exceedingly rare. Although allegations of voting fraud have been widely publicized in the media, most all of these have evaporated upon closer investigation. We found a handful of documented instances of disenfranchised felons voting, but almost all of these appear to be people who did not know that they were prohibited from voting. Few documented cases of voter fraud exist, and, in the rare instances when it does occur, such fraud is of the "retail" (isolated incidents) rather than the "wholesale" (systemic) variety.[52] Almost all the documented incidents of ineligible voting, including both fraud and mistake, involve people who are ineligible due to felony convictions.

After allegations of fraud surfaced during the November 2004 election, a joint task force of the Milwaukee County District Attorney's Office, the Milwaukee Police Department, the U.S. Attorney's Office, and the Federal Bureau of Investigation began an inquiry.[53] The probe included allegations of double voting and of voting by felons who had not completed probation or parole.[54] After nearly a year of investigation, the task force found only a handful of isolated cases and no evidence of any broad conspiracy to engage in fraud. The U.S. Attorney's Office ultimately brought fourteen prosecutions for suspected violations in Milwaukee, twelve percent of all federal voting fraud cases brought in the country. The government won only five of those cases, failing to secure a conviction in every case where double voting was alleged.[55] The Milwaukee district attorney's office reports prosecuting two cases of felon voting arising from the 2004 election, obtaining convictions in both. This makes seven substantiated cases of ineligible people knowingly casting votes that counted, all of them felons.[56] In 2005, the Republican Party of Wisconsin made additional allegations of voting fraud in connection with the 2004 election, but the U.S. Attorney's Office for the Eastern District of Wisconsin found "no evidence" of voting fraud by any of the individuals accused.[57]

Professor Lorraine Minnite of Columbia University conducted a study of fraud allegations in Wisconsin and other EDR states. Looking at the three federal election cycles between 1999 and 2005, Minnite documented only one instance of registration fraud, one incident of multiple voting, and one instance of absentee voting fraud in Wisconsin. There were no documented instances of voter impersonation in the state.[58]

Attorneys from the Milwaukee district attorney's office, including former D.A. Michael McCann, confirmed that they have not found evidence of organized voting fraud. Certain types of election fraud, including voting more than once, are punishable as Class I felonies, while less severe infractions like electioneering are punishable as misdemeanors.[59] After the 2006 election, the State Elections Board requested that the Milwaukee D.A.'s office investigate twenty-eight "potential" cases of election fraud from that election.[60] On August 22, 2007, a Milwaukee jury found Michael Zore guilty of having voted twice,

after officials caught him through the new statewide registration database,[61] and two other cases of alleged double voting in 2006 are pending.

State prosecutors in Milwaukee have documented no case of anyone going to the polls pretending to be someone else, and no prosecutions on these grounds appear to have been brought anywhere in the state in recent memory. There is no evidence from which to conclude that Wisconsin faces a widespread or concerted effort to commit voting fraud. As former Milwaukee D.A. McCann put it, when charges are brought against suspects in any kind of wrongdoing, the "coin of the realm" in the D.A.'s office is for them to provide incriminating information on others in an effort to reduce their own vulnerability. Were there an organized and systematic effort to commit voter fraud, he believes it would have come to light.[62] Election officials likewise expressed the view that it is very difficult to engage in voter fraud without getting caught.

There have been some incidents of unlawful voting – most commonly by ineligible ex-felons or those who have not yet attained citizenship – which do not constitute fraud, a crime that requires proof of intent. The *Milwaukee Journal-Sentinel* reported that 361 ineligible felons voted in the 2000 election. Even assuming that the *Journal-Sentinel's* figure is correct, the likelihood of ineligible felons' votes affecting the result is small in a state where almost three million people turned out to vote in the 2004 general election. More serious are the Milwaukee Board of Elections' serious problems in recordkeeping, which account for most of the allegations of unlawful voting in Milwaukee in 2004.[63]

Wisconsin's experience is consistent with that of other EDR states. Professor Minnite's investigation of six EDR states over a six-year period found only ten cases of alleged voter fraud that "appeared to have some merit." Of these, only one was a case of voter impersonation at the polls, which was unrelated to that state's EDR law. Minnite also surveyed county prosecutors, who reported only a handful of documented cases of voter fraud. She concluded that "the collective evidence suggests that there has been very little vote fraud in EDR states over the past several election cycles." In fact, far from facilitating fraud, EDR may actually help discourage it by "bring[ing] the registration process into the polling place where it is conducted under the eyes and authority of election officials on one day, Election Day."[64] Whether or not one agrees that EDR deters fraud, there is little evidence – in Wisconsin or other EDR states – that the practice has increased it.

Occurring against this backdrop of concerns over fraud is a vigorous debate over whether to require government-issued photo identification, such as a driver's license, in order to vote. Since 2003, Wisconsin's Republican-majority legislature has enacted three bills to require government-issued photo ID, all of which were vetoed by Democratic Governor Jim Doyle.[65] One election official described voter identification as something constantly hanging over debates regarding election administration in the state. As in other states, proponents of voter identification argue that it is necessary to curb fraud, while opponents argue that it will disproportionately exclude certain groups of voters from participating.

Wisconsin has more evidence than any other state on the types of potential voters who lack identification. A report prepared in 2001 for the Carter-Ford Commission estimated that, nationwide, 6-10% of eligible citizens do not have official state photo identification.[66] In Wisconsin, much more precise data is available in the form of a study released in 2005 by John Pawasarat of the University of Wisconsin-Milwaukee. Pawasarat's study found stark differences in who has photo identification based on race, ethnicity, age, income, and geography. Statewide, over 80% of Wisconsin residents had a valid driver's license. By contrast, only 45% of African American males and 51% of African American females had a license. The results were even more dramatic for young adults. Pawasarat found that only 22% of African American men 18-24 had a valid license.[67] This study provides reasons for concern about the possible consequences of imposing a photo identification requirement on Wisconsin voters, particularly given the slender evidence that voter fraud is widespread and the fact that a stricter identification requirement would do nothing to stop disenfranchised felons from voting, by far the most frequent reason for ineligible votes being cast.

STATEWIDE VOTER REGISTRATION SYSTEM

One of the most significant changes required by the Help America Vote Act ("HAVA") was that every state institute a statewide voter registration list.[68] Prior to that, local election officials had responsibility for maintaining voter lists in most of the states, including Wisconsin. HAVA's requirement arose from evidence of serious problems with the way that registration lists had been administered before 2002, the year of HAVA's enactment. An influential report prepared by the Caltech/MIT Voting Technology Project estimated that 1.5 to 3 million votes were lost due to registration problems in 2000,[69] probably more than the number of votes lost due to faulty voting equipment.

Congress believed that moving responsibility for registration lists from the local to the state level would improve their accuracy. In addition, Congress thought that the statewide registration list requirement would cut down on voting fraud, making it more difficult for people to register and vote in more than one place. Describing Congress' overriding objectives in passing the law, one of its principal co-sponsors, Representative Steny Hoyer, articulated it this way: to make it "easier to vote" but "harder to cheat."[70] Statewide voter registration lists, Congress thought, would simultaneously achieve both objectives. They would make it easier to vote by reducing registration glitches that had resulted in the failure to count many correctly cast votes. They would make it harder to cheat by increasing the likelihood that those engaged in voting fraud would be caught.

In practice, the transition to statewide registration lists has been much more difficult than Congress anticipated. Wisconsin exemplifies these difficulties. After HAVA's enactment, the Wisconsin State Elections Board contracted with Accenture to create the software for its Statewide Voter Registration System ("SVRS"). The state allocated $27.5 million of its federal funds for this transition. Accenture did not have experience in creating a statewide voter registration database, but did engage in extensive discussions with state and local election officials aimed at developing a system that would meet both their needs and the requirements of HAVA. Accenture also secured contracts with the states of Kansas, Wyoming, Pennsylvania, and Colorado, but only Wisconsin ultimately retained Accenture's services.[71]

Wisconsin's transition to a statewide voter registration system has not gone smoothly. As one election official put it, the problems getting the system up and running properly have led to "profound frustration" on the part of many clerks.[72] Among the problems they have experienced are:

- Slowness of the system for officials trying to enter data, particularly in peak-use periods prior to elections.

- High costs to local government for workers required to enter data, partly due to the slowness of the system.

- Data entry errors, resulting in some newly registered voters not being placed on the list for the appropriate precinct.

- Inability of the system to generate lists of registered voters in a district ("walk lists," for candidates running for office).

- Difficulties in "mapping" specific addresses to particular electoral districts.

- The failure of the system to check against motor vehicle records, as required by HAVA.

- Ongoing delays in the system being able to check voting lists against state records of deaths and felons.

- Serious ongoing problems in the absentee voting module, which continues to function poorly and which some clerks find difficult to use.[73]

Some local elections officials attribute these problems to Accenture promising more than they could deliver. They "tried to build a

Cadillac," as one election official put it, but ended up with something that does not yet satisfy the state's needs. To date, the state's system is still not fully compliant with HAVA.

Wisconsin's implementation of the SVRS was made more difficult because its elections are primarily administered at the municipal level, and because most of the state's municipalities did not even have voter registration prior to 2006. As noted above, under state law municipalities with fewer than 5,000 people were not required to have voter registration lists before then, and only 312 of the state's 1,851 municipalities (less than 17%) actually had registration lists before 2006.[74] While other states could combine existing local lists in order to meet HAVA's requirements, Wisconsin election officials had to start from scratch in most municipalities. In Wisconsin, the sheer number of local governmental entities, along with the absence of pre-existing registration lists, made the transition especially challenging.

What added to these difficulties, some officials believe, was the fact that the transition to the SVRS was taking place at the same time as the transition to new voting technology. Making these dramatic changes in election administration overtaxed their already thin time and resources. Local election officials voiced mixed opinions as to whether the deadlines imposed by HAVA were realistic. Whatever the reason, the unresolved issues with the state registration database remain a persistent source of frustration.

Despite the difficulties that the state has experienced, there is reason to hope that the SVRS will ultimately make Wisconsin's system function better than it has in the past. A fully functional SVRS would substantially diminish the likelihood of voting fraudulently without getting caught. In fact, the SVRS has already resulted in the detection and conviction of at least one double-voter.[75] While one conviction does not erase the serious difficulties that state and local election officials continue to experience, it does provide a ray of hope that Wisconsin's SVRS may ultimately achieve the goals that Congress envisioned.

POST-ELECTION DISPUTES

It is widely accepted that the United States dodged a bullet in 2004, in that a very close presidential election did not result in the protracted post-election fight similar that had occurred four years earlier. Much of the attention focused on Ohio, where President Bush prevailed by some 119,000 votes, effectively sealing his re-election. Less commonly recognized is that, had Ohio gone for Senator Kerry instead, *Wisconsin* likely would have been the site of a lengthy and bitter post-election fight. In fact, Kerry's margin of victory in Wisconsin's 2004 general election was 11,384 votes or approximately 0.4%,[76] much smaller than Bush's 2.1% margin of victory in Ohio. If Kerry had taken Ohio, he still would have needed to carry Wisconsin to secure an Electoral College victory. It is therefore possible, even probable, that the Bush-Cheney campaign would have sought to challenge a Kerry victory in Wisconsin.

Considering how Wisconsin would have handled such a post-election dispute is a valuable thought experiment. Much, of course, would have hinged upon the basis upon which the losing candidate challenged the election. The five states discussed in this study each have their own ways of handling different types of election disputes, including those involving absentee ballots, voters who failed to sign in, or provisional ballots.[77]   Regardless of the subject matter of the dispute, however, two significant problems would likely have arisen, had Wisconsin's presidential election been contested. To be sure, these difficulties are not unique to Wisconsin. Nor are they unique to presidential elections, although, for reasons explained below, there are special reasons for concern in the event of a post-election presidential fight.

The first concerns the institution(s) responsible for handling post-election disputes. As an initial matter, election inspectors (or poll workers) have responsibility for tallying votes at their respective locations.[78] The county board of canvassers must then complete a canvass, and would be responsible for conducting a recount of a presidential election, should the appropriate petition be filed. In Wisconsin, each county board of canvassers consists of the county clerk – elected on a partisan basis – and two people appointed by the clerk to serve for two-year terms. Those appointed must be "qualified electors of the county," and at least one must "belong to a political party other than the clerk's."[80]   The practice has been for county clerks to appoint one Democrat and one Republican.

Wisconsin has substantial experience with conducting recounts over the years, most of which have been resolved amicably with minimal litigation. In fact, it is common for candidates not to hire lawyers for recounts in local elections. In the event of a contested presidential election, however, it is easy to imagine this process breaking down. This is particularly true given that each three-member board of canvassers can be expected to have either two

Democrats or two Republicans, depending on the party of the county clerk. Even if everyone involved makes a sincere effort to act in a nonpartisan and neutral manner, representatives of one party's candidate could be expected to charge unfairness in counties where the clerk – and therefore a majority of the board of canvassers – is of the other party. The consequence could thus be a replay of Florida's messy 2000 recount, in which the public comes to doubt the neutrality of local officials conducting recounts, therefore undermining the integrity of the result.

The second conceivable problem concerns the timetable for resolving disputed presidential elections. Under federal law, states must choose their presidential electors on the first Tuesday after the first Monday in November – Election Day.[81] All states now select their electors through statewide elections on this date, which in 2004 fell on November 2. Federal law further requires the electors chosen on this date to "meet and give their votes [for president and vice president] on the first Monday after the second Wednesday in December"[82] – that is, 41 days after the presidential election. This is the date on which the electors meet in each of the states, which in 2004 fell on December 13. Congress then convenes to open the votes cast by the electors and formally determines the president and vice president. In the 2004 election, the date for Congress' convening was January 6, 2005.[83]

What happens in the event of a disputed election within a state? Federal law does not dictate how such disputes are resolved. Instead, it is up to the states to determine the procedures for resolving disputes over who won their presidential election. Federal law does, however, provide a so-called "safe harbor" date, six days before the electors meet in their states. In 2004, the "safe harbor" date was December 7. The relevant statute provides:

> If any State shall have provided, by laws enacted prior to the day fixed for the appointment of the electors, for its final determination of any controversy or contest concerning the appointment of all or any of the electors of such State, by judicial or other methods or procedures, and such determination shall have been made at least six days before the time fixed for the meeting of the electors, such determination made pursuant to such law so existing on said day, and made at least six days prior to said time of meeting of the electors, shall be conclusive, and shall govern in the counting of the electoral votes as provided in the Constitution, and as hereinafter regulated, so far as the ascertainment of the electors appointed by such State is concerned.[84]

What this means is that a state must reach a final determination of post-election disputes by the "safe harbor" date in order to be sure that this determination will be "conclusive" when its electoral votes are counted in Congress. Put negatively, a state that *fails* to reach a conclusive determination by the safe harbor date cannot be assured that the votes cast by its citizens will count. It would instead be up to the House of Representatives to decide who won that state's electoral votes.

A close look at Wisconsin's election law leads to some doubt that the state could have reached a conclusive determination by the safe harbor date of December 7 – or even by December 13, the date of the Electoral College meeting – had the result been challenged in

2004. Under Wisconsin law, a recount petition may not be filed before the "time of completion of the canvass."[85] This date would fall in mid-November, two weeks after the election.[86] The recount would not begin until 9:00 a.m. on the morning after the last day for filing a recount petition and has to be completed within thirteen days after the recount is ordered. That means that a recount would probably extend through early December, before any judicial review can take place.[87]

No matter how quickly a recount is conducted, it would be difficult for there to be a final judicial resolution of any remaining disputes by the safe harbor date of December 7, 2004. Under Wisconsin law, the process for seeking review of a recount decision is to file an appeal in the appropriate circuit court, Wisconsin's trial court, within five business days.[88] Once the circuit court decides the matter, a dissatisfied litigant has thirty days to file an appeal with the appropriate court of appeals[89] – and after that, to seek review in the Wisconsin Supreme Court. By that time, of course, the safe harbor date, the date for electors' meeting, and probably even the counting of votes in the U.S. House would have long since passed.

Wisconsin is certainly not the only state in which we can imagine such a scenario.[90] It does, however, present an especially troubling example, given that boards of canvassers effectively function as the court of first resort. As a matter of state law, it would appear to be impossible for a dissatisfied litigant – specifically, a presidential candidate – to secure adequate judicial review of an election dispute prior to the safe harbor date. That is true whether the dispute involves allegations of absentee ballots mistakenly not counted, ineligible felons' votes being counted, faulty software on electronic voting machines, or ballot stuffing in a jurisdiction using paper ballots. While previous recounts in Wisconsin have proceeded without incident, it is not difficult to imagine a contested presidential election in the state getting thrown to Congress.

This possibility should not lead to panic, but instead to serious attention to the question of how the system for resolving post-election disputes can be adjusted so as to avoid a meltdown in 2008, or some future election. As we suggest in Chapter 9, it would be helpful for Congress to intervene by pushing back the safe harbor date. While the problem is particularly acute for presidential elections, given the safe-harbor and Electoral College dates prescribed by federal law, the state's scheme for resolving post-election disputes could lead to problems in other elections as well. It is quite conceivable, for example, that fighting over a close gubernatorial contest could extend past the prescribed inauguration date. The fact that these problems have not yet occurred does not mean that they could not happen.

REFERENCES

1. Wisconsin Historical Society, *Lies, Bribes and Capitol Stationary*, 1856, Wisconsin State Journal, available at www.madison.com. For more on the Bashford-Barstow election, see Richard N. Current, THE HISTORY OF WISCONSIN, VOLUME II: THE CIVIL WAR ERA, 1848-1873, at 226-30 (1976). For discussion of the LaFollette era of progressive politics in Wisconsin, see Robert C. Nesbit, WISCONSIN: A HISTORY 399-434 (2d ed. 1989).

2. James K Conant, WISCONSIN POLITICS AND GOVERNMENT: AMERICA'S LABORATORY OF DEMOCRACY 160-61 (2006); Robert C. Nesbit, *supra* note 1, at 399-434.

3. In 2006 there were 2,161,700 votes cast for governor of 3,448,767 registered voters (62.7%). *See* Wisconsin State Elections Board, 2006 Election Cycle, *available at* http://elections.state.wi.us/subcategory.asp?linksubcatid=592 &linkcatid=631&linkid=155&locid=47 (last visited Oct. 8, 2007).

4. WIS. STAT. ANN. § 6.55(2)(a).

5. WIS. STAT. ANN. § 15.61 (creating Wisconsin State Elections Board); WIS. STAT. ANN. § 5.05 (2006) (defining the duties of the Board). In 2007, as discussed more fully below, the Wisconsin Legislature passed Act 451 which granted the powers previously held by the State Elections Board to a Government Accountability Board. *See* WIS. STAT. ANN. § 5.05 (2007).

6. Wisconsin State Elections Board, 2006 Fall Election Cycle, Voter Turnout and Registration, http://elections.state.wi.us/docview.asp?docid=11077&locid=47 (last visited Sep. 24, 2007). This figure includes all early registrations, late registrations, and Election Day registrations.

7. WIS. STAT. ANN. § 7.15.

8. WIS. STAT. ANN. § 7.15.

9. WIS. STAT. ANN. § 7.15(e).

10. Wisconsin State Elections Board, *supra* note 6. This figure includes all early registrations, late registrations, and Election Day registrations.

11. *See* City of Milwaukee Election Commission, Election Information, *available at* http://www.city.milwaukee.gov/router.asp?docid=1717.

12. City of Milwaukee Election Task Force, *Official Report* 14 (June 27, 2005).

13. U.S. Census Bureau, State & County Quick Facts, *available at* http://quickfacts.census.gov/qfd/states/55000.html (last visited Sep. 24, 2007).

14. WIS. STAT. ANN. §7.20.

15. WIS. STAT. ANN. § 7.20(2).

16. *See* James K. Conant, *supra* note 2, at 17.

17. WIS. STAT. ANN. § 7.10(1)(b).

18. WIS. STAT. ANN. § 9.01.

19. Wisconsin Legislative Reference Bureau, WISCONSIN BLUE BOOK 254 (2007), *available at* http://www.legis.wisconsin.gov/lrb/bb/07bb/pdf/249-258.pdf

20. Dane County Clerk Bob Ohlsen formerly served as Clerk for the Village of Waunakee.

21. For a party to qualify to select a member of the Elections Board, it must have qualified for a separate ballot in the most recent primary, and have received at least 10% of the vote in the most recent gubernatorial election. WIS. STAT. ANN. § 5.62(1)(b). Under this standard, only the Democratic and Republican parties currently qualify to select a member of the board.

22. WIS. STAT. ANN. § 5.61.

23. WIS. STAT. ANN. § 5.05 (2006). From December 2002 to May 2007, the board also had a Libertarian Party member, because that party's gubernatorial candidate received a sufficient percentage of the vote to quality for a position on the board.

24. WIS. STAT. ANN. § 5.05(4) (2006).

25. WIS. STAT. ANN. § 5.05 (2007).

26. WIS. STAT. ANN. §§ 15.07, 15.60 (2007); 2007 Wisconsin Act 1 § 209(4). The initial GAB members need only be confirmed by a majority of the legislature (three by the State Assembly and three by the State Senate).

27. Wisconsin Legislative Reference Bureau, ETHICS REGULATION REFORM, LEGISLATIVE BRIEF 07-1.

28. "All full-time equivalent positions in the elections board are transferred to the government accountability board." Wisconsin Act 1, § 209(2)(b) (Feb. 2, 2007). S.B. 1 § 209(3)(b).

29. *Six Retired Judges Prepare for Service on New Government Accountability Board*, Jul. 10, 2007, *available at* http://www.wicourts.gov/news/archives/2007/gab071007.htm.

30. *See* Memorandum from Terry C. Anderson, *Interim Director, to Members, Government Accountability Board* (Aug. 16, 2007) (regarding the first meeting of the new board), *available at* http://elections.state.wi.us/docview.asp?docid=11715&locid=47.

31. *Id.*

32. James K. Conant, *supra* note 2, at xv-xvii.

33. The others are Idaho, Maine, Minnesota, New Hampshire, Wisconsin, Wyoming, Iowa, Montana, and North Carolina, the last three of which only recently adopted EDR. Iowa's HF 653 goes into effect on Jan. 1, 2008. North Carolina's HB 91/S195 was signed into law on July 20, 2007 and precleared by the DOJ on Aug. 8, 2007. *See* R. Michael Alvarez & Jonathan Nagler, *Same Day Voter Registration in North Carolina*, DEMOS (BRIEFING PAPER) (July 16, 2007); *see* also Election Day Registration Legislation State Legislatures, Demos, *available at* http://www.demos.org/pubs/ EDR%20legislation%20Aug%2016%202007.pdf.

34. WIS. STAT. ANN. § 6.55.

35. WIS. STAT. ANN. § 6.34.

36. WIS. STAT. ANN. § 6.55(2)(b).

37. *See* Mark J. Fenster, *The Impact of Allowing Day of Registration Voting on Turnout in U.S. Elections from 1960 to 1992*, 22 AM. POLITICS RESEARCH 74 (1994); *see* also Benjamin Highton, *Easy Registration and Voter Turnout*, 59 JOURNAL OF POLITICS. 565, 568 (1997) (finding turnout about 10% higher in EDR states); Craig L. Brians & Bernard Grofman, *Election Day Registration's Effect on U.S. Voter Turnout*, 82 SOC. SCI. QUARTERLY 170, 176-77 (2001) (finding a 6% increase with EDR, compared to states with a 30-day closing date for registration, with a persistent advantage in EDR states even in comparison to state with shorter closing dates)

38. This excludes North Carolina which only recently adopted its EDR system and thus has limited data as to its effect in that state.

39. Demos, *Voter Win with Election Day Registration: A Snapshot of Election 2006* (2007), *available at* http://www.demos.org/pubs/voters_win_web.pdf.

40. Michael Alvarez, et al., *Election Day Voter Registration in the United States: How One-Step Voting can Change the Composition of the American Electorate*, CALTECH / MIT VOTING TECHNOLOGY PROJECT (2002); but see Craig L. Brians, *supra* note 37, at 170-71 (finding that EDR raised turnout, but resulted in only modest increases in the composition of the electorate).

41. *See* Benjamin Highton, *supra* note 37 (finding a turnout gap between most and least educated of 41% in non-EDR states and 30% in EDR states).

42. *See* Stephen Knack & James White, *Election-Day Registration and Turnout Inequality*, 22 POLITICAL BEHAVIOR 29 (2000); Benjamin Highton, *supra* note 37, at 572.

43. *See* R. Michael Alvarez, et al., *How Hard Can It Be: Do Citizens Think It Is Difficult to Register to Vote*, VTP Working Paper #48, at 20 (2006).

44. 42 U.S.C. § 1973gg-2(b)(2).

45. 42 U.S.C. § 1973gg-6.

46. *Wisconsin State Elections Board, What Is a Provisional Ballot and Who Is Entitled to A Provisional Ballot?, available at* http://elections.state.wi.us/ faq_detail.asp?faqid=259&locid=47. The requirement that voters cast a provisional ballot if they do not have their driver's license is the result of an exchange between the U.S. Department of Justice ("DOJ") and the State Election Board. Previously, the state allowed a voter who could not produce his or her driver's license number to instead provide the last four digits of his or her Social Security number. In a June 13, 2006 letter to the Elections Board, DOJ took the position that this policy did not comply with HAVA. The Board subsequently adopted Emergency Rule ElBd 3.04, requiring that voters cast provisional ballots in these circumstances, to be counted if the driver's license number is provided by 4:00 p.m. on the day after the election. DOJ subsequently acknowledged that this rule resolved its concerns, and the rule became permanent in January 2007. *See* Memorandum from George A. Dunst, *Legal Counsel, State Board of Elections, to Elections Board* (Oct. 4, 2006) (relating to Election-Day Voter Registration - ElBd 3.04); Wisconsin Elections Board, *Wisconsin Election Day Voter Registration Clarified* (Aug. 9, 2006); Memorandum from George A. Dunst, Legal Counsel, State Board of Elections, to Elections Board (June 23, 2006) (regarding providing a driver's license number for purposes of voter registration).

47. Kimball W. Brace & Michael P. McDonald, *Final Report of the 2004 Election Day Survey*, 6-9, Tab 6A (2005) (reporting only 274 provisional ballots cast statewide in Wisconsin's 2004 general election).

48. *See*, e.g., Steven Walters, *Senate approves voter ID measure*, JS ONLINE, Apr. 14, 2005, *available at* http://www.jsonline.com/story/index.aspx?id=318206; Voting Rights Group Denounces Attempts to Push Voter ID in Wisconsin Legislature, DEMOS (June 28, 2005) *available at* http://www.demos.org/page339.cfm.

49. *See* e.g., Greg J. Borowski, *Inquiry finds evidence of fraud in election*, JS ONLINE, May 11, 2005, http://www.jsonline.com/story/index.aspx?id=324933.

50. WIS. STAT. ANN. § 5.05(11).

51. WIS. STAT. ANN. § 12.13(1).

52. *See* e.g., Eric Lipton and Ian Urbina, *In 5-Year Effort, Scant Evidence of Voter Fraud*, N.Y. TIMES, April 12, 2007.

53. Steve Schultze, *No Vote Fraud Plot Found: Inquiry Leads to Isolated Cases*, Biskupic Says, MILWAUKEE JOURNAL-SENTINEL, Dec. 6, 2005.

54. *See* WIS. STAT. ANN. § 6.03(b).

55. *See* Eric Lipton & Ian Urbina, *In 5-Year Effort, Scant Evidence of Voter Fraud*, N.Y. TIMES, Apr. 12, 2007. These prosecutions have been linked to pressure exerted by the DOJ on some U.S. Attorneys to prosecute fraud cases more aggressively. *See also* Dan Eggen & Amy Goldstein, *Voter-Fraud Complaints by GOP Drove Dismissals*, WASH. POST, May 14, 2007 (reporting that Milwaukee's U.S. Attorney Steve Biskupic was targeted for potential dismissal after complaints by Karl Rove that he was being insufficiently aggressive in prosecuting voter fraud); Jacob Stein, *Report: Biskupic Was on the Chop List; He Got a Reprieve and Wasn't Fired, A Report Says As Congress Probes Firings of U.S. Attorneys*, WIS. STATE JOURNAL, Apr. 15, 2007 (reporting that Biskupic's name appeared on a list of prosecutors to be fired).

56. Brennan Center for Justice, *Wisconsin, 2004*, *available at* http://www.truthaboutfraud.org/case_studies_by_state/wisconsin_2004.html.

57. Letter from Steven M. Biskupic, *U.S. Attorney, to Rick Wiley, Republican Party of Wisconsin*, Aug. 22, 2005 (regarding alleged double voting).

58. *See* Lorraine Minnite, *Election Day Registration: A Study of Voter Fraud Allegations and Findings on Voter Roll Security* 6-9 (2007), *available at* http://www.demos.org/pubs/edr_fraud_v2.pdf.

59. See WIS. STAT. ANN. § 12.13.

60. Stacy Forster, *State Elections Board Finds 82 Possible Vote Fraud Cases*, MILWAUKEE JOURNAL-SENTINEL, Apr. 13, 2007.

61. Derrick Nunnally, *Man Convicted of Double Voting*, MILWAUKEE JOURNAL-SENTINEL, Aug. 22, 2007.

62. Some evidence exists of registration forms being turned in with names or addresses that do not exist, in cases where registration-gatherers are paid by the form. *See* Derrick Nunnally, *Two Plead Guilty to Election Crimes*, MILWAUKEE JOURNAL SENTINEL, Feb. 14, 2006 (reporting that two voter registration workers had been convicted of turning in bogus registration forms prior to the 2004 election). But there is no evidence of people actually attempting to vote under these bogus registrations. In response, the Wisconsin legislature enacted a statute prohibiting registration-gatherers from being paid for each registration they submit. WIS. STAT. ANN. § 12.13(3)(ze). Election officials and prosecutors believe that this has largely solved the problem, resulting in fewer false registration forms in the 2006 election cycle.

63. *See* Loraine Minnite, *The Politics of Voter Fraud* 35, *available at* http://projectvote.org/fileadmin/ProjectVote/Publications/Politics_of_Voter_Fraud_Final.pdf (citing

evidence that "Milwaukee's Board of Elections was overwhelmed by its own incompetence and understaffing on Election Day [in 2004], resulting in massive record-keeping problems").

64. Lorraine Minnite, *supra* note 58, at 3-4.

65. General Assembly Bill 111 (Wis. 2003); General Assembly Bill 63 (Wis. 2005); Senate Bill 42 (Wis. 2005).

66. *See* John Mark Hansen, VERIFICATION OF IDENTITY, TASK FORCE ON THE FEDERAL ELECTION SYSTEM 4 (July 2001); *see also* Brennan Center for Justice, *Citizens Without Proof: A Survey of Americans' Possession of Documentary Proof of Citizenship and Photo Identification* (Nov. 2006) (finding that 11% of those surveyed did not have current and valid government-issued photo ID).

67. John Pawasarat, *The Driver's License Status of the Voting Age Population in Wisconsin* (June 2005), *available at* http://www.uwm.edu/Dept/ETI/barriers/DriversLicense.pdf.

68. 42 U.S.C. § 15483.

69. Caltech MIT Voting Technology Project, VOTING WHAT IS WHAT COULD BE 9 (2001).

70. *See* Daniel Tokaji, *Early Returns on Election Reform: Discretion, Disenfranchisement, and the Help America Vote Act*, 73 GEO. WASH L. REV. 1206, 1213 (2005).

71. Patrick Marley, *Delays Plague State Lists of Voters: Missing Deadline Will Add to Costs*, MILWAUKEE JOURNAL-SENTINEL, Mar. 23, 2006.

72. Annysa Johnson & Patrick Marley, *State's Voting System Faulted: Election Officials Say New Database Not Trustworthy*, MILWAUKEE JOURNAL-SENTINEL, Mar. 5, 2007 (quoting Neil Albrecht, Assistant Director, Milwaukee Election Commission).

73. For a discussion of these problems, see Letter from Susan Edman, Executive Director, Milwaukee Election Commission, to Barbara Hansen, Project Director, Statewide Voter Registration System, State of Wisconsin Elections Board, May 31, 2007 ("Edman Letter").

74. Electionline.org, *Holding Form: Voter Registration 2006* (July 2006), *available at* http://www.electionline.org/Portals/1/Publications/ERIPBrief13.final.pdf.

75. *See College Student Accused of Voting Twice in Primary*, A.P., Aug. 11, 2004; *Plea Deal Ends in Probation for Voting in Appleton*, Eau Claire, A.P., Jan. 10, 2005.

76. *See* Wisconsin State Elections Board, Canvass Summary, *Fall General Election, President & Vice President*, Nov. 2, 2004, *available at* http://165.189.88.185/docview.asp?docid=1416&locid=47.

77. Edward B. Foley, *The Analysis and Mitigation of Electoral*

Errors: Theory, Practice, Policy, 18 STAN. L. & POL'Y REV. 350 (2007).

78. WIS. STAT. ANN. § 7.51.

79. WIS. STAT. ANN. § 9.01; *Wisconsin State Elections Board, Election Recount Procedures* (Nov. 2006). As noted above, a municipal board of canvassers has responsibility for canvassing an election taking place within its jurisdiction, while a county board of canvassers would have responsibility over federal, state, or county elections. There are no automatic recounts in Wisconsin; however, if the appropriate petition is filed by any elector (if a referendum) or candidate (if election for office) and the difference between the leading candidate and the next vote earner is less than 0.5% the recount shall be done at no cost. WIS. STAT. ANN. § 9.01(1)(ag). A flat fee of $5 per ward is assessed for recounts with a vote difference of 0.5% to 2%. WIS. STAT. ANN. § 9.01(1)(1m). If the difference is over 2% the party requesting the recount shall pay the actual costs of conducting it. WIS. STAT. ANN. § 9.01(1)(2).

80. WIS. STAT. ANN. § 7.60(2).

81. 3 U.S.C. § 1.

82. 3 U.S.C. § 7.

83. The description of the process that appears in this paragraph and the one that follows draws heavily on Peter M. Shane, *Meshing State and Federal Presidential Election Law: The Need for Reform*, Nov. 30, 2004, http://moritzlaw. osu.edu/electionlaw/analysis/2004/041130.php.

84. 3 U.S.C. § 5.

85. WIS. STAT. ANN. § 9.01(1).

86. *See* WIS. STAT. ANN. § 7.60(5)(a)(county clerks to certifiy no later than 14 days after general election); *see also* 2007-08 Wisconsin Election Calendar, *available at* http://elections. state.wi.us/docview.asp?docid=11170&locid=47.

87. Election Recount Procedures, *supra* note79, at 7,15.

88. WIS. STAT. ANN. § 9.01(6)(a).

89. WIS. STAT. ANN. § 9.01(9).

90. *See* Peter M. Shane, *supra* note 83; Steven F. Huefner, *Reforming the Timetable for the Electoral College Process*, ELECTION LAW @ MORITZ WEEKLY COMMENT, Nov. 30, 2004, http://moritzlaw.osu.edu/electionlaw/comments/ 2004/041130.php.

Wisconsin:
NINE AREAS

INSTITUTIONAL ARRANGEMENTS

Primary authority for running Wisconsin elections lies in the state's 1,851 cities, villages, and townships. Municipal clerks, who may be elected or appointed, serve as the chief election official in most jurisdictions. Wis. Stat. Ann. § 7.15. They are also responsible for convening boards of canvassers, which have authority over municipal recounts. Wis. Stat. Ann. § 9.01(1)(ar). Counties with populations over 500,000 must also have a board of election commissioners, consisting of three members. Wis. Stat. Ann. §7.20. County clerks have more limited election responsibilities, but are responsible for providing ballots and other supplies, and for convening county canvassing boards, which have authority over recounts for federal, state, and local elections that cross municipal lines. Wis. Stat. Ann. §§ 7.10, 9.01. At the state level, the Wisconsin legislature recently overhauled the structure of election administration to create a Government Accountability Board ("GAB"), which took over responsibilities formerly performed by the State Elections Board ("SEB")effective September 1, 2007. 2007 Wisconsin Act 1 ("Act 1"). The GAB consists of six former judges, each of whom was approved by a two-thirds super-majority of the state senate. The GAB is authorized by statute to employ an elections division administrator, who will execute the election administration functions formerly executed by the executive director of the state board of elections.

VOTER REGISTRATION/STATEWIDE DATABASE

Since 1976, Wisconsin law has allowed Election Day Registration ("EDR"). Wis. Stat. Ann § 6.55. Eligible voters may register at the polls on Election Day, so long as either 1) they provide documentary proof of residence, such as a current and valid driver's license, utility bill, or bank statement, or 2) an eligible elector from the same municipality corroborates the registrant's address. Wisc Code Ann. §§ 6.34(3), 6.55. Eligible voters may also register by mail twenty days or more before the election, Wisc. Stat. Ann § 6.30, or in person at a municipal clerk's office until 5:00 p.m. (or the close of business) on the day before the election, Wis. Stat. Ann § 6.29(2). Proof of residence is required for those who register after the third Wednesday before an election. Wisconsin contracted with Accenture to create the software for its Statewide Voter Registration System ("SVRS"), and the state has had well-publicized problems in getting the system up and running properly. As described more thoroughly in the accompanying text, the statewide registration database still suffers from serious problems, including slowness, data entry errors, problems generating lists, poor functioning of the absentee voting module, and inability to cross-check against felon, death, and motor vehicle records.

CHALLENGES TO VOTER ELIGIBILITY

A Wisconsin voter's eligibility may be challenged in two ways: 1) during the registration process, and 2) at the polling place when voting. The burden of proof is on the challenger to disqualify an elector and ineligibility must be shown beyond a reasonable doubt. Wis. Stat. Ann. § 6.325. For a registration challenge, the challenger must submit a complaint-like affidavit. Both the challenger and the challenged voter then are asked to appear before the municipal clerk, who makes a ruling following a hearing. In jurisdictions with over 500,000 people (currently only Milwaukee), challenges to a registered voter must be made by the last Wednesday before the election. Wis. Stat. Ann. § 6.48. Polling place challenges may be made by an election inspector (poll worker) or by another voter. Wis. Stat. Ann. §§ 6.92, 6.93. Challenges may be made on the basis of age, citizenship, residency, or disqualification from voting. Election Day Manual at 48 (April 2006). Citizens disqualified from voting include those who are "unable to understand the objective of the election process" and felons who have not finished their sentences, including probation and parole. Wis. Stat. Ann. 6.03.

PROVISIONAL VOTING

Provisional ballots are rare in Wisconsin because of EDR. They are used under two circumstances: 1) if the voter registered by mail before an election and did not provide the documentation required by HAVA at the time of registration and also does not do so at the time of voting, or 2) if the voter has a driver's license but cannot provide the driver's license number when registering, as required by HAVA. Wisconsin State Elections Board, FAQs, http://elections.state.wi.us/faq_detail.asp?faqid=259&locid=47 (last visited Sep. 8, 2007). Voters who lack the required documentation or driver's license number may vote a provisional ballot, which will be counted if they provide the missing information by 4:00 p.m. on the day after the election. Wis. Admin. Code. [ElBd] 3.04.

EARLY AND ABSENTEE VOTING

Wisconsin allows people to vote absentee if they are unable or unwilling to appear at the polls for any reason. Wis. Stat. Ann. § 6.20. Although the state legislature has defined absentee voting as a "privilege" that "must be carefully regulated to prevent fraud or abuse," Wis. Stat. Ann. § 6.84(1), the state effectively has a "no-reason" absentee voting system. Absentee ballots may be obtained through applications filed by mail, fax, email, in person, or through an agent for voters who are hospitalized. Wis. Stat. Ann. § 6.86(1). Accompanying the absentee ballot sent to each voter is an envelope with postage prepaid. Wis. Stat. Ann. §6.87(3)(a). The voter must cast his or her absentee ballot in the presence of a witness, who must sign to verify that the elector was really the one casting the ballot. Wis. Stat. Ann. § 6.87(4). People who are disabled or non-English proficient may vote their absentee ballots with assistance from a third party. Wis.

Stat. Ann. § 6.87(5). Absentee ballots are available 21 days before an election (30 days before fall elections) and may be returned by mail or in person. Voters may request and mark an absentee ballot at their municipal clerk's office until 5:00 p.m. the day before the election.

VOTING TECHNOLOGY

Decisions about what voting technology to use are made at the municipal level, and Wisconsin uses a mix of optical-scan and direct record electronic ("DRE") voting equipment. The state received money under Title I of HAVA, and was therefore required to eliminate the punch card systems formerly used in some municipalities, and the state enacted legislation specifically prohibiting the use of punch cards. Wis. Stat. Ann. § 5.91(14). All voting equipment used in Wisconsin must allow for straight-party ticket voting. Wis. Stat. Ann. § 5.91(2). Electronic voting machines must generate a voter verifiable paper record that may be used in a manual recount. Wis. Stat. Ann. § 5.91(18). Vendors of electronic voting machines must also place software components in escrow, which are to be made available in the event of a valid recount petition in a jurisdiction that uses electronic voting equipment, subject to confidentiality requirements. Wis. Stat. Ann. § 5.905(4). Wisconsin allocated $18 million in HAVA funds to accommodate people with disabilities. The accessible equipment used by Wisconsin's municipalities includes: 1) DRE systems with attached printers, 2) hybrid systems, which have a DRE-like interface that generates a paper ballot that may be read by an optical scan system, and 3) the Vote-PAD ("Voting-on-Paper Assistive Device"), a paper ballot with tactile indications for voters with visual impairments.

POLLING PLACE OPERATIONS

Wisconsin polling places are open from 7:00 a.m. until 8:00 p.m. and voters are entitled to three hours off in order to vote. Wis. Stat. Ann. § 6.78. Wisconsin law refers to poll workers as "election inspectors." Each polling place using paper ballots must have seven election inspectors, and each polling place using electronic voting machines must have five. Wis. Stat. Ann. § 7.30. Inspectors are supposed to be identified by the parties and, when a vacancy occurs, it is supposed to be filled from lists submitted by the parties. Wis. Stat. Ann. § 7.30(2)(b). The majority party (the one that received the most votes in the last presidential or gubernatorial general election in the wards served by the polling place) is entitled to one more inspector than the minority party. Wis. Stat. § 7.30(2)(a). In practice, the parties do not commonly submit lists of names, leaving it to municipal clerks to find poll workers. Although Wisconsin missed the Help America Vote Act's ("HAVA's") January 1, 2006 deadline for having an accessible voting machine in every polling place, ninety-five percent of polling places were reported accessible as of May 1, 2006. Wisconsin State Elections Board, Polling Place Accessibility Survey, http://elections.state.wi.us/docview. asp?docid=3081&locid=47 (last visited Sep. 8, 2007). The State Board of Elections requested a compliance plan from the remaining jurisdictions to ensure accessibility by September 1, 2006.

BALLOT SECURITY

Election fraud, bribery, and threatening an elector are felonies under Wisconsin law, punishable by up to 3.5 years in prison and a $10,000 fine. Wis. Stat. Ann. §§ 12.09, 12.11, 12.12. As described in the accompanying text, state and federal prosecutors in Wisconsin have been vigorous in investigating and prosecuting voting fraud. The newly created Government Accountability Board ("GAB") will consolidate procedures for investigating and prosecuting election law violations. Its legal counsel or a prosecutor is empowered to prosecute civil violations of law, or to refer criminal matters to the appropriate district attorney. Wis. Stat. Ann. §§ 5.05(2m)(c)(4) & (11). The law establishing the GAB also creates a penalty of $10,000 and up to nine months imprisonment for board members, investigators, prosecutors, or employees who leak information about an investigation. Wis. Stat. Ann. § 12.13(5). Although voting fraud is rare, there have been instances of bogus registration forms being submitted, mainly by third-party registration collectors being paid per returned form. Under a recently enacted law (Act 451), municipal clerks are required to forward to the GAB the names of all registration collectors, referred to as Special Registration Deputies ("SRDs"). SRDs may no longer be paid on a "rate that varies relative to the number of registrations obtained," and they must include their name on all registrations. Wis. Stat. Ann. §§ 6.26(4), 12.13(3)(ze). Violations are punishable by fines of $1,000 and up to six months in jail. SRDs are also required to attend training once every two years. Wis. Stat. An. § 7.315(1)(b).

POST-ELECTION PROCESSES

Election inspectors have the first responsibility for tallying votes cast at each polling place. Wis. Stat. Ann. § 7.51(2). Ballots and electronic voting equipment are then sent to the municipal clerk's office under seal. Wis. Stat. Ann. § 7.51(3)(a). The municipal board of canvassers is responsible for canvassing returns from elections taking place within a municipality. Wis. Stat. Ann. § 7.53. For federal, state, and county elections, the canvass is performed by the county board of canvassers. Wis. Stat. Ann. § 7.60. Following the county canvass, the clerk is required to certify the results of county-level elections and send ballots to the state level to be examined by the state board of elections (now the GAB). Wis. Stat. Ann. § 7.60. After the results are ascertained, the chair is to release the total votes for federal and state elections, certify a winner, and transmit results to the governor. Wis. Stat. Ann. § 7.70(3)(d) & (5)(a)-(b). A recount may be requested by any candidate or, for referenda, by anyone voting for or against the measure in question. Wis. Stat. Ann. § 9.01(1). A recount is initiated through the filing of a recount petition, stating the reasons why a recount is believed necessary. Wis. Stat. Ann. § 9.01(1). Fees are required, depending on the margin of victory. Wis. Stat. Ann. § 9.01(1)(ag). The recount process is open to the public and to be performed by the same canvassers who completed the initial count. Wis. Stat. Ann. § 9.01(3). In effect, the board of canvassers functions as the court of first resort. The results of a recount may then be appealed to circuit court, with further appellate review available after that. Wis. Stat. Ann. § 9.01(6) & (9).

CHAPTER 7: MINNESOTA'S ELECTION ECOSYSTEM
A MODEL TODAY, BUT WILL IT LAST?

OF THE FIVE STATES in this study, Minnesota appears to have the healthiest election ecosystem at present. Indeed, Minnesota has the highest percentage of voter participation in the nation (60.8% of the eligible electorate in 2006, 76.8% in the presidential year of 2004[1]), with virtually no evidence of unlawful voting (only eleven ballots cast by non-citizens in 2004,[2] out of a total of 2,842,912 ballots cast[3]).[4] A mandatory audit of the November 2006 election showed the state's optical scan machines to be "very accurate," in the words of the watchdog group Citizens for Election Integrity Minnesota, which monitored the audit.[5] Moreover, the process of casting ballots at polling places in both 2004 and 2006 was widely regarded as having gone smoothly throughout the state, with only a minimal amount of the kind of problems – long lines, ballot shortages, missing supplies, technology failures, disruptive challenges, poll worker confusion, and mistakes – that plagued many precincts in other states.[6]

Yet in the recent past the state also has weathered some serious criticism that its election officials, particularly its elected secretary of state, have behaved in an excessively partisan fashion.[7] And its underlying culture of cooperative decisionmaking and civic engagement may be waning, thus increasing the chances that the state's election processes may become a casualty – or weapon – of partisanship. This would be a profound loss for a state that, in a previous generation, produced two competing candidates for governor who, in a remarkable accord, developed their own procedure for resolving a razor-thin Election Day voting margin.

This chapter seeks to capture the relative strength of Minnesota's election ecosystem, while also identifying its present challenges. An underlying concern of this discussion is the extent to which Minnesota's admirable achievements are replicable elsewhere. The discussion begins with an overview of the mutually reinforcing character of the state's political culture and its election laws. The chapter then describes more specifically the extraordinary story of the state's 1962 gubernatorial contest, when the two principal candidates superseded the existing judicial structure to work out their own mechanism for resolving their close race. Next, it discusses the central role that the Minnesota Secretary of State plays in the state's election administration, the importance to the state of its system of Election Day voter registration ("EDR"), and its statewide use of an optical scan voting system. The chapter strives to make clear that each of these attributes of the state's election ecosystem comes with both some benefits and some burdens. The chapter then identifies several additional potential vulnerabilities in the state's election ecosystem, including its shortage of poll workers, its prospects for absentee ballot abuse, its growing political polarization, and the risk of increasing judicial activism in election matters. Finally, the chapter concludes with some reflections on the state's ability to serve as a model for others.

THE MUTUAL ROLES OF LAW
AND CULTURE

Minnesota's successes in election administration can be attributed in part to the state's laws and in part to its political culture, although it is difficult to determine the precise proportion of credit attributable to each factor. For instance, consider first the impact of a number of the key legal frameworks that shape Minnesota elections. Election Day Registration undoubtedly facilitates voter participation,[8] while it also avoids the potential of contentious post-voting disputes over the eligibility of provisional ballots. Minnesota's centralized voter registration database, developed prior to the HAVA requirement (in part to make sure that the state's EDR option is not abused),[9] helps detect the few incidents of unlawful voting.[10] The state's decision to mandate optical scan balloting in all precincts (with the AutoMARK™ device available in every polling place for voters needing or wishing technological assistance in marking their optical scan ballots),[11] has facilitated Election Day operations considerably: long lines and other sorts of problems are avoided, as most voters can continue to fill out their paper ballots while poll workers attend to the relatively few technological glitches that intermittently occur. And the use of optical scan ballots also facilitates the state's new mandatory post-voting audit, as well as any potential recount, avoiding the need for a separate (and unwieldy) voter-verified paper audit trail. The mandatory audit, moreover, serves to reinforce Minnesotans' high degree of public confidence in their election system.[12]

Indeed, the audit may be one of the most important recent innovations in Minnesota's election laws. Enacted in 2004, the new law requires a manual recount of ballots in two to four percent of randomly selected precincts, depending upon a jurisdiction's population.[13] If discrepancies are found, additional precincts are randomly selected. The first audit, conducted in November 2006, was successful not only for demonstrating the accuracy of the vote count, but also for the speed and efficiency with which the audit was conducted.[14] In this respect, the audit contrasts with the otherwise successful recount of the 1962 gubernatorial election, which took until March of 1963 to complete.[15] It also offers some hope in the event of another disputed statewide election, in which it would be highly desirable – and in a presidential race essential, for reasons discussed in previous chapters – for any recount to be complete by early December (within five weeks after Election Day).

Yet even as these and other laws establish an infrastructure favorable to successful voting administration, the laws alone cannot fully account for the state's achievements. Citizens must take advantage of the easier electoral opportunity that EDR provides. Likewise, even though state law has mechanisms to detect and deter voting by ineligible individuals, Minnesota's low incidence of unlawful voting also is a product of the state's longstanding commitment to clean elections. And the use of optical scan machines does not guarantee smooth operations at polling places, particularly given that any paper ballot system can result in ambiguous markings that do not occur with direct recording electronic ("DRE") equipment. Rather, a state needs intelligent and well-trained poll workers to implement polling place procedures properly. Whatever type of voting equipment is used, post-voting disputes can turn ugly and corrosive if partisan polarization in a state prevents cooler heads from resolving those disputes in a way that preserves public acceptance of the legitimacy of the electoral process.

In Minnesota, a tradition of nonpartisanship is not merely an ethos, but a practice. Not only was the legislature elected on a formally nonpartisan basis from 1914 through 1972 (meaning no party endorsement or affiliation appeared on a ballot next to a candidate's name until the 1974 elections),[16] but in 1998 Minnesota famously elected independent Jesse Ventura as its governor. Minnesota has shown its deviation from the conventional two-party model of politics in other ways as well. For example, because historically most Minnesota voters were not locked into a rigid bipolar partisan framework, many political parties flourished under a distinctive multi-party approach. Although this tradition has diminished considerably in recent years, it remains reflected in the fact that the Democrats in Minnesota still call themselves the Democratic-Farmer-Labor, or DFL, Party, although it has been over sixty years since the state's Democratic Party merged with its Farmer Labor Party.

In terms of fostering nonpartisan election administration, a political environment with vibrant multi-party or independent candidates presents challenges as well as opportunities. In one respect, it may be easier to structure inherently neutral institutions in a strictly two-party world: guarantee that each of the two parties has equal say concerning the membership of the institution. (Other states, as we have seen, take this approach with respect to the composition of their local election boards or canvassing boards.) Even for an institution with an odd number of members, evenhandedness between two parties is guaranteed if both parties must agree on the identity of the individual who will cast the tie-breaking vote.

In a world of multiple parties or independents with an equal claim on the fairness of the administrative agency, it may be harder to structure the body in a way that is both evenhanded and perceived as such with respect to all of these claimants. Perhaps the best that can be done would be to have some kind of threshold requirement for the right to equal participation in the selection of the institution's members. For example, any political party that has five percent of the seats in either chamber of the state's legislature, or whose candidate for governor polled five percent in the last gubernatorial election, might get to exercise an effective veto over the governor's nominees for this institution. (Independents are specifically represented under this scheme if the governor is independent.) But one need not dwell on this interesting issue as long as Minnesota's political culture is one in which its administrative bodies and election officials will be scrupulously fair to all political parties, large or small, and to independents also.

Likely tracing to its long-standing tradition of civic engagement and solidarity,[17] Minnesota has a political culture that places a high value on the fairness of the political process. Even political partisans typically respect their opponents' equal entitlement to a fair system. Indeed, as the authors of a recent study of Minnesota politics and government wrote, following Daniel Elazar's typology of political cultures:

> Minnesota is the archetypical example of a state informed and permeated by the moralistic political subculture: both the general public and the politicians conceive of politics as a public activity centered on some no-

tion of the public good and properly devoted to the advancement of the public interest. The tone set by the state's political culture permeates Minnesota's civil society, its politics and government, giving Minnesota a "clean" image.[18]

This tradition has contributed historically not only to high voter turnout, but also to an adequate supply of well-qualified poll workers and local election officials, willing and able to operate elections whose integrity and accuracy go largely unquestioned by the public and losing candidates. Compared to other states (Illinois, for example), Minnesota appears to have had fewer judicially contested elections over the last several decades, even though Minnesota's laws are not unfavorable to such challenges.[19] Moreover, when such contests do occur in Minnesota, they seem to be disposed of with less residual rancor than comparable controversies elsewhere.[20]

EXHIBIT A: THE 1962 GOVERNOR'S RACE

Perhaps most emblematic of Minnesota's tradition is the resolution of the 1962 gubernatorial election. Out of more than 1.2 million votes cast, initial election returns that year showed only a 58-vote difference between the two leading candidates, Karl Rolvaag and Elmer Anderson.[21] The two sides quickly ended up in the Minnesota Supreme Court, fighting over the authority of local election boards to submit amended returns. After the court unsatisfactorily decided this preliminary issue by a 3-2 partisan vote,[22] the two camps realized that they needed a better means of handling the inevitable recount to follow.

With the goal of devising a recount process that the public would view as fair and neutral, the two sides sat down and hand-picked three mutually agreeable judges to form a special recount tribunal.[23] Having negotiated the rules for this self-created court, the competing candidates then narrowed the scope of disputed ballots for the judges to review: although 97,834 ballots were disputed at the beginning of the recount process, three subsequent rounds of negotiation and compromise (including one in the midst of the recount trial itself) left only 967 ballots subject to judicial determination.[24] Moreover, the disputes centered almost exclusively on determinations of voter intent based on ambiguous markings on the ballots themselves. Although initial stages of the recount included allegations of election improprieties in four precincts, in the end the parties "could not find even a trace of fraud," and only one minor instance of mishandling of ballots was identified.[25]

Although the final recount ruling did not occur until March 21, 1963 (135 days after the election), the fairness of the recount process validated both its own outcome as well as the conduct of the original election. As the authoritative book on this recount concluded: "Long regarded and publicized throughout the country as a state having 'clean politics,' . . . Minnesota more than lived up to its reputation."[26] The 1962 gubernatorial election in this state thus stands in sharp contrast to the 1982 gubernatorial election in Illinois, which ended with a divisive 4-3 state supreme court decision and findings of widespread fraud after federal investigation.

The question inevitably arises whether Minnesota would fare as well again if another important statewide race produced initial returns as close as those in the 1962 gubernatorial election. Is the Minnesota tradition of integrity, administrative competence, and bipartisan fairness as strong today as then? Would the two sides be willing and able to agree upon a mutually – and publicly – acceptable procedure for resolving disputes arising from a razor-thin statewide vote? Would both sides then use this process in order to achieve an outcome widely perceived to be accurate and legitimate? We are less sanguine about whether a similarly close race today would be settled as amicably. Although certain newer features of the state's election ecosystem presumably decrease the bases for a judicial contest of a close election, other features may continue to provide grounds for an election contest, particularly as partisanship increases in the state. Important to our assessment of the likelihood that Minnesota can continue to avoid serious electoral malfunctions is a deeper understanding of other basic components of Minnesota's contemporary election ecosystem.

THE CENTRAL ROLE OF THE SECRETARY OF STATE

One factor that contributes to Minnesota's success in election administration is the relatively strong role played by the secretary of state in assisting local election officials. This assistance includes advising and training the local officials with respect to Minnesota's standardized statewide voting procedures.[27] In this respect, Minnesota contrasts with Wisconsin and Illinois, which both have relatively weak state election boards vis-à-vis local election authorities. Meanwhile, Minnesota is similar to Wisconsin (as well as to Michigan), in the critical role that municipal officials play in administering elections, although in Minnesota county officials also have significant responsibilities. In con-

trast, elections in Ohio and Illinois are administered largely at the county level (with the major exception of Chicago). Yet the distinction between municipal and county control, on the one hand, seems less significant than the distinction between a strong secretary of state and a weak state elections board, for Minnesota has not suffered from the local difficulties and local variability that has surfaced in Wisconsin and, even more, in Illinois. Table 5 contains a simplified comparison of the structural features of the election ecosystems of the five states.

To be sure, a strong secretary of state cannot fully explain Minnesota's successes. Ohio has a secretary of state with the power to remove local election officials, a power that Minnesota's counterpart lacks, and still Ohio's many election administration problems have included too much variation among local practices as well as local noncompliance with state rules. Nevertheless, when local election officials in Minnesota are asked why their state fares better in voting administration than Wisconsin, a neighboring state with many similarities, they attribute the difference to the stronger centralized guidance in Minnesota, including authoritative information, good training, and effective coordination of the work of local officials. From their perspective across the border, for example, Minnesota election officials observe that Milwaukee historically has been able to operate largely as its own fiefdom, a practice that would not be tolerated by Minnesota's legislature (which would either write rules or give the secretary of state authority to rein the city in).

In addition to the secretary of state's formal role assisting local election officials, the legacy of that central office's working relationship with localities also is a significant presence in the current landscape. Joan Growe served as Minnesota Secretary of State for twenty-four years, after winning office in 1974, until she retired at the end of 1998. By widespread acknowledgment, she supervised the state's elections with "energy, integrity, and enthusiasm,"[28] establishing an excellent rapport with local election officials regardless of partisan affiliation. Although Growe ran for office as a Democrat, once on the job she received acclaim for administering it professionally, without partisan bias. For instance, in one dramatic event, in 1990 the Republican candidate for governor withdrew amid scandal less than two weeks before the election. Growe

TABLE 5
ELECTION ADMINISTRATION SYSTEMS

	chief election officer	Local Election Authority	State Supreme Court
ILLINOIS	State Board of Elections (appointed, bipartisan[1])	*Default:* county clerk (elected) *DuPage County:* county BOE (bipartisan[3]) *Chicago and 7 other municipalities:* Municipal BOE (bipartisan[4])	7 members, elected R (3) D (4)
MICHIGAN	Secretary of State (elected)	Municipal clerks (elected, appointed, partisan or non-partisan, depending on the charter of each city)	7 members, elected R (3) D (4)
MINNESOTA	Secretary of State (elected)	County auditor (elected or appointed) Municipal clerk (appointed)	7 members, elected
OHIO	Secretary of State (elected)	County BOE (appointed, bipartisan)	7 members, elected R (7)
WISCONSIN	Government Accountability Board (appointed[2])	*Default:* Municipal clerk (elected or appointed[5]) *Counties/cities with population over 500K:* County/municipal BOE Commissioners (bipartisan[6])	7 members, elected R (4) D (3)

Table 5 Notes:

1. The Illinois governor appoints the eight state BOE members, four Republicans and four Democrats, subject to the advice and consent of the state senate. 10 ILL. COMP. STAT. 5/1A-2, 5/1A-4.

2. The Wisconsin governor appoints the six members of the GAB, subject to senate confirmation by a 2/3 vote, from among individuals nominated by a nominating panel consisting of retired judges. WIS. STAT. ANN. § 15-60.

3. In Illinois, county boards of elections are appointed by the chairman of the county board. Each BOE has three members, at least one Republican and at least one Democrat. 10 ILL. COMP. STAT. 5/6A-3.

4. Illinois municipal boards of elections are appointed by the local circuit court. Each BOE has three members, at least one Republican and at least one Democrat. 10 ILL. COMP. STAT. 5/6-21, 5/6-22.

5. The default is that town clerks are elected, but they may be appointed by a majority of the town board if the town board enacts an ordinance to that effect. WIS. STAT. ANN. § 60.30. Village clerks are elected. WIS. STAT. ANN. § 61.19. City clerks are elected or appointed. WIS. STAT. ANN. § 62.09.

6. These boards have three members. The mayor or county executive appoints two from the largest political party in the county or city, and one from the second largest party. WIS. STAT. ANN. § 7.20.

was lauded for her prompt actions to help the party get a replacement candidate, Arne Carlson, on the ballot, who then defeated the incumbent. At the end of Growe's six-term tenure, Governor Carlson offered these words of praise for her: "It's been a pleasure to work with her – she's gracious, hard-working and has been a superb public servant."[29]

The situation changed in 1999, when Mary Kiffmeyer was elected secretary of state upon Growe's retirement. Her eight-year tenure was marred by controversy, as Kiffmeyer was accused of politicizing the office, particularly for engaging in practices and promoting policies that (at least in the eyes of some) were designed to suppress voter participation in order to help Republican candidates.[30] She advocated a photo identification requirement for all in-precinct voters despite the virtual nonexistence of polling place fraud in Minnesota,[31] and her decision to forbid the use of tribal-issued identification for Native American voters using EDR in precincts outside reservations was enjoined by a federal court.[32]

Even more disconcerting than these accusations was the extent to which Kiffmeyer's relationship with local election officials deteriorated over time. Communication from her office became poor and erratic.[33] In sharp contrast to Growe's administration, in Kiffmeyer's tenure there was instability, and even incompetence, as she went through five election directors in her eight years in office. The complaints about her professional shortfalls, moreover, were bipartisan. Many local election officials who initially had supported her, including a number of Republicans, opposed her reelection in 2006, and localities were even in revolt against her as her second term moved towards its conclusion.

Not surprisingly, after Mark Ritchie defeated Kiffmeyer's bid for reelection in 2006, he entered office in 2007 as the beneficiary of prospective goodwill from all those local officials welcoming a change in administration. In keeping with Minnesota's tradition of democratic experimentalism and not resting on its laurels,[34] he quickly embarked on an across-the-board review and analysis of the health of the state's democracy, as well as specifically promoting the innovation of automatic voter registration ("AVR") to supplement Election Day Registration.[35] Governor Pawlenty vetoed the AVR proposal passed by the legislature,[36] but had it been adopted, it would have created a system whereby the state itself registered voters based on its own review of driver's license records, unless a citizen chose to opt out.[37]

Ritchie faces challenges of his own, however. There is a risk that he, too, will be accused of partisanship in the opposite direction if he pushes too hard and too fast on proposals seen as favoring Democrats. For instance, Governor Pawlenty's rejection of Ritchie's AVR proposal may fit in this category. Even if Ritchie genuinely believes that his proposals are nonpartisan and motivated solely by the desire to promote the public interest, others may not share his perception, and in this context perception is as important as reality. His administration must be perceived to be impartial and fair, as well as actually being so.

In this respect, one of the potential challenges facing Minnesota's election ecosystem concerns the inherent partisanship of any elected chief election officer. Minnesota benefits from the advantages of a relatively powerful central elections figure in its secretary of state. But is it necessary for this office to be elective for it to have this degree of influence over the localities? Would it be possible, instead, for Minnesota to have the best of both worlds by combining the power of a secretary of state with the transparent impartiality of a state elections board whose members are selected on an inherently nonpartisan basis? Illinois and Wisconsin have nonpartisan state election boards, but they lack sufficiently effective power in relation to local authorities. Would making Minnesota's Secretary of State a nonpartisan position – say, by having the officeholder appointed by the governor, perhaps drawn from several nominees submitted to the governor by a bipartisan commission, and subject to approval of three-fourths of each legislative chamber[38] – necessarily dilute the office's effective power? Fortunately, Minnesota need not grapple with these difficult questions if, as a practical matter, Mark Ritchie restores the tradition that Growe nurtured, administering the office in an obviously nonpartisan manner notwithstanding the fact that the office is elective.

Yet in this regard, Ritchie faces a more difficult climate than Growe did. As described in greater detail below, Minnesota politics are more polarized now than they were in previous decades, and this polarization is especially true in the area of election administration. Ritchie will need to bend over backwards to build confidence, among Republicans as well as Democrats, that he is fair to both sides. Unfortunately, there is some chance that even if he gives his best effort, the political environment may already be too polluted for him to succeed. But he should persist nonetheless because one of Minnesota's most precious political resources historically has been its culture of nonpartisan

fairness. It would be a terrible shame if this culture were further eroded or irretrievably lost.

MINNESOTA'S OPTION OF ELECTION DAY REGISTRATION

Another principal feature of Minnesota's election ecosystem is its use of Election Day Registration ("EDR"). Minnesota is one of a growing number of states (presently nine[39]), including Wisconsin, that allows its eligible voters to register at the polls on Election Day. Indeed, Minnesota's success with Election Day Registration has contributed to its replication elsewhere. Moreover, EDR's ongoing success in Minnesota is one reason that Governor Pawlenty gave for refusing to experiment with Secretary Ritchie's Automatic Voter Registration proposal, described above.

To take advantage of EDR, Minnesota residents must provide poll workers with evidence of residency, either with appropriate documents or by "vouching," a process by which another (registered) voter vouches for the residence and general eligibility of the Election Day registrant.[40] In 2004, almost 600,000 (or over twenty percent) of the state's voters took advantage of this option, as did almost 300,000 (or over thirteen percent) in 2006.[41] Yet as previously noted, the state still has a very low number of ballots cast by ineligible voters. Among its benefits, EDR eliminates provisional voting, and therefore frees Minnesota from the risks of litigation over uncounted provisional ballots. EDR thus is one part of the legal infrastructure now in place in Minnesota that reduces the kinds of problems that are likely to provide a basis for contesting an election.

Nevertheless, two relatively minor issues associated with Minnesota's EDR system merit discussion. First, Minnesota fails to keep data on the number of individuals who attempt to utilize EDR but are unable to do so because they fail either to have the necessary identification or to get another voter to vouch for them. State law obligates localities to collect this data, but this requirement is often overlooked, and the secretary of state neither retains the information that is selectively collected nor prods the noncompliant jurisdictions to fulfill this obligation. Although anecdotally this number is thought to be very low – some individuals, when denied EDR, simply return to the polls later in the day with either identification or a vouching compatriot – it would be useful to enforce the existing data collection requirement. One reason is that this data would enable comparisons between EDR in Minnesota and provisional voting elsewhere, in terms of the role they play as "insurance policies" for voters mistakenly omitted from the state's registration database.

Second, also from the standpoint of tracking the impact of EDR (and polling place operations generally), one recent interlude in state law was unwelcome. At Secretary of State Kiffmeyer's request (although she explained that she was simply passing along the supplications of local election officials), in 2004 the state legislature revised the election code to give local officials control over whether to grant news media access to polling places to observe balloting there, and then only with prior approval and for no more than fifteen minutes.[42] Fortunately, this restrictive provision was quickly rewritten in 2005 to ensure that media representatives are allowed to observe indefinitely at the polls, provided that they do not interfere with the conduct of the election.[43] Although obviously the right of each individual to cast a secret ballot must be protected, the conduct of poll workers concerning the administration of EDR and the handling of ballots before and after they are voted are matters of utmost public importance that should be transparent. The media, acting as the public representatives, should be able to view and report on this quintessentially public function of democracy.

One more attribute of Minnesota's EDR system also merits brief mention. As in other states, erroneous purging of voters from the registration rolls also can occur in Minnesota, particularly because the state denies incarcerated felons and those still on parole or probation the right to vote (and recent legislative efforts to soften the state's felon disenfranchisement laws have been unsuccessful).[44] In 2004, there were a few complaints that some individuals were wrongly excluded from the state's voter registration database – much to the surprise of these voters when they arrived at their precinct.[45] But with EDR as a failsafe, it appears that virtually all of these individuals nonetheless were able to vote a traditional ballot. These are voters who in many other states either would have voted a provisional ballot, or perhaps would have been denied any opportunity to vote. In 2004 there also were some complaints about the eligibility of voters being challenged at their polling places, but again these challenges (and thus the complaints) seemed to fizzle as either identification documents or vouching established the eligibility of these challenged voters, thereby enabling them to cast regular ballots without significant difficulty or delay.[46]

OPTICAL SCAN BALLOTS AND SOUND PROCEDURES

Minnesota's exclusive use of optical scan ballots, combined with its sound procedures for implementing that technology, also provide some advantages. While optical scan ballots have their limitations, as discussed at greater length in Chapter 9, they avoid contestable issues associated with touchscreen machines, like those arising in the 2006 election for Florida's thirteenth congressional district.[47] Furthermore, because of Minnesota's procedures for administering its optical scan system, there is less likelihood of a serious breach that could provide the basis for contesting the outcome.

A key aspect of Minnesota's system that furthers the goal of election integrity is its procedure for checking in voters. As discussed in our Ohio chapter, in November 2006 approximately 12,000 individuals were erroneously permitted to cast ballots in Cuyahoga County without verification of their registration, in violation of Ohio law. In Minnesota, state law similarly prohibits individuals from casting ballots unless either their previous registration was verified or they complete the EDR process, which as described above itself requires evidence of residency (either by documentation or "vouching"). Were such a breach of required procedure ever to occur in Minnesota, the state election code and Minnesota Supreme Court precedent support the proposition that, if the ballots cast by unverified voters might make a difference in the outcome of the election, then election officials must randomly remove from the offending precincts' returns the same number of ballots as those that were unverified.[48] Thus, imagine Al Franken defeating Senator Norm Coleman's

2008 reelection bid by less than 1,000 votes, and election officials in Hennepin County having to randomly withdraw 12,000 unverified ballots from its precincts, where Franken perhaps outpolled Coleman sixty percent to forty percent.

Fortunately, such a nightmare scenario is highly unlikely, given Minnesota's procedures for administering its voting process. A predicate for Cuyahoga County's large number of unverified ballots was a problem associated with a very different procedure. In Cuyahoga County, after verification of their registration, voters were supposed to receive a computerized card that, when inserted into the DRE machine, would activate it, thereby enabling them to vote. In several precincts, however, during periods of high voter turnout, a shortage of these cards occurred. In the ensuing confusion, individuals were permitted to stand in the line to use a DRE machine – and receive the next available card – without first standing in the separate preliminary line to verify their registration.[49]

In Minnesota, by contrast, individuals must first receive a paper "voter receipt" indicating that they are registered to vote before they are given a ballot. (They receive this paper "voter receipt" either as a result of standing in the line for verifying their previous registration or, alternatively, by standing in the line for completing the EDR process.) Voters then proceed to a separate line to exchange this "voter receipt" for a ballot. (In a pinch, if a Minnesota precinct failed to receive the pre-printed "voter receipts," any kind of paper could serve as a substitute, thereby permitting the polling places to open without unreasonable delay.[50]) Because of the simplicity and straightforwardness of this process, there is much less chance of a widespread breakdown of procedures that would lead to thousands of individuals casting a vote without first obtaining – and presenting to the appropriate precinct official – the requisite "voter receipt."

Minnesota's system similarly protects against the kind of problem that crippled Maryland's primary election in 2006, where again computerized cards necessary for activating DRE machines were the predicate for the fiasco.[51] In that situation, election officials had failed to include the necessary cards in the bag of supplies delivered to precinct workers, with the consequence that polling places were unable to open, causing the disenfranchisement of thousands of eligible voters. Were that kind of scenario to occur in Minnesota – say if the ballots themselves were not present in the polls when they opened on Election Day – there is again precedent for the proposition that the courts would provide some type of remedy, perhaps even voiding the tainted election and ordering a new one.[52] But that prospect does not arise if the problem never occurs in the first place. Of course, problems also can occur with optical scan voting, such as delivering the wrong ballots to a voting location, or calibrating the scanning equipment in a way that results in some votes being misread or not counted. Yet it may be less likely that the ballots themselves will be overlooked than that activation cards for DRE machines will be overlooked.

SOME POTENTIAL PITFALLS

Minnesota's contemporary ability to handle a litigated contest of a close statewide election, such as occurred in 1962, may never be tested if there are no tenable grounds for contesting the

election. But as sound as Minnesota's electoral infrastructure appears to be, it is not impervious to difficulties. Some of its more likely problems include a shortage of poll workers, potential absentee ballot fraud, and difficulties that may flow from the state's increasing political polarization. It also is worth reflecting on how well the state judiciary is positioned to handle any major election litigation, were it to occur.

A Shortage of Poll Workers. Like all states, Minnesota's biggest challenge is the "graying" of its poll workers and the need to recruit, train, and retain a new cadre of committed citizens. Minnesota's challenge in this regard may be somewhat easier than other states.[53] But much of the difficulty of poll worker recruitment and retention is demographic: new generations of two-wage-earner families (or single parents) result in fewer individuals able to commit the time necessary to serve as poll workers, and even among those individuals with available time, those who have grown up "bowling alone" (or simply sitting at home with all the entertainment options there) are less inclined to sign up as a poll worker simply out of a sense of duty to engage in public service. While the public-spirited tradition of Minnesota may make it more resistant to these demographic trends, the state cannot escape them altogether. It is therefore conceivable that in some future Minnesota election a shortage of well-trained poll workers will cause precinct-based problems that lead to either (1) voter disenfranchisement or (2) breaches in procedure that serve as the basis for contesting an election – or both.

Absentee Ballot Abuse. Like any other state, Minnesota is also vulnerable to the risk of absentee ballot fraud or abuse. Although in early

2007 the governor vetoed the legislature's adoption of no-excuse absentee voting, the state retains absentee voting for the traditional bases of need (infirmity, absence, etc.), and recent election cycles have seen an increased use of absentee ballots.[54] Moreover, as a corollary to EDR, Minnesota law permits individuals to register and cast an absentee ballot simultaneously.[55] Although voters using this process must provide evidence of residency, this requirement could be easily evaded by the unscrupulous, especially as one permissible form of evidence – analogous to "vouching" for EDR voters – is the signature of another registered voter who attests to the absentee voter's residency.[56] One would hope that Minnesota's tradition of honesty in elections would prevent any widespread form of absentee ballot abuse from occurring, but there is no guarantee. In a 1994 tribal election on a Native American reservation within the state, for example, leaders of one tribal faction forged hundreds of absentee ballots (and were convicted in federal court of crimes arising from this fraud).[57] Therefore, one cannot rule out the possibility that a future election in the state could become clouded by absentee ballot improprieties, with a judicial contest occurring over whether or not to overturn the outcome of the election. Regrettably, too, the precedent from the Minnesota Supreme Court is ambiguous about how it would resolve a case involving absentee ballot improprieties. The court's ultimate decision likely would be highly dependent on the exact nature and extent of abuse, particularly in relation to the winning candidate's margin of victory.

Increased Political Polarization. Were such an election contest to occur, it is not clear that the leadership of Minnesota's two major polit-

ical parties would be able to agree upon a process for resolving the contest that the public would widely perceive as transparently fair, comparable to what happened in the 1962 gubernatorial election. Electoral politics in the state are more polarized and divisive now than they were then. Some attribute this undesirable trend to the increasing influence of national politics over the conduct of business within the state capitol. One example cited in support of this contention involves recent deliberations over revisions to the rules for "vouching" in the context of EDR. While Statehouse politicians on both sides ultimately were able to reach a compromise on this issue,[58] it was not without overcoming substantial resistance from national figures with their own agendas, who sought to derail a state-based agreement.

Whatever the causes of the increased partisan polarization, it also is evident in recent debates over voter identification and voter registration. In 2006, Governor Pawlenty, a Republican, advocated introducing a photo identification requirement for polling place voting within the state, but he was unable to get the measure through the legislature, one house of which at the time was controlled by the Democrats. After the November 2006 elections, the Democrats took solid control of both houses of the legislature, but came short of veto-proof margins in each. In the same veto that blocked the legislature's adoption of no-excuse absentee voting, Governor Pawlenty also rejected other legislative reforms of the electoral process, including Secretary Ritchie's plan, discussed above, to introduce a form of "automatic voter registration" ("AVR") based on driver's license records. In his veto message, Governor Pawlenty objected that driver's license records might be inaccurate with respect to an individual's citizenship and, in any event, AVR was unnecessary given the existence of EDR.[59]

It is perhaps of some ironic consolation to Minnesotans that the state's polarized debate over election reform has many Republicans defending EDR, whereas Republicans elsewhere oppose that longstanding (and by all accounts successful) practice in Minnesota. But purely in the scientific interest of observing a democratic experiment, it would have been interesting (and likely illuminating) if Governor Pawlenty had agreed to let the state serve as a laboratory for testing the idea of AVR. In any event, his veto of the legislature's package of election reforms demonstrates the current inability of the state's political leadership to reach a bipartisan agreement on what rules should govern the voting process.

Whether that inability to achieve bipartisan compromise would carry over to the context of adopting procedures for resolving a post-voting dispute over the outcome of a close election, no one can know for sure, but it is generally thought harder to achieve a bipartisan agreement once ballots have been cast (which is why the 1962 bipartisan agreement over the recount process is so remarkable). And if the election contest concerned absentee ballot improprieties facilitated by relatively lax rules for authenticating the eligibility of absentee voters, a topic which has been part of the polarized legislative debate leading up to the governor's veto, the possibility of a bipartisan basis for resolving the litigated contest seems especially remote.

Is the State's Judiciary Sufficiently Non-Partisan? In the absence of an ability to achieve a bipartisan dispute resolution process like the one adopted in 1962, Minnesota would need to rely on its existing judicial procedures for adjudicating any litigated election contest. Recall that in 1962 the two parties developed their own mutually agreeable procedures in large part to avoid the inadequacies of the then-existing judicial process, which was perceived as insufficiently neutral or nonpartisan. In any future judicial contest of an important statewide race, there is reason to fear that the fairness or neutrality of the judiciary would again be questioned.

Although Minnesota's judiciary has largely (and deservedly) been held in high regard over the last few decades, recent pressures threaten to undermine public respect for this institution. Minnesota's judges are themselves elected (although often initially appointed to a vacancy by the governor), and although the state's canons of judicial ethics have attempted to insulate these judges from partisan politics, these canons recently have been invalidated as violating the First Amendment's protection for free speech.[60] Accordingly, it is increasingly doubtful that the state's supreme court will be viewed as sufficiently nonpartisan and neutral to resolve fairly a post-voting dispute over which party's candidate won a close and important statewide race. Indeed, if it were a race for one of the seats on the Minnesota Supreme Court itself, reliance on this institution to resolve the contest would be particularly problematic, as neither the rules governing such contests nor the rules concerning judicial recusals specify how to handle this situation.

Minnesota elections are not frequently disputed in court, but state law permits its judiciary to nullify the results of an election based on a taint in the electoral process. Indeed, indicative of its insistence on clean elections, Minnesota is exceptional in authorizing its courts to void a candidate's victory if the candidate engaged in prohibited campaign activities, including disseminating deliberately false campaign literature.[61] In the increasingly litigious environment surrounding voting administration practices since 2000, it is conceivable that, in a closely fought campaign in an important future Minnesota election, one side or the other will attempt to seek a favorable result in court when they could not obtain it – at least not decisively – at the polls.

Moreover, in an important decision involving replacement absentee ballots after the death of Senator Paul Wellstone just eleven days before the November 2002 election, the Minnesota Supreme Court ruled that it violated the U.S. Constitution's Equal Protection Clause for the state to refuse to mail a replacement absentee ballot to voters who previously received an absentee ballot by mail, and to permit these voters to obtain a replacement absentee ballot only in person.[62] The court thought it entirely unjustifiable to make the absentee voter obtain a replacement ballot in person when the reason that they had received an absentee ballot by mail was their inability to go get one themselves. The decision illustrates the Minnesota Supreme Court's willingness to flex its judicial muscle when the court perceives a fundamental injustice in the state's electoral practices, notwithstanding the content of the state's election laws.

The possibility that the court will do so again hovers over any close and disputed election. And the court's intervention might not necessarily involve a more "liberal" understanding of what fundamental justice requires than the views reflected in the state's statutes or administrative practices. Instead, as in *Bush v. Gore*, it might be a more "conservative" court finding an Equal Protection violation in practices that "liberals" thought to be fair. (In the dispute over the "dimpled" and "hanging" chads in the presidential election of 2000, liberals tended to favor a generous "discern the intent of the voter" standard, even if its vagueness led to uneven application, whereas conservatives thought that equality required a more rigid standard, even though it would result in more discarded ballots.) Thus, if a major contested election occurred in the near future, a majority of the Minnesota Supreme Court might view matters differently than the new secretary of state, with the court invoking Equal Protection to supersede the secretary's authority.

Because of this background uncertainty over the Minnesota Supreme Court's willingness to exercise any ultimate authority over matters of election administration, the legislature should undertake a review of its election statutes in an effort to minimize this risk. This kind of "election code audit" would be valuable in any state, as all of them have ambiguities and gaps in their election statutes, which create uncertainty and thereby invite litigation. Minnesota is no exception, as perfect clarity and specificity in a state's election code is unattainable. Indeed, a review of past litigation in Minnesota (even if relatively infrequent) reveals spots where the state's election statutes previously fell short.[63] Minnesota, however, could do itself a favor (by reducing the risk of elections resolved in court) and also exercise national leadership if it became the first state to establish an institutional mechanism for periodic (perhaps quadrennial or decennial) review of its election statutes.[64] This innovation would be consistent with the general excellence that Minnesota historically has maintained in election administration.

POTENTIAL CONVERGENCES: POSITIVE OR NEGATIVE?

A basic theme of this chapter is Minnesota's historical exceptionalism: it performs the function of election administration differently, and for the most part better, than elsewhere. (In this respect, this chapter is similar to many other observations concerning different aspects of governance in Minnesota.) In the future, however, it is quite possible that Minnesota's performance in voting administration will look more like other states.

This potential convergence, however, could go in either of two directions, depending upon what factor predominates in the coming years. One possibility, the rosier scenario, is that other states will learn to emulate Minnesota's successes, especially if Minnesota exerts more of a leadership role in national policy discussions concerning election administration. The other possible scenario, decidedly less optimistic, is that Minnesota will increasingly resemble other states, as Minnesota demographically moves closer to national norms and its politics become increasingly polarized in ways that mirror the high degree of partisanship elsewhere. We do not venture to guess which version of convergence is more likely; we hope only that raising this issue here will help forces within the state shape the future in the better direction.

Go It Alone, or Participate in National Debates on Election Administration? Because Minnesota has excelled in administering its voting process, and because this excellence stems in large measure from Minnesota's distinctively virtuous political ethos, some have suggested that Minnesota historically has felt little need to participate in broader national discussions about improving election administration. How much could Minnesota really learn from these conversations, which were largely devoted to preventing problems that arise in poorly performing states? Minnesota understandably could have concluded that participation in these discussions was not worth the effort and decided instead to continue refining its own voting process independently.

But, as part of Secretary Ritchie's review of his office's practices, Minnesota is turning away from this isolationist attitude. One reason is that, because Congress has intensified its regulatory scrutiny of state practices in this area, Minnesota no longer can act entirely on its own. In many ways, HAVA was an unwelcome intrusion for Minnesota, which perceives that piece of legislation as a defective compromise that, in some respects, is counterproductive. The consequence of a national standard adopted in response to the egregiousness of the worst offenders, aspiring to bring them up to the level of the median states, can be a "dumbing down" of states like Minnesota, at the other end of the spectrum. Minnesota may have been unprepared for this consequence of HAVA (having been largely immune, because of its Election Day Registration, from the requirements of the National Voter Registration Act, which was Congress's earlier and less intrusive foray into this field). Accordingly, Minnesota now sees potential value in becoming much more proactive in national discussions on election administration. Perhaps Minnesota can even become a leader of these discussions, using its own successful experiences to elevate national standards in the process.

Diminishing Homogeneity. One question arises, however, about the prospect of Minnesota's taking a lead in national discussions on the improvement of voting administration. If Minnesota's successes stem in any large measure from its distinctive cultural traditions, what use are the state's experiences for states that have different traditions? This question, in turn, prompts an even more vexing and delicate one: if Minnesota's distinctive cultural traditions are partly a product of its particular characteristics, then is it possible even to replicate its political culture elsewhere?

Historically, Minnesota has had an especially high degree of cultural homogeneity. The state also been isolated geographically from other states to a considerable degree, in part because of its northern location and frigid climate. Some have attributed its community spirit and fair-minded political culture in part to these factors, and some political scientists have raised the question whether Minnesota's traditional political values will be affected by changes occurring in the states.[65]

We would align ourselves with the view of those who predict that Minnesota can maintain its political traditions, on the basis that the values of nonpartisanship, community spirit, and evenhandedness can be cultivated in any environment, as long as they are promoted and nurtured by political leaders in those jurisdictions. Minnesota itself may soon become a testing ground for this proposition, as its demographics are changing. With these changes,

will Minnesotans gradually come to reflect the broader political culture of the U.S., which is more individualistic and less communitarian than Minnesota's, or instead will they continue to embrace and embody Minnesota's distinctive political culture? Optimists expect the latter will hold true, counting on the state's educational system and other transmitters of political values to inculcate those distinctive values in future generations of Minnesotans. If it does hold true, it obviously would bode well for spreading to other states the strengths found in Minnesota's election ecosystem.

Rather than wait, however, there are lessons to be learned today, not only from Minnesota but from all the states in this study, lessons that may be transferable to a variety of political cultures. It is to those lessons that we turn in the remaining chapters.

REFERENCES

1. http://elections.gmu.edu/ Voter_Turnout _2004.htm; http://elections.gmu.edu/ Voter_Turnout_2006.htm.

2. *See* Bill Salisbury, *Pawlenty Urges Voter ID Changes*, ST. PAUL PIONEER PRESS, Sept. 28, 2006, at 5B.

3. http://elections.gmu.edu/ Voter_Turnout_2004.htm.

4. The virtual nonexistence of unlawful voting in 2004 reflects the state's general history in this respect. "Election fraud is not an issue [in Minnesota]: same-day registration has existed since 1973, and no serious incidents have been reported concerning voter fraud and abuse." Daniel J. Elazar, Virginia Gray & Wyman Spano, MINNESOTA POLITICS & GOVERNMENT 208 (1999).

5. *See* Citizens for Election Integrity Minnesota, REPORT AND ANALYSIS OF THE 2006 POST-ELECTION AUDIT OF MINNESOTA'S VOTING SYSTEMS, Apr. 4, 2007, at 7, *available at* http://www.ceimn.org/files/CEIMNAuditReport. pdf. Even with respect to the small percentage of discrepancies discovered by the audit (ranging from 0.1% for one congressional race, to 0.01% for another), "the overwhelming majority" of these discrepancies were caused by voter, not machine, error. *Id*. at 5.

6. *See* Bill Salisbury, *Election Day Fears Fizzle, Balloting Smooth as Kiffmeyer Proves Her Critics Wrong*, ST. PAUL PIONEER PRESS, Nov. 13, 2004, at B1; Nathan Cemenska, *Overview of Minnesota Voting Process in November 2006*, http://moritzlaw.osu.edu/electionlaw/election06/MinnesotaEl ectionOverviewNovember2006.php.

7. *See, e.g., Editorial*, (MINNEAPOLIS) STAR-TRIBUNE, Oct. 21, 2006, at 18A ("Her policies and practices have had the steady effect - some would say the partisan intent, as well - of discouraging voter participation.").

8. *See* sources cited *supra* Chapter 6, notes 40-43.

9. *See* MINN. STAT. ANN. § 201.022.

10. *See* Dane Smith & Conrad deFiebre, *State Republicans Turn Spotlight on Immigrants*, (MINNEAPOLIS) STAR-TRIBUNE, Sept. 28, 2006, at 6B.

11. *See Keeping an Eye on the Machines that Count Minnesotans' Votes*, ST. PAUL PIONEER PRESS, Oct. 24, 2006, *available at* http://www.votetrustusa.org/ index.php?option=com_content&task=view&id=1925&Itemi d=113.

12. *See also* Sean Greene, *Minnesota Performs First Post-Election Review*, ELECTIONLINE WEEKLY, Dec. 14, 2006, http://www.wheresthepaper.org/ electionline061214MinnPerformsFirstPostElectionReview.ht m; Brad Swenson, *Post-Election Review Checks Accuracy of*

Voting Machines, BEMIDJI PIONEER, Nov. 17, 2006, available at http://www.ceimn.org/news/ post_election_review_checks_accuracy_voting_machines.

13. *See* MINN. STAT. ANN. § 206.89.

14. *See* Sean Greene, *supra* note 12; Citizens for Election Integrity Minnesota, *supra* note 5, at 7.

15. *See* Ronald F. Stinnett & Charles H. Backstrom, RECOUNT 1 (1964).

16. *See* Daniel J. Elazar, et al, *supra* note 4, at 96.

17. *See id*. at 20.

18. *Id*. at 19.

19. For a separate analysis of the Minnesota judiciary's likely response to election litigation, *see* Edward B. Foley, *The Analysis and Mitigation of Electoral Errors: Theory, Practice, Policy*, 18 STAN. L. & POL'Y REV. 350, 361-74 (2007).

20. Washington State, in its own contested gubernatorial election of 2004, failed to develop a bipartisan dispute resolution process comparable to Minnesota's in 1962. (Minnesota's experience in 1962 is discussed in detail in the immediately next paragraph in the text.) As a consequence, Washington State suffers much greater ongoing resentment of the 2004 election having been resolved unfairly in contrast to what Minnesota experienced in the aftermath of 1962. The same comparison could be made between Minnesota in 1962 and Illinois in 1982. Like Washington in 2004, Illinois in 1982 developed no mutually acceptable bipartisan dispute resolution process.

21. *See* Ronald F. Stinnett & Charles H. Backstrom, *supra* note 15, at 3.

22. *See id*. at 81.

23. The two sides were also likely motivated by a self-interested fear that they might end up before an inhospitable trial judge, whose factual findings would be largely insulated from supreme court review (even if that review might be more favorable). But precisely because the Republicans faced somewhat better odds than the Democrats if they rolled the dice with the then-existing judicial system, given their initial partisan victory in the supreme court, it is to their credit that rather than gambling they settled upon a process equally and transparently fair to both sides.

24. *See id*. at 159.

25. *Id*. at 138-39.

26. *Id*. at 139; see also Daniel J. Elazar, et al., *supra* note 4, at 208:

Even when Minnesota courts spent five months deciding what appears to be the closest gubernatorial election in

American history, the Rolvaag-Anderson contest of 1962, serious vote fraud was not an issue. The only question about the outcome – determined by a margin of ninety-one votes – concerned voter intention, not political chicanery.

27. Minnesota law authorizes the secretary of state, among other powers, to "prepare and transmit to the county auditors and municipal clerks *detailed written instructions* for complying with election laws relating to the conduct of elections, conduct of voter registration and voting procedures." MINN. STAT. ANN. § 204B.27 (emphasis added).

28. *Editorial*, ST. PAUL PIONEER PRESS, Sept. 14, 1997, at 22A.

29. Gary Dawson, Secretary of State Joan Growe Retiring; Voting Rights Crusader Won't Run in '98, ST. PAUL PIONEER PRESS, Sept. 12, 1997, at 1A.

30. *See, e.g., Editorial*, (MINNEAPOLIS) STAR-TRIBUNE, Oct. 21, 2006, at 18A; Mark Brunswick, *Kiffmeyer Takes Flak, Pushes On*, (MINNEAPOLIS) STAR-TRIBUNE, Sept. 25, 2004, at 1A.

31. *See Legislative Round-Up*, ST. PAUL PIONEER PRESS, July 6, 2001, at B3.

32. *See ACLU of Minnesota v. Kiffmeyer*, 2004 WL 2428690 (D. Minn. 2004). The federal court ruled that Kiffmeyer's decision, by selectively disallowing tribal ID in some circumstances but not others, and at the same time permitting some other comparable forms of ID, was unjustified discrimination in violation of the Equal Protection Clause of the U.S. Constitution. The ruling came in the context of an emergency motion filed by the ACLU shortly before the November 2004 presidential election.

33. *See* Bill Salisbury, *Election Officials Criticize Glitches; Kiffmeyer Defends Voter Registration*, ST. PAUL PIONEER PRESS, Oct. 1, 2004, at B1.

34. *See* Daniel J. Elazar, *et al.*, *supra* note 4, at 171.

35. *See* Dane Smith, *A New Push to Open Up Voter Signup*, (MINNEAPOLIS) STAR TRIBUNE, Feb. 25, 2007, at 1B.

36. *See* Charley Shaw, *No Election Changes This Year in Minnesota*, ST. PAUL LEGAL LEDGER, May 29, 2007, 2007 WLNR 10252824.

37. *See* Mark Ritchie, *Commentary: Keep Minnesota #1 in Elections*, Mar. 13, 2007 (Press Release); Letter from Secretary of State Mark Ritchie to Governor Tim Pawlenty, May 8, 2007, *available at* http://www.sos.state.mn.us/docs/replytogovsvetomsg.pdf.

38. *See, e.g.,* Richard L. Hasen, *Beyond the Margin of Litigation: Reforming U.S. Election Administration to Avoid Electoral Meltdown*, 62 WASH. & LEE L. REV 937, 983-84 (2005); Commission on Federal Election Reform (Carter-Baker Commission), *Building Confidence in U.S. Elections*, Sept. 2005, at 50.

39. *See* Lorraine Minnite, *Election Day Registration: A Study of Voter Fraud Allegations and Findings on Voter Roll Security*, Sept. 6, 2007, at 5 n.3, *available at* http://www.demos.org/pubs/edr_fraud_v2.pdf.

40. *See* MINN. STAT. ANN. § 201.061 subd. 3(a)(4).

41. *See* Minnesota General Election Statistics 1950-2006, *available at* http://www.sos.state.mn.us/docs/election_result_stats.pdf.

42. *See* 2004 MINN. LAWS ch. 293, art. 2, § 24.

43. *See* MINN. STAT. ANN. § 204C.06 subd. 8.

44. *See* Rubén Rosario, *They Did The Time. Now Let Them Vote*, ST. PAUL PIONEER PRESS, October 16, 2006, at 1B.

45. *See Some Minnesota Voters Upset They Weren't Registered*, DULUTH NEWS TRIBUNE, Nov. 13, 2004.

46. *See* Chuck Frederick, *Charges Prove Duluth's Role as Battleground*, DULUTH NEWS TRIBUNE, Nov. 4, 2004, at 7A.

47. *See* Amy Green & Ben Arnoldy, *Election Controversy Hits Florida, Again*, CHRISTIAN SCIENCE MONITOR, Dec. 8, 2006, at 3.

48. *See* MINN. STAT. ANN. § 204C.20 subd. 2; *Johnson v. Trnka*, 154 N.W.2d 185, 188 (Minn. 1967).

49. *See* Joan Mazzolini, Thousands Voted Illegally; *Cuyahoga Failed To Ensure Signatures*, (CLEVELAND) PLAIN DEALER, Dec. 5, 2006, at A1: "[P]oll workers were trained to give voters the cards to operate voting machines at the table where voters signed the election books. But as polling places backed up with voters, poll workers did not have enough cards to give to everyone, and they might have lost track of [who had, and had not, signed in]." However it specifically happened, the bottom line is that "poll workers assigned to give voters computer cards to operate the touch-screen voting machines failed to make sure that the voters had signed in and showed identification."

50. All that would be necessary is that the pollworker who hands out ballots be able to recognized as authentic a "voter receipt" submitted by a voter after receiving it from the poll worker who verified the voter's eligibility. Some sort of mutually agreed upon mark, signature, or convention could be quickly established by these poll workers to convert scratch paper into make-shift official "voter receipts."

51. *See* Editorial, *Primary Debacle*, BALTIMORE SUN, Sept. 13, 2006, at 22A.

52. *See, e.g., In re Contest of Vetch,* 71 N.W.2d 652, 660 (Minn. 1955) (voiding an election where administrative breaches "cast doubt and suspicion upon the election and impeach the integrity of the vote").

53. *See, e.g., California Secretary of State's Ad Hoc Touch Screen Task Force, Report,* § 3, item 6, *available at* http://www.sos.ca.gov/elections/taskforce_report_3.htm (raising concern that complex equipment mght make poll worker recruitment more difficult).

54. *See* John C. Fortier, ABSENTEE AND EARLY VOTING 92-93, (2006).

55. *See* MINN. STAT. ANN. § 203B.04.

56. The risk of detection appears less under Minnesota's approach than if absentee voting is limited only to those citizens who have previously registered. The reason is that, when previous registration is required, the fraudulent absentee voter must impersonate the previously registered voter (or commit a two-stage fabrication of a nonexistent citizen). By contrast, in Minnesota, when submitting fake absentee ballots, the perpetrator can simply invent fictitious names, addresses, and signatures, hoping that these ballots will be counted and, even once the fraud is discovered, leaving no way of identifying the perpetrator. Somewhat more daring, but still easier than the two-stage process in other states, the perpetrator could obtain a list of real but unregistered individuals and fraudulently submit absentee ballots – and simultaneous registration forms – on behalf of them.

57. *See* Molly Guthrey, *Wadena Gets More Than Four Years In Jail Plus Hefty Fine,* ST. PAUL PIONEER PRESS, Nov. 22, 1996, at 1B.

58. *See* 2005 MINN. LAWS ch. 156, art. 6, §§ 15, 42, 43.

59. "Minnesota's current system of same-day voter registration makes the need for the automatic government registration of individuals unnecessary." Governor Pawlenty's Veto Message, May 7, 2006, in STATE OF MINNESOTA, JOURNAL OF THE SENATE, 85TH LEGISLATURE, 3724, 3726 (May 8, 2006), *available at* http://www.senate.leg.state.mn.us/journals/2007-2008/20070508064.pdf#Page6.

60. *See Republican Party of Minnesota v. White,* 536 U.S. 765 (2002).

61. *See Matter of Contest of Election,* 344 N.W.2d 826 (Minn. 1984) (4-3 decision).

62. *See Erlandson v. Kiffmeyer,* 659 N.W.2d 724 (Minn. 2003).

63. For example, the statute concerning the remedy for "excess ballots" – more ballots cast in a precinct than registered voters who signed the pollbook – needed amendment to clarify the distinction between circumstances in which pollworkers have initialed ballots, as they are required to do, from those situations in which they have not. *See* MINN. STAT. ANN. § 204C.20 subd. 2. Similarly, the statute providing for when it is possible to challenge the eligibility of absentee ballots because of improprieties in the handling of those ballots has caused confusion in the past and remains in need of further clarification. *See* MINN. STAT. ANN. § 204C.13, *Bell v. Gannaway,* 227 N.W.2d 797 (Minn. 1975).

64. For further discussion of this proposal, *see* Edward B. Foley, *supra* note 19, at 375-76.

65. *See* Daniel J. Elazar, *et al., supra* note 4, at 12.; Carolyn M. Shrewsbury, *Minnesota: A Decade of Demographic Change,* in PERSPECTIVES ON MINNESOTA GOVERNMENT AND POLITICS 13 (Steven M. Hoffman, *et al.,* eds. 2003).

Minnesota:
NINE AREAS

INSTITUTIONAL ARRANGEMENTS

Minnesota's chief election officer is its secretary of state. Minn. Stat. Ann. § 204B.27. In addition to responsibility for general management and coordination of the state's elections, the secretary also has specific duties prescribed by the state election code concerning voter registration, examination and approval of voting machines, training, and other areas. Minn. Stat. Ann. § 206.57. At the county level, elected or appointed county auditors help manage the state's voter registration database, Minn. Stat. Ann. § 201.121; 201.022, conduct absentee voting, Minn. Stat. Ann. § 203B.04, adjudicate pre-election registration challenges, Minn. Stat. Ann. § 201.195, provide poll worker training, Minn. Stat. Ann. § 204B.25, and oversee equipment testing, Minn. Stat. Ann. § 206.83; 206.89. Meanwhile, responsibility for overseeing actual polling place operations is shared between county auditors and municipal clerks. See Minn. Stat. Ann. §§ 203B.04; 204B.14; 204B.16; 204B.21.

VOTER REGISTRATION/STATEWIDE DATABASE

Minnesota permits Election Day Registration, as well as advance voter registration. Voters register in advance by filling out a form and submitting it to the county auditor or secretary of state either in person or by mail. Minn. Stat. Ann. § 201.054. At the polls on Election Day, voters submit a similar form and proof of residence to the poll workers, and voters without proof of residence may still vote if another voter "vouches" for their residence. Minn. Stat. Ann. § 201.061. Minnesota also allows voters to register when sending in their absentee ballots. Minn. Stat. Ann. § 203B.04.

The secretary of state must attempt to verify information in incoming voter registration applications, including Election Day applications, against information contained in either the state motor vehicles database or the federal social security database. Minn. Rule 8200.9310. Only applications that exactly match the information in the outside databases are considered verified. Minn. Rule 8200.9310. When the secretary cannot verify an application, it goes to the county auditor, who attempts to contact the applicant and will verify the application if the auditor can "reasonably conclude" that the two sets of information "relate to the same person." Minn. Rule 8200.9310. The auditor must investigate EDR applications that cannot be verified, and in suspicious circumstances may refer the matter to the county attorney for prosecution. Minn. Rule 8200.5500(2).

CHALLENGES TO VOTER ELIGIBILITY

Challenges to specific voters' eligibility may be brought either before or on Election Day. Any registered voter may initiate a pre-election challenge against any other voter in the county by filing a petition with the county auditor, who then must decide the challenge, subject to an appeal to the secretary of state. Minn. Stat. Ann. § 201.195. Election Day challenges may be brought at the polls by challengers assigned there by political parties if they have personal knowledge of a basis for a challenge, or by poll workers themselves. Poll workers must make Election Day challenges for a variety of reasons, including when the individual attempting to vote has already voted absentee, Minn. Stat. Ann. § 203B.12, when a registration confirmation postcard was returned undeliverable, Minn. Stat. Ann. § 201.12, and when a previous incoming voter registration application – including Election Day Registration applications from previous elections – could not be verified against outside databases, Minn. Rule 8200.5500. Marks are placed in the poll books ahead of time to notify poll workers of voters who should be challenged for these or other reasons. Poll workers question the challenged voter and decide whether the challenge is valid, in which case (or if the voter refuses to answer), the voter cannot vote. Minn. Stat. Ann. § 204C.12. There is no appeal.

PROVISIONAL VOTING

Minnesota does not have provisional voting. Instead, it has Election Day Registration.

EARLY AND ABSENTEE VOTING

Minnesota permits absentee voting only for voters who reasonably expect that they will be unable to go to their polling place on Election Day because of absence from the precinct, illness, disability, religious discipline or holiday, service as an election judge in another precinct, or other factors. Minn. Stat. Ann. § 203B.02. Voters may vote an absentee ballot in person prior to Election Day at the office of the county auditor or at any other polling place designated by the county auditor, Minn. Stat. Ann. § 203B.081, but only if they meet the requirements for absentee voting set forth in Minn. Stat. Ann. § 203B.02. Otherwise, Minnesota does not have early voting.

VOTING TECHNOLOGY

Minnesota uses precinct-count optical scan ballots statewide, with all but a handful of the state's eighty-seven counties using the ES&S Model 100 optical ballot reader as their primary equipment (with the ES&S AutoMARK for disability access). Before voting machines may be used, they must be tested and certified by the secretary of state and an independent testing authority. Minn. Stat. Ann. § 206.57. The machines must be tested again within fourteen days before each election, and since 2006 a random manual audit of ballots also must be performed after each state general election. Minn. Stat. Ann. § 206.83; Minn. Stat. Ann. § 206.89; Minn. Rule 8220.1550. If the machines fail the audit, it can trigger a full manual recount and decertification of the machines until they are brought up to standards. Minn. Stat. Ann. § 206.89. This new audit feature is discussed in greater detail in the accompanying chapter.

POLLING PLACE OPERATIONS

At least three poll workers must be present at all times in each precinct polling place (and, in state primary or general elections, at least four workers in any precinct that had more than 400 voters in the last similar election). Minn. Stat. Ann. § 204B.22. Poll workers are nominated by the major political parties and appointed by the municipal governing body or the county board of elections. Minn. Stat. Ann. § 204B.21. To serve as poll workers, individuals must complete a two-hour training course at least once every two years. Minn. Rule 8240.1300. On Election Day, voting begins at 7:00 a.m. and ends at 8:00 p.m., although any person standing in line at the close of polls is allowed to vote. Minn. Stat. Ann. § 204C.05; 204C.08. The number of voting machines available must be adjusted for the number of eligible voters in the precinct, and there must be 100 ballots for every 85 individuals who voted in the precinct in the last election of the same kind. Minn. Stat. Ann. § 204B. Disabled voters are entitled to assistance either from two poll workers of different political parties or, alternatively, with certain exceptions, any person of their choice. Minn. Stat. Ann. § 204C.15.

BALLOT SECURITY

Minnesota law contains numerous chain of custody provisions. The critical feature of most of these rules is that their violation will not necessarily provide a basis for challenging a concluded election (although while the voting and canvassing process remains ongoing, an aggrieved party may obtain an injunction to enforce the rules, see Minn. Stat. Ann. § 204C.39; Green v. Independent Consol. School Dist. No. 1 of Lyon County, 89 N.W.2d 12, 16 (Minn., 1958)). Instead, as the state supreme court explained: "in the absence of fraud or bad faith or constitutional violation, an election which has resulted in a fair and free expression of the will of the legal voters upon the merits will not be invalidated because of a departure from the statutory regulations governing the conduct of the election" unless a specific statutory provision at issue clearly provides that it's observance is mandatory to a valid election. Green v. Independent Consol. School Dist. No. 1 of Lyon County, supra, at 17.

POST-ELECTION PROCESSES

Because Minnesota's optical scan ballots are generally scanned through the tabulating machine by the voter, poll workers do not themselves physically count Election Day ballots (although they do feed absentee ballots into the tabulating equipment). Nevertheless, if there are more ballots cast than voters who signed in to vote, poll workers are directed to randomly exclude a sufficient number of ballots to equalize the counts. Minn. Stat. Ann. § 204C.20. Returns then are delivered to the county auditor, and the county canvassing board canvasses the returns and determines the winner of county races. Minn. Stat. Ann. § 204C.27. The state canvassing board determines the winner of multi-county and statewide races. Minn. Stat. Ann. § 204C.32, 204C.33.

For statewide elections, congressional and state legislative elections, and judicial elections, Minnesota has automatic recounts whenever the margin of victory is less than one-half of one percent of the vote total, or is ten votes or less and the total number of votes cast is 400 or less. Minn. Stat. Ann. § 204C.35. The same margins in local races entitle losing candidates to request a recount at state expense if they desire. Minn. Stat. Ann. § 204C.36. For larger margins of victory, any candidate in any race can obtain a recount at the candidate's own expense. Minn. Stat. Ann. § 204C.35; 204C.36. Recounts are conducted by reviewing individual ballots to identify the "voter's intent." Minn. Stat. Ann. § 204C.22; Minn. Rule 8235.0800.

Election contests generally must be filed within seven days after the canvass is completed, but the deadline is delayed in the event of a recount, which is to be completed "as soon as possible." Minn. Stat. Ann. § 209.021, Minn. Stat. Ann. § 204C.35; 204C.36. A candidate may contest the result of an election "over an irregularity in the conduct of an election or canvass of votes, over the question of who received the largest number of votes legally cast, . . . or on the grounds of deliberate, serious, and material violations of the Minnesota election law," Minn. Stat. Ann. § 209.02, see Hahn v. Graham, 225 N.W.2d 385, 386 (Minn., 1975). There is no required timetable for completing the contest.

PART III: LESSONS LEARNED

Chapter 8: General Observations

Chapter 9: Recommendations for Nine Areas of Election Administration

Chapter 10: Specific Reforms for the Five States

CHAPTER 8
GENERAL OBSERVATIONS

OUR EXAMINATION of Ohio, Illinois, Michigan, Wisconsin, and Minnesota yields valuable insights for election administration across the United States, as well as more specific advice for these five states. The experiences described in the preceding chapters should therefore be taken into consideration as election reform deliberations proceed in other states and in Congress. In some areas, these five states provide examples worthy of emulation; in others, they provide warnings of what to avoid; in still others, they suggest the need for further research.

We divide our discussion of lessons learned into three chapters. This chapter offers a set of general observations from our research that should guide state and federal policymaking. In Chapter 9, we offer a set of specific recommendations for each of the nine areas of election administration around which this study is organized. Chapter 10, the final chapter, offers particularized reforms tailored to each of the five states in the study.

1. STATE ELECTION ECOSYSTEMS ARE CRITICAL TO FEDERAL ELECTIONS.

Each of the five states in this study has structured its political system so as to advance the three democratic values that we identified at the outset of this study: access, integrity, and finality. Each state recognizes that every citizen's vote should be viewed as equally valuable, not merely as a constitutional requirement of one-person-one-vote but also as a political norm. The election ecosystems of all five states seek to promote this

principle to some degree, through practices designed to facilitate participation by all eligible citizens. They also include features designed to ensure that the results obtained are reliable and that disputes can be resolved fairly and without undue delay. At the same time, it is clear that there is room for improvement in how the election ecosystems of all the subject states advance the values of access, integrity, and finality.

From a national policymaking perspective, one of the questions that must be considered is how to prioritize the various reforms that are needed, not only in these five states but also throughout the country. We suggest that, under our federal system, there is a particular need for attending to problems in those states upon which the federal elections – including the presidential election – are likely to turn. In this regard, there is no denying the fact that Ohio, because of its past and probably future significance in presidential elections, receives more attention to matters of its election administration than other states. We think this is appropriate. Given our federal structure, the election ecosystems of each state function to serve not just each state's needs, but also the needs of the nation as a whole. This reality should be kept in mind in establishing priorities.

For instance, considered on their own, the need for reform in Illinois might be considered just as urgent as in Ohio. Looking at the recent history of each of these states in isolation, Ohio does not seem any more mismanaged than Illinois. But an electoral disaster in Ohio is more likely to have national implications than one in Illinois. It therefore makes sense to devote special attention to whether Ohio can improve the administration of its elections by 2008, especially in Cuyahoga County. That is not to say that election administration problems in Chicago or East St. Louis, Illinois should be ignored but rather that, from a national perspective, problems in swing states should be considered especially urgent. The states, in other words, can be compared on two dimensions: 1) the vulnerability of their election ecosystems, and 2) their significance in federal elections. The first dimension is the one that matters for internal purposes, while both matter for national purposes. Both perspectives are legitimate and, indeed, necessary for policymakers to take into consideration as they attempt to set priorities for reform.

Even aside from their importance to federal elections, there is another reason why state election ecosystems are a matter of national importance. Election administration, although historically an exclusively state matter, is today becoming more and more federalized. This reality affects all states, even those with relatively smooth-running systems. Federal statutes in this area – most notably the National Voting Registration Act ("NVRA") and the Help America Vote Act ("HAVA") – reflect Congress' awareness of the central role that state and local election administrators play in federal elections. These laws have given rise to a federal infrastructure that, although presently quite limited, will assume increasing importance in years to come.

To be clear, we do not advocate the federalization of election administration, in the sense of putting federal officials in charge of the day-to-day operations involved in running elections. State and local control over election administration is the reality and is likely to remain so for the foreseeable future. We do, however, think it necessary for there to be a stronger set of guiding principles that will enhance election fairness and uniformity throughout the nation. This will also necessarily mean that Congress will have to assume some responsibility for funding the administration of federal elections on an ongoing basis, rather than simply leaving states to their own devices as it did before HAVA.

The need for this federal infrastructure also means that state and local officials must be active participants in national policy debates. Even states like Minnesota, which in many respects has an exemplary system, cannot simply go it alone. Instead, as Secretary of State Ritchie has recognized, Minnesota and other states need to participate in and contribute to the development of federal policy. If through this process states can export some of their electoral successes to other states, that would be an enormous contribution.

2. INDIVIDUAL VOTERS' PRIORITIES AND SYSTEMIC PRIORITIES WILL SOMETIMES DIVERGE.

Any state's election ecosystem can be evaluated from multiple perspectives. As we have just discussed, it can be viewed from either a state or a national perspective. It can also be viewed from either an individualistic or a systemic perspective. The individualistic perspective considers how well the system serves needs of the individual voter, in allowing people to register easily, cast their votes conveniently, and have those votes counted accurately. The systemic perspective, by contrast, focuses on how well the state's system aggregates individual voter preferences into a reliable outcome. This requires not only that all eligible citizens have equal access to the polls, but also that the process be transparent, fair, and timely in its resolution of election disputes. The systemic perspective must therefore take into account the values of access, integrity, and finality.

Although the individualistic and systemic perspectives are usually reinforcing, they occasionally are not. For example, individual voters might prefer the convenience of no-excuse absentee voting by mail. From a systemic perspective, however, such a policy may pose problems – such as voter errors in submitting absentee ballots, administrative mistakes in their handling, or fraudulent use of such ballots – that may call election results into question. More significantly, the individualistic and systemic perspectives may give rise to a different order of priority for potential reforms, even when both perspectives would put the same reforms on the list.

The extent to which any state adopts the individualistic or systemic perspective depends on a variety of factors, including its place in the national landscape. In states like Ohio and Wisconsin, because of their prominent place in presidential elections today, the systemic perspective is particularly important. Such states should therefore make a special effort to ensure fairness and transparency in their processes for conducting elections and resolving disputes that arise afterwards. Moreover, in keeping with our first observation, federal policymakers – including Congress – must adopt a systemic perspective in their ongoing attempts to improve the federal infrastructure of elections.

3. A STATE'S POLITICAL CULTURE AFFECTS THE HEALTH OF ITS ELECTION ECOSYSTEM

From the outset we approached this study with the expectation that the specific background and traditions of each state would substantially influence its election ecosystem, especially in how the system's practical operation differed from its theoretical design. We had not anticipated, however, the close correlation between the relative health of each state's election ecosystem and a pre-existing framework for classifying a state's political culture – namely, the typology of political scientist Daniel Elazar, which we discuss beginning in Chapter 5. Professor Elazar describes three dominant types of political culture in American states: individualist, moralist, and traditionalist.[1] Although some scholars have criticized this classification scheme,[2] we believe it is instructive to compare how these political cultures map onto the election ecosystems of this study.

The order of the five state chapters in Part II reflects our rough evaluation of each state's relative electoral health, with Ohio's election ecosystem being the weakest and Minnesota's the strongest. After making this evaluation of electoral health, we were intrigued to discover that the healthiest state election ecosystems were in states whose political cultures Elazar has described as predominantly "moralist." In his original work, Elazar labeled Minnesota, our strongest state, as almost entirely moralist, and Wisconsin, our next strongest state, as largely moralist with a hint of individualist culture. In contrast, Elazar identified Michigan as having more of a mix of (primarily) moralist and (secondarily) individualist cultures, while Illinois and Ohio were largely individualist (with pockets of moralist and traditionalist cultures).[3]

The underlying characteristics upon which Elazar focused in classifying a state's political culture as "moralist" or "individualist" are useful in thinking about how political culture influences election administration. In oversimplified terms, Elazar describes a moralist culture as one in which government is viewed positively as a shared enterprise to enhance community well-being.[4] It is not surprising to find that this culture is associated with a commitment to nonpartisan and professional election administration. Such states are likely to have an easier time functioning in nonpartisan or bipartisan administrative structures because administrators see their positions as an opportunity and an obligation to serve the public interest. This in turn entails a commitment to procedural fairness and transparency in the conduct of elections. In contrast, Elazar describes an individualist political culture as one in which government is viewed ambivalently as a marketplace for responding to competing demands.[5] It is not surprising that states where this culture predominates may be less attentive to procedural fairness, and may sometimes lose sight of the public interest in matters of election administration.

To be clear, these generalizations certainly do not describe all election officials in any given state. In the course of our research, we have encountered election officials deeply committed to procedural fairness and the public interest in each state. Our focus here is not on the integrity of individual administrators, but rather on the overall health of a state's election system. Elazar's typology captures an important contributing factor to the functioning of each state's ecosystem.

4. CENTRAL LEADERSHIP AND COMMUNICATION MAKE A GREAT DIFFERENCE

The health of a state's election ecosystem also depends on the presence of an effective state elections authority. Yet while central leadership plays a crucial role in the smooth operation of an election ecosystem, the mere presence of strong central leadership is not sufficient. This chief elections bureau or officer must use the power of that position *effectively*. This requires at least three things: 1) asserting vigorous leadership to promote statewide consistency and uniformity where appropriate, 2) avoiding conduct that would give rise to any appearance of bias, and 3) providing meaningful assistance and guidance to local election officials.

It is also essential that a state's central election authority foster excellent communication with other election officials around the state, constantly earning and confirming their trust. This requires both a comprehensive knowledge of what is occurring at the local level and the ability to provide authoritative guidance to local officials. For guidance to be authoritative, the state election authority must also have the means to make sure that state policies are actually followed. This partly depends on enforcement authority, a subject we discuss in Chapter 9, but a strong relationship between state and local authorities is at least as important to a healthy state ecosystem.

5. STATEWIDE EQUALITY SHOULD GENERALLY TRUMP LOCAL AUTONOMY.

In the field of election administration, as in other areas of public policy such as education, an inevitable tension exists between the values of local autonomy and statewide equality. Preserving some degree of local control over election administration is important, not merely because of tradition but also because local variation can foster experimentation, which in turn yields greater knowledge about innovative best practices. One good example from Illinois is DuPage County's technological innovation involving electronic protocols for when poll workers should use provisional rather than regular ballots. Such experimentation should be encouraged, because it will eventually benefit the system as a whole.

It is nevertheless critical for states to accord equal treatment to all their citizens, especially with respect to the casting and counting of ballots. The exercise of the franchise is one sphere in which equality of citizenship must be the paramount concern. Therefore, although each state ought to do more to foster local experimentation, this should occur only within a framework that guarantees the essential equality of the right to vote. A certain degree of statewide uniformity in election practices and procedures is helpful, and in some cases necessary, to ensure equality.

There is no obvious or easy way to properly promote equality while protecting innovation, but all five states – and especially Illinois and Ohio – have room to improve in this respect. In particular, the wide variation in provisional voting rates across Ohio (as discussed in more detail in the Ohio Provisional Voting Supplement to Chapter 3), and the extent to which Ohio's local elections officials have operated without statewide standards in recent elections, provide evidence of unequal treatment that might give rise to an Equal Protection claim under the principles of *Bush v. Gore*.

Whether or not such variations violate the law, the practical effect of such disparities is to undermine the ideal of democratic equality. Our examination of Illinois similarly reveals a lack of statewide standardization in many areas of its election administration. In contrast, Michigan, Wisconsin, and Minnesota have achieved a greater degree of statewide consistency, and thus appear closer to the ideal of equal treatment of all citizens regardless of where in the state they happen to live.

6. THE STATE JUDICIARY PLAYS A SIGNIFICANT ROLE IN AN ELECTION ECOSYSTEM, AND NOT ALWAYS A CONSTRUCTIVE ONE.

Each state's judiciary plays a significant role in determining the law that actually is put into effect, usually in circumstances where the judicial interpretation of the law has the potential to make a real difference in the outcome of an election. It is not uncommon to see state judicial decisions in which rules are interpreted creatively, or overturned as unconstitutional, by courts not fully attentive to the rules' application in particular circumstances. The content of any state's election laws is much more amorphous and unsettled than what any examination of the state's statutes would indicate.

This observation in turn leads to two related comments: First, it suggests the value of drafting the rules and procedures of election administration with as much clarity and specificity as possible. The less ambiguity in a rule, the fewer discretionary judgments that administrators and judges will have to make. Second, where such ambiguity inevitably remains, it points to the tremendous importance of the particular individuals who sit at the apex of a state's judiciary, its supreme court. The ultimate authority to define the meaning and application of a state's election laws lies in their hands, except to the extent that the U.S. Supreme Court intervenes based on a conflict with federal law, as it did in *Bush v. Gore*.

The interpretation of any state's election laws thus depends in part on the identity and personal philosophies of the individuals who constitute that state's supreme court. The implications of this observation are significant. Consider Ohio, where all of the current state supreme court justices are elected Republicans. In any significant election law controversy, there is a realistic chance that a majority of these current justices would clash with the Ohio Secretary of State, an elected Democrat – as they did in a recent case involving the timetable and procedures for vetoing state legislation.[6] The members of that court might view themselves as simply interpreting the state's constitution and statutory laws as objectively as they can. But when in a given case there is a Democratic interpretation vying with a Republican interpretation, it is difficult for the elected justices to claim convincingly that they are transcending party allegiance if they adopt the Republican interpretation. The situation could get ugly in October or November 2008 if, for example, the Democratic secretary of state and the Republican-controlled state legislature become embroiled in a dispute that winds up before the Republican state supreme court, over the meaning of Ohio's rules regarding provisional voting or voter identification.

The same point applies in Michigan. There, a state supreme court that is bitterly divided along party lines has already made a spectacle of itself on various matters, and was deeply divided in adjudicating the state's voter identification measure. It is doubtful that many people would trust that court to operate "above the partisan fray" if an important election law issue came before it in October or November 2008, with Democrats and Republicans on opposite sides. The "perfect storm" in Michigan in 2008 would be if the race to be the state's chief justice is close and contested and, in order to resolve it, the Michigan judiciary is called upon to review a potentially determinative issue of state law.

Regrettably, there has been no effort in any of these five states to develop a bipartisan or nonpartisan institutional arrangement, even if only temporary, to handle a partisan election dispute that might arise in the heat of battle. None of these states has in place a court with the institutional credibility needed to resolve such a dispute in a manner that both sides would perceive as fair. In that sense, all of these states – and probably most states in the country – have failed adequately to prepare for the next election. The U.S. Supreme Court might try to step in and perform that role. In fact, this may be what the Court thought it was doing in *Bush v. Gore*, and what the Court thinks it is doing by agreeing to review the dispute over Indiana's voter identification requirement in early 2008. But some doubt remains about whether the U.S. Supreme Court would be accepted as an evenhanded tribunal guaranteed to deliver a fair result in a partisan election dispute.

It is therefore incumbent on the states to rise to the occasion, by creating institutions capable of fairly resolving disputes over the administration of elections. One possibility is a specialized election court whose members are selected through a mechanism that will ensure bipartisan consensus, something we discuss in Chapter 9's treatment of post-election processes and in Chapter 10 with reference to Ohio and Illinois. The need to resolve election disputes fairly may also be a factor counseling in favor of merit selection of state judges, rather than partisan judicial elections. While the best solution is debatable, there is an undeniable need for bipartisan leadership to address this systemic weakness.

7. SYSTEMWIDE RISK ASSESSMENT AND MANAGEMENT IS CRITICAL.

There can be no question that the field of election administration remains underdeveloped, both as a profession and as a subject of research.[7] We need greater professionalization and, in turn, better research to direct the profession. One approach to this need would be the development of a science of risk management, comparable to that which one might learn in business school. No state can determine what requires attention without identifying and weighing the various risks that it confronts.

Currently, only Secretary of State Brunner in Ohio seems to have adopted a risk management approach to election administration, perhaps in large part because she feels the glare of the national spotlight on her. But even her office has not yet fully come to terms with all of the various risks that Ohio faces, like abuses of no-excuse absentee voting and partisan decisionmaking by the state supreme court. Even more problematic is that, without the benefit of much research on "election risk management," a conscientious secretary of state has little choice but to operate on the fly in

attempting to mitigate risks. Nor has the state legislature, ultimately responsible for lawmaking and funding in the state, stepped in to assist. This may be one situation where the separation of powers, with its diffusion of authority, facilitates buck-passing and the inability of government to tackle an issue for the benefit of the citizenry. Still, it is only because Secretary Brunner will be held primarily accountable if things go wrong in Ohio in 2008 that there has been any progress in an effort to get a systemwide handle on the health of the state's election ecosystem.

Although nothing comparable appears to be occurring elsewhere, Illinois has taken a positive step to identify certain kinds of election administration problems, in the form of its requirement of a partial audit (five percent) of its vote tallies. Specifically, for two decades the Illinois code has tasked the state board of elections with randomly identifying five percent of each jurisdiction's precincts, after the election is over, in order for the jurisdiction then to recount the ballots in those precincts (using the paper trails in the case of DRE voting, and rescanning the ballots in the case of optical scan ballots). The results of the audit then can be compared with the official results, to identify equipment or other problems in vote counting. This is a welcome innovation, although Illinois needs to ensure compliance with it more rigorously than it appears to have done to date. This kind of post-voting audit of the process has real value and importance in identifying some kinds of system failures that affect voting machine accuracy, and all states should be implementing some similar form of post-election audit. Minnesota, too, has much more recently adopted its own post-voting audit procedure, and the one time that it has been implemented so far (November 2006) was successful. While more needs to be done, these steps are examples of how states might act to reduce the risks of an Election Day meltdown.

8. POLICYMAKING IN THE AREA OF ELECTION ADMINISTRATION IS OVERLY PARTISAN.

In the course of conducting this study, it has been disconcerting to learn the extent to which the mindset of elected policymakers is not on how to design the voting process for the public's benefit, but rather on how to advance one's candidacy or party. Perhaps it is too much to expect state legislators and other political actors to think about the public interest, rather than their own interests, when it comes to the administration of elections. The cynic will say that politicians will always think and act like politicians. We believe, however, that legislators and other elected officials have the capacity to rise above their narrow political interest and act like "statesmen." It may not happen often, but when it does – as in the case of Wisconsin's legendary governor and senator Robert LaFollette, Sr. – the history books reward them. Each of the states we have studied needs leaders from both major political parties to transcend narrow-minded partisanship and work together to strengthen their state's election ecosystem for the benefit of the people whom they are sworn to serve.

9. URBAN ELECTIONS POSE SPECIAL CHALLENGES.

Some of the most serious problems in the administration of elections are in large cities like Detroit, Cleveland, Chicago, and Milwaukee. Greater attention therefore should be devoted to the special challenges of running elections in urban localities. Social scientists need to study this problem more systematically and learn from studying other urban social systems, such as schools, hospitals, and libraries. Among other challenges, elections in an urban setting require massive logistical coordination at the precinct level for what is a large but one-day event, staffed by volunteers. This makes running elections different from running a school or hospital, which is kept in continuous operation day after day through permanent employees.

The role of the poll workers looms large in any jurisdiction, as discussed in more detail in Chapter 9, but nowhere is the need for an adequate number of qualified poll workers greater than in urban precincts. Indeed, with election processes increasingly complicated, staffing the polls is an issue approaching crisis levels. To an even greater extent than other public functions, the fair administration of elections depends on following procedures that may make it difficult to recruit enough poll workers. The need for bipartisan processes at each polling place, for example, imposes a legitimate constraint on poll worker recruiting in some jurisdictions – such as the requirement that they cannot all be of the same party. Our research also suggests that the education level of poll workers is a factor in the quality of service provided to voters. To the extent that a locality's public education system lags behind the mean, it is likely to have difficulty staffing its polls adequately. While there is no magical solution, there is an undeniable need for greater attention to the significant challenges that urban electoral jurisdictions face in running elections.

REFERENCES

1. *See* Daniel J. Elazar, AMERICAN FEDERALISM: A VIEW FROM THE STATES 114-142 (3d ed. 1984).

2. *See, e.g.*, Rodney E. Hero & Caroline J. Tolbert, *A Racial/Ethnic Diversity Interpretation of Politics and Policy in the States of the U.S.*, 40 AM. J. POL. SCI. 851 (1996); John Kincaid, *Political Cultures of the American Compound Republic*, 10 PUBLIUS 1 (1980).

3. *See* Daniel J. Elazar, *supra* note 1, at 124-25.

4. *See id.* at 117-121.

5. *See id.* at 115-121.

6. *See State ex rel. Ohio General Assembly v. Brunner*, 872 N.E.2d 912 (Ohio 2007).

7. *See* Daniel P. Tokaji, *The Birth and Re-Birth of Election Administration*, 6 ELECTION L.J. 118, 126-31 (2007).

CHAPTER 9
RECOMMENDATIONS FOR NINE AREAS OF ELECTION ADMINISTRATION

HAVING SET FORTH general observations in the preceding chapter, we now turn to policy recommendations for the nine areas of election administration around which this study is structured. To some extent, these nine divisions are artificial. As we have emphasized, election administration in any state should be understood as an ecosystem, consisting of numerous interdependent components. Changing one part of a state's ecosystem – whether it is the equipment used for voting, the way in which registration lists are kept, or the institution with oversight authority – will necessarily affect others. Thus, our recommendations in each subject-matter area will have implications for the entire state ecosystem. We also emphasize that these recommendations are not meant to be a comprehensive recipe for national election reform, something that would require a broader inquiry than the geographically limited one presented here. Still, the experience of the states we have studied suggests some key improvements that can be made in how elections are conducted across the country.

INSTITUTIONAL ARRANGEMENTS

1. State election authorities must establish clear lines of communication with local officials.

The five states we have examined all run their elections differently. At the state level, an elected secretary of state has authority over elections in Michigan, Minnesota, and Ohio. In Wisconsin and Illinois, on the other hand, oversight responsibility is entrusted to bipartisan or nonpartisan state boards. There are also consid-

erable differences in how local authority is distributed. In Ohio, for example, local authority rests primarily with county officials; in Michigan and Wisconsin, by contrast, municipal officials have primary responsibility over elections.

We do not believe that our study provides a clear basis for preferring either a particular state administrative structure or a particular allocation of authority among local entities. There are clearly some disadvantages inherent in electing a state's chief election official on a partisan basis, foremost among them the danger of real or perceived bias in favor of that official's party. Ohio's former Secretary of State Ken Blackwell served as the poster child for such concerns in the 2004 and 2006 election seasons. Although many recent allegations of partisanship have surrounded Republican officials, the new Democratic secretaries of state in Ohio and Minnesota are already facing criticism for partisan decisionmaking. How these two states move forward will likely provide some useful information, given the partisan tensions that exist within them.

While elected chief election officials present some inescapable problems, there can also be serious problems of accountability with appointed boards like Illinois' and Wisconsin's. The inertia built into a multi-member policymaking body can make it difficult to take decisive action when it is needed. When those bodies are split along ideological or partisan lines, it can also lead to gridlock.

One alternative to both of these predominant models would be to move to an appointed chief election officer with professional experience administering elections, selected through a mechanism that ensures bipartisan consensus. We discuss this idea further in Chapter 10 in connection with our recommendations for Ohio, where the problems of an elected chief election officer have been greatest, and our recommendations for Illinois, where the problems of an appointed state board are most apparent.

As is the case with state election authorities, there is no obvious answer to the question of how best to allocate authority among local entities. There are advantages and disadvantages to allocating authority to municipal officials rather than county officials, as Wisconsin and Michigan do, and as Minnesota also does to a lesser extent. The relatively small size of municipalities may make them easier to manage. On the other hand, smaller towns are likely to have very limited staffs and budgets, making it hard to perform the tasks essential to running twenty-first century elections. In addition, entrusting authority to municipalities rather than counties multiplies the number of local authorities running elections, thereby increasing the difficulty of managing a state election system in a manner that ensures equal treatment to all voters throughout the state. Wisconsin exemplifies the tradeoffs of municipal election administration. While the small size of most municipalities makes it easier for the local clerk to keep track of individual voters, it is difficult to ensure consistency across the 1,851 municipalities in the state – particularly when many of their clerks do not even have email access.

Despite their variations, there is one important feature that well-run election systems share:

strong lines of communication exist between the state election authority and the localities with direct responsibility for running elections. It is vitally important that state officials be ready and willing to answer questions from local officials promptly and consistently. This has been an attribute of Wisconsin's and Michigan's election systems for many years, probably because of the long tenure and professionalism of the appointed state officials with responsibility for election administration in both states. By contrast, Ohio and Minnesota have both experienced serious problems in this area in recent years, though their newly elected secretaries of state have expressed a commitment to making improvements. Illinois probably has the furthest to go of the five states in making sure that there is consistency in the administration of elections across the state.

No democratic value is more important than a state's obligation to treat its citizens equally. Consistency in the administration of elections is essential to achieve this value, yet every state has some room for improvement in this area. However authority is allocated among the components of state and local government, it is critical that the state's chief election authority provide clear guidance to local authorities on how election laws are to be administered.

2. State legislatures must give their election officials the tools to enforce consistency in the application of state law across counties and municipalities.

While communication is important, it is not sufficient to ensure equality among a state's electoral jurisdictions and their voters. State law must also ensure that state authorities have the means to enforce consistency in the application of election laws across the state. There is little use in having policies on how elections are to be run, however clear they may be, if those policies are not followed.

There are different ways of enforcing localities' compliance with state policies, involving both carrots and sticks. Perhaps the most obvious method is to entrust state officials with authority to grant or withhold funds based on local authorities' compliance with state rules. Another alternative is to give the state's chief election authority power to commence litigation against noncompliant localities. A more drastic approach still is to vest the state's chief election authority with the power to discharge local election officials who fail to discharge their duties, as Ohio's Secretary of State recently did with the Cuyahoga County Board of Elections. While giving the state's chief election official this power has the value of allowing this official to ensure local jurisdictions comply with state policies, it is a blunt tool with a significant downside. Especially if the state's chief election official is a secretary of state elected on a partisan basis, firing local officials can have a polarizing effect, casting doubt on whether the law is being administered in an evenhanded fashion.

While this example demonstrates a need for caution, it does not detract from the pressing need for state legislatures to give the state's chief election officials the means by which to enforce compliance with state policies. If state officials do not have this authority – or fail to exercise it appropriately – they run the risk of lawsuits alleging unequal treatment under *Bush v. Gore* and other voting rights cases, like those which have already been filed in Ohio.

3. States should regularly audit their laws and consult with officials from peer states to keep pace with a rapidly changing election environment.

One of the most noteworthy aspects of election administration in all five states is the degree of change that has occurred in the past several years. Much of this is attributable to HAVA, which imposed new requirements with respect to voting technology, provisional ballots, registration databases, and voter identification. Implementation of these new federal requirements presented a major challenge to states, given that the new rules did not always fit neatly with the preexisting election ecosystems. An example is provisional ballots, which were and remain seldom used in Michigan, Minnesota, and Wisconsin because those states have other ways of dealing with the problems that HAVA's provisional voting requirement was designed to remedy.

It is unlikely that the period of dynamism in the administration of elections will end anytime soon. There will instead be continuing change, as technology and other factors continue to alter the way in which democracy functions.

After reviewing the five states' election laws, it became clear that state legislatures have not entirely kept pace with the changing election environment. Some aspects of state election laws seem designed for an era in which hand-marked ballots were counted at a central location, something that no longer predominates in any of our states. Another area in which state laws need updating involves the disconnect between state post-election processes and the federal timetable for presidential elections. As discussed below in our recommendations for post-election processes, this is particularly difficult to understand given that Florida's 2000 experience provided states clear notice of this problem. To solve this problem, we encourage state legislatures to work with state election administrators to engage in top-to-bottom audits of state election statutes on a regular basis.

We also believe that the states have much to learn from one another. There is great value in state election officials communicating with each other about what has worked in their states, from Michigan's statewide registration database to Wisconsin's and Minnesota's Election Day Registration systems. Accordingly, we suggest that election officials have periodic meetings organized on a regional basis, as a means by which to exchange information. This already happens at the national level, through such organizations as the National Association of State Elections Directors, and the National Association of Secretaries of State, as well as with the U.S. Election Assistance Commission's standards board. We believe that there are common characteristics to Midwestern states (and perhaps characteristics common to states in other parts of the country) that would make regional meetings – for example, an annual summit of Midwest state election officials – particularly useful.

VOTER REGISTRATION

4. States should work to improve both access and accuracy by relaxing barriers to registration and complying with existing federal laws governing registration.

State registration requirements can sometimes serve as a barrier registration. To be sure, there are good reasons for having a voter reg-

istration requirement – as all states in the country except North Dakota do – including the prevention of double-voting and voting by those who are ineligible. Onerous registration requirements, however, can impede participation. By contrast, making it easier to register is one of the few reforms that has been demonstrated to increase voter turnout.[1]

Congress recognized the link between registration and turnout fourteen years ago when it enacted the National Voter Registration Act ("NVRA"), requiring that states provide an opportunity to register at state motor vehicle and welfare offices. More recently, HAVA required that states implement statewide registration databases, partly as a way of improving access by increasing the accuracy of voter registration lists. Unfortunately, there is reason to believe that many states are not fully complying with these laws. Several states, including some of those studied in this report, are not yet in full compliance with HAVA's statewide registration database requirement.[2] Particularly troubling is evidence that states are not complying with the NVRA's requirements that states provide voter registration opportunities at public assistance agencies, such as state offices that provide services to people with disabilities.[3] Thirty-one states reported a decrease in registered voters between 2004 and 2006.[4] It is important that the federal government enforce these requirements and that states follow them, in order to ensure that voters are allowed to register and that their names will be on the rolls when they come to vote.

Complying with federal law, while a necessary precondition to improving voter registration, is not sufficient. States should also work to find other ways by which to make registration easier for the voter. One of the best ways of doing this is Election Day Registration ("EDR"), a reform that has achieved great success in increasing participation Minnesota, Wisconsin, and the other states in which it has been implemented. EDR also has the side-benefit of virtually eliminating the need for provisional ballots. Eligible citizens whose names do not appear on the list when they come to the polls need no longer vote provisionally, but can instead register on the spot. While opponents of EDR sometimes argue that it leads to greater voting fraud, our five-state analysis shows no evidence that this is the case. Consistent with other research on the topic, we find no reason to believe that voter fraud is more common in EDR states than in other states.[5]

For states that remain wary of moving to EDR, Michigan provides an intriguing example of a half-step that may achieve some of the same goals. Michigan allows voters to cast an affidavit ballot if they swear under oath that they registered before the deadline, despite the fact that their names do not appear on the list. This eliminates the problem created when a mistake is made by a third party, such as groups conducting registration drives, NVRA agencies that fail to transfer registration forms to election authorities, or election officials who make a data entry error. While Michigan's affidavit ballots are technically a form of provisional ballot, they are presumptively counted, absent subsequent proof that the voter is ineligible. This eliminates the need for additional verification, which exists in states like Illinois and Ohio that do not have a comparable procedure. Of course, Michigan's process does not do anything for voters who develop an interest in politics late in the campaign season, after the deadline for

registration has passed, and therefore cannot sign the required affidavit. Still, it does avoid the risk that voters will have their votes denied due to an administrative error. And one option to serve voters who did not attempt to pre-register would be a form of "provisional" EDR, permitting new registrants at the polls to cast provisional ballots that would count upon subsequent verification of their registration information.

Other possibilities include expanding online registration, as in Arizona and Washington. John Anderson and Ray Martinez have urged "automatic voter registration" for all high school seniors, and Minnesota Secretary of State Mark Ritchie supported a bill (vetoed by the governor) that would automatically register eligible citizens applying for a driver's license unless they declined.[6] In keeping with the notion of states as laboratories for democracy, this seems a worthwhile experiment for Minnesota and other states.

Finally, states should continue working to improve their statewide registration databases. One uniformly desirable feature would be the ability to correct and update the database from each precinct on Election Day. However, in addition to the technological obstacle of having sufficient electronic equipment, such a system would pose difficult security problems, as it would entail providing thousands of volunteer poll workers with access to the official database. But short of such real-time updating of their voter databases, states still could employ electronic poll books, rather than paper ones, that could share information with each other across precincts about who has voted, even if they did not allow changes to the registration information itself. Working with one such master state list, and following consistent statewide standards of voter identification in the process, would reduce problems and make it even more difficult to engage in Election Day fraud.

CHALLENGES TO VOTER ELIGIBILITY

5. If states allow challenges, they should implement procedures that protect individual voters and prevent bottlenecks at the polls.

Of the nine areas of election administration we have considered, challenges to voter eligibility is the area that has yielded the least information. Procedures for challenging the eligibility of voters vary from state to state, but the two basic types are 1) registration challenges brought before Election Day, and 2) Election Day challenges, brought once the voter enters the polls.

A commonplace in all five states is that these procedures are not frequently used and, when used, seldom successful at disqualifying any voters. The Republican Party did pursue pre-election challenges to voters in Ohio and Wisconsin in October 2004. In Wisconsin, the Milwaukee election board unanimously rejected the 5,619 challenges on a bipartisan vote, finding they lacked evidence.[7] In Ohio, a federal court enjoined the Republican Party's pre-election challenges to some 35,000 voters on due process grounds.[8]

Although there was considerable concern that state challenge processes would be abused on Election Day in 2004, that did not in fact happen. Of course, it may be that the litigation surrounding voter challenges – especially in Ohio, where four separate cases were brought regarding the Election Day challenge process

– is one reason that they did not become a significant problem in 2004. It is thus possible that overly aggressive challenges could still become a problem in future elections, exacerbating polling place lines or even being used to intimidate voters. Another concern is that challenges could be used for so-called "vote caging," in which mass mailings are sent to registered voters and those returned as undeliverable are used as a basis for challenges. Our research has uncovered very little evidence of ineligible voters attempting to vote, as might justify broad-based challenges to voter eligibility. At the same time, the mere existence of a challenge process, even if seldom used, could be important in deterring voter fraud or other improper attempts to influence elections. Accordingly, there may be some justification for some form of challenge procedure.

If states permit challenges to voter eligibility, the challenge process needs several features if it is to serve its purposes while also protecting the rights of individual voters. First, the process should be designed to resolve as many cases as possible before Election Day. A large number of challenges on Election Day could easily prove disruptive, and make poll workers' already difficult job even more difficult. Second, any challenge procedure must provide adequate due process to voters, including an opportunity to present evidence demonstrating their eligibility to vote. Third, the process must deter an overly aggressive use of challenges. For example, poll workers might be empowered to limit the number of challenges that any one person could lodge on Election Day, or to report anyone who made several unwarranted challenges for some form of post-election punishment.

PROVISIONAL VOTING

6. States should provide clear guidance to local officials and poll workers on the circumstances under which provisional ballots should be issued and counted.

Enormous differences exist in how provisional ballots are used among the five states studied here. Ohio, for example, makes extensive use of provisional ballots – using them not only for voters whose names do not appear in the polling book at the precinct in which they claim to be registered, but also for some voters who have moved from one location to another. In other states, provisional ballots are seldom used. The EDR system in place in Minnesota and Wisconsin, for example, eliminates or sharply reduces the need for provisional ballots, since voters whose registration forms have been mishandled can simply show up at the polls on Election Day and re-register on the spot.

In general, we believe a system that reduces the need for provisional ballots is preferable to one that relies extensively on them. A large number of provisional ballots increases the risk that a close election will turn into a protracted post-election fight. Improving the registration process – both by easing registration and by increasing the accuracy of voter registration lists – is one way that states can reduce their reliance on provisional ballots.

Regardless of how extensively a state relies on provisional ballots, it is essential that the state set clear rules for both 1) who should receive a provisional ballot and 2) the circumstances under which provisional ballots will be counted. As part of the second set of rules, each state must clearly specify all the procedural steps to be taken in determining whether a provisional voter was in fact registered as required by state law. For example, it should specify whether local election officials are to check with the state motor vehicle office or other registration locations. It should also set clear rules for when a provisional ballot should be counted, notwithstanding some registration mistake. Each state also should specify, for example, whether a provisional ballot should be counted when it is discovered that a third-party registration group (like the League of Women Voters or ACORN) made a mistake in processing the voter's form.

Equally important is that local authorities follow the rules for counting provisional ballots that the state has set. This is necessary to ensure that voters are treated consistently across jurisdictions within the state. Thus, local authorities should not be permitted to adopt their own standards or procedures for verifying provisional ballots, whether they are more generous or more stringent than those prescribed by the state. While local officials in Ohio and Illinois appear to have implemented their own processes, in some cases out of an understandable desire to make sure that all eligible voters have their votes counted, it is absolutely critical that voters be treated equally across counties. It is also critical that the process for verifying and counting provisional ballots be transparent, so that the public is assured that fair and equal processes are being followed across the state.

EARLY & ABSENTEE VOTING

7. States seeking to promote voter convenience should consider in-person early voting instead of no-excuse mail-in absentee voting.

In recent decades, states have increasingly liberalized their early and absentee voting rules. Allowing some form of pre-election voting can both make the process more convenient for voters and take the pressure off the polls on Election Day. Mail-in absentee voting, in particular, has become increasingly popular in recent decades. Ohio is among the states that have moved to "no excuse" absentee voting.

While there are undoubtedly some advantages to pre-election voting, some words of caution are in order. The most commonly recognized risk is the greater potential for voter fraud, given that the individual voter need not appear at the polls in order to cast an absentee ballot. There is, accordingly, no way of being sure that the registered voter is in fact the one who cast the ballot, or that the voter was not intimidated or coerced into voting a particular way. Also significant, although less commonly recognized, are the mistakes that voters can make when voting by mail. When voting from home, voters do not have the advantage of notice technology now available at polling places that can alert them that they have overvoted (and thus spoiled) their ballot. In addition, voters can make mistakes such as failing to sign forms, omitting necessary identifying information, returning their ballots late, or using insufficient postage, all of which may result in absentee ballots not being counted.[9]

Notwithstanding these risks, some form of pre-election voting has some undeniable advantages. Although there is little evidence that expanded early or absentee voting will substantially increase turnout,[10] these practices do enhance voters' convenience. In addition, they can take the pressure off the polls on Election Day, thus minimizing both the lines that other voters face and the difficulties that poll workers face.

Accordingly, we suggest that jurisdictions interested in promoting voter convenience consider in-person early voting. Because in-person early voters have the advantage of notice technology, there is less risk of their inadvertently overvoting or undervoting. It also reduces the risk of fraud. Finally, early voters avoid some of the things that can go wrong with mail voting – like failing to include enough postage or returning the ballots too close to the deadline, resulting in their exclusion from the tallies.

VOTING TECHNOLOGY

8. States must ensure that localities provide an adequate number of ballots or machines, that equipment is thoroughly tested before Election Day, and that poll workers are properly trained.

The years since the 2000 election have seen a massive transformation in the equipment used for voting. Like most other states, the five states we have examined now use either direct record electronic ("DRE") or precinct-count optical scan equipment for polling place voting. Nationwide, jurisdictions moving to DRE equipment saw the sharpest decline in the number of uncounted votes (combined overvotes and undervotes), although both types of equipment considerably improve accuracy.[11] There have of course been well-publicized problems with the implementation of DRE equipment in some places. Most notable among the states we have studied are problems in Cuyahoga County, Ohio, which implemented a DRE system with a voter verifiable paper trail.

Optical-scan systems have arguably been easier to implement, particularly in those jurisdictions (like Ohio and Wisconsin) that require a voter verifiable paper record. They are not, however, without limitations. They are difficult to use for in-person early voting and vote centers, in comparison to DREs, which can more readily accommodate multiple ballot styles at a single location. DREs also are more easily adapted to last-minute changes in the ballot – for example, court orders requiring that a certain candidate's name be added to or omitted from the ballot. DREs can also accommodate multilingual and disabled populations more easily than optical scan systems. Relatedly, DREs can accommodate an unexpected increase in the number of voters at a particular location without the need for printing additional ballots – something that is of special concern in EDR states, given the difficulty of predicting how many people will show up to vote at each precinct. With optical scan or other paper ballots, by contrast, it is necessary to print an excess of ballots in advance of the election, some of which will ultimately go to waste, although when turnout is unexpectedly heavy, voters waiting to use DRE equipment may suffer longer lines than those voting on optical scan ballots. Finally, DREs eliminate the problem of ambiguously marked ballots (which can still arise with optical scan systems), and with it one potential source of post-election litigation.

Given that both optical scan and DRE systems have advantages, we do not make any definitive recommendation on the type of equipment that should be adopted. In fact,

decisions about which equipment works best may well vary from jurisdiction to jurisdiction. In addition, the limited funds available for voting technology mean that most jurisdictions are likely to continue using the type of equipment currently in place, at least for now. It is quite possible that there will be a need to make further changes in voting technology – and that the technology itself will be vastly different – in the next five or ten years, a problem that requires more study than has been possible in this report.

Whatever type of equipment is used, election officials can and should take steps to minimize the risk of problems. One obvious step is for state and local officials to make sure that an adequate number of machines are in place to deal with the number of voters that can reasonably be expected to appear on Election Day. Some urban precincts experienced severe problems with lines in 2004 because there were not enough voting machines in place, and it is essential to avoid this in 2008. Second, there must be adequate pre-election testing of hardware and software. One possibility is the approach presently being taken in Ohio, with a testing process that has both bipartisan consensus on methodology and bipartisan oversight of how it will proceed, in the form of an advisory committee of county elections officials.[12] Third, poll workers must be trained in how the equipment is to be used and, importantly, in what to do if problems arise on Election Day.

One area for which training is essential is the accommodation of people with disabilities. HAVA requires that a disability-accessible voting machine be made available at every polling location. But if voters are not aware that this equipment is available, or are unsure of how to use it, then it is likely to go unused. If HAVA's promise of independent voting is to be made a reality, poll workers also should receive specific instruction on how to use the accessible equipment, as well as training on how to use the regular voting equipment.

POLLING PLACE OPERATIONS

9. State and local officials must experiment with ways of recruiting qualified poll workers and training them to perform the difficult tasks that we expect of them.

Among the greatest challenges facing all five states is the difficulty in staffing polling places with an adequate number of sufficiently trained workers. This problem, exacerbated by changing technologies and procedures, creates the conditions in which any number of things could go wrong in the administration of the voting process: late openings of polling places, excessive machine failures, lost supplies, breaches in chain-of-custody procedures, and so forth. Larger, economically depressed urban areas like Chicago, Detroit, Milwaukee, and Cleveland are especially likely to have more difficulty in adequately staffing polling places, and at the same time more likely to be vulnerable to Election Day pressures and problems. One reflection of the added challenges facing urban precincts are

TABLE 6A
PROVISIONAL VOTING IN LARGE JURISDICTIONS
OHIO, ILLINOIS, AND MICHIGAN

November 2004

Ohio Jurisdiction	Total Ballots Cast	Provisional Ballots Cast	% PB Cast Total Cast	PB Counted	% PB Counted	% PB Counted/ Total Cast
Cuyahoga Cty (Cleveland)	687,255	25,309	3.68%	16,750	66.18%	2.437%
Franklin Cty (Columbus)	533,575	14,462	2.71%	12,124	83.83%	2.272%
Hamilton Cty (Cincinnati)	433,063	14,564	3.36%	11,035	75.77%	2.548%
Ohio State Total	**5,722,443**	**158,642**	**2.77%**	**123,548**	**77.88%**	**2.159%**
Illinois Jurisdiction	Total Ballots Cast	PB Cast	% PB Cast Total Cast	PB Counted	% PB Counted	% PB Counted/ Total Cast
Chicago	1,056,830	22,611	2.14%	13,838	61.20%	1.309%
Cook Cty	1,024,867	10,425	1.02%	5,425	52.04%	0.529%
Illinois State Total	**5,350,493**	**43,464**	**0.81%**	**22,238**	**51.16%**	**0.416%**
Michigan Jurisdiction	Total Ballots Cast	PB Cast	% PB Cast Total Cast	PB Counted	% PB Counted	% PB Counted/ Total Cast
Wayne Cty (Detroit)	874,861	2,244	0.26%	918	40.91%	0.105%
Michigan State Total	**4,875,692**	**5,610**	**0.12%**	**3,227**	**57.52%**	**0.066%**

Source: Ohio Secretary of State, Michigan Secretary of State, and Illinois State Board of Elections

the higher rates at which provisional ballots are often cast there, as shown in Table 6A and 6B.

Legislatures in each state have not done enough to address this critical need. Rather, they seem content to let local officials muddle through, election after election, in the face of increasing difficulty staffing the polls. In this regard state legislatures also seem to be relying instead on the election officials' prayer of "God, let this not be a close election." Unfortunately, absent greater leadership, states will resolve this problem only in response to the occurrence of some major failure, rather than preventing it in the first place.

One possibility is to move toward more aggressive reliance on high school students. Some of the election officials we interviewed report success in this regard. Another possibility is to consider making Election Day a school holiday. This would allow the recruitment of both teachers and students as poll workers. But resolving the poll worker crisis is also likely to require that more money be devoted to recruiting and paying poll workers. While the solutions to the poll worker crisis are not obvious, it is clear that this is a severe problem that demands innovation. Local entities should be encouraged – and funded – to experiment with new ways of attracting poll workers.

TABLE 6B
PROVISIONAL VOTING IN LARGE JURISDICTIONS
OHIO, ILLINOIS, AND MICHIGAN

November 2006

Ohio Jurisdiction	Total Ballots Cast	Provisional Ballots Cast	% PB Cast Total Cast	PB Counted	% PB Counted	% PB Counted/ Total Cast
Cuyahoga Cty (Cleveland)	469,930	17,656	3.76%	11,683	66.17%	2.486%
Franklin Cty (Columbus)	385,863	19,612	5.08%	16,973	86.54%	4.399%
Hamilton Cty (Cincinnati)	296,420	12,569	4.24%	10,331	82.19%	3.485%
Ohio State Total	**4,186,207**	**129,432**	**3.09%**	**104,581**	**80.80%**	**2.498%**
Illinois Jurisdiction	Total Ballots Cast	PB Cast	% PB Cast Total Cast	PB Counted	% PB Counted	% PB Counted/ Total Cast
Chicago	670,222	7,464	1.11%	1,308	17.52%	0.195%
Cook Cty	680,693	3,275	0.48%	1,381	42.17%	0.203%
Illinois State Total	**3,587,676**	**15,875**	**0.44%**	**5,874**	**37.00%**	**0.164%**
Michigan Jurisdiction	Total Ballots Cast	PB Cast	% PB Cast Total Cast	PB Counted	% PB Counted	% PB Counted/ Total Cast
Wayne Cty (Detroit)	650,109	1,361	0.21%	483	35.49%	0.074%
Michigan State Total	**3,852,008**	**2,426**	**0.06%**	**952**	**39.24%**	**0.025%**

Source: Ohio Secretary of State, Michigan Secretary of State, and Illinois State Board of Elections

BALLOT SECURITY

10. State election integrity efforts should focus on "insider" fraud.

One encouraging aspect of our study is that it found little contemporary evidence of voter cheating. While Illinois in particular has a sordid history of election fraud, those incidents appear to be diminishing. The statewide registration databases required by HAVA should further decrease the risk of voter fraud, by allowing detection of those attempting to register and vote in multiple jurisdictions.

That does not mean that corrupt election practices are entirely a thing of the past. Both Michigan and Illinois have experienced recent incidents of insider corruption. This decade, Illinois has prosecuted vote buying schemes, and Michigan and Illinois have each seen local elected officials run programs of improperly influencing absentee voters. There is a corresponding need to promote rigorous adherence to procedures designed to ensure ballot integrity. Foremost among those procedures are the investigation of cases in which a large number of absentee ballot requests come from a single address. States should also make sure to verify signatures on absentee ballots with those submitted on registration forms. Also important are chain-of-custody rules, both for electronic voting technology and for paper ballots.

States should be cautious, however, in instituting practices that might constitute barriers to participation in the name of preventing fraud. Rather, any new voting requirements should be tailored to documented instances in which ineligible people have voted. The identification requirements in Michigan and Ohio are particularly worth watching in 2008, especially in terms of their impact on voter participation.

POST-ELECTION PROCESSES

11. States should re-examine their post-election procedures to ensure the evenhanded and prompt resolution of disputes.

There is perhaps no more worrying area of election administration than the processes for resolving close and disputed elections. Each of the states we examined would benefit from a thorough analysis of their post-election procedures. This area can be broken down into three parts: 1) the procedures used for canvasses, recounts, and contests, 2) the institutional mechanism available for judicial review, 3) the timetable for resolving post-election disputes.

On the first point, it is of utmost importance that the process for counting votes and conducting recounts be above reproach. That means that it be conducted either by nonpartisan officials or by bipartisan teams. In either event, the transparency of the process should be paramount. That includes having procedures that will allow for the transparent resolution of post-election disputes over ballot security. A good example is Wisconsin, which recently enacted a law allowing for the disclosure of the electronic voting system's source code (subject to confidentiality requirements) in the event of a disputed election. This would avoid the ongoing controversy over the 2006 race for Florida's 13th Congressional District, in which the losing candidate has been denied access to the software code that could have shed light on the nature of the problem that caused over 18,000 undervotes in Sarasota County.

Second, states should consider restructuring the forum for judicial review of post-election disputes. Ideally, judges resolving election disputes should be above the partisan fray. But as explained above, it is doubtful whether the state judiciaries in any of our subject states could live up to this ideal in the event of a disputed statewide election. When a state's supreme court is dominated by members of one party, or has a reputation for voting on party lines, and especially when those judges are themselves subject to re-election or retention, there will always be questions about their impartiality. Although federal judges are appointed for life, it is not at all clear that the federal courts – including the current Supreme Court – will provide the sort of neutral arbiter that is needed either. One possibility is for states to consider creating specialized election courts to deal with post-election disputes. One of us has proposed that such an institution might consist of four sitting judges, designated to serve on the election tribunal at set intervals by the leaders of the state legislature's two largest parties in both chambers, with these four judges in turn unanimously selecting a fifth member of this special tribunal.[13] We offer further thoughts on this in Chapter 10, in discussing potential reforms in Ohio and Illinois.

Finally, states should attend to the timetable for resolving post-election disputes. This is especially important for presidential elections, given the safe harbor and Electoral College meeting dates detailed at the end of Chapter 6. Several states have failed to consider the "safe harbor" timing problem, something that is particularly difficult to excuse given that states have been on notice of this problem since 2000. Yet the contest timetable is not exclusively a presidential election problem. In any race it is quite possible to imagine post-election disputes being left unresolved for months after those elected are supposed to be sworn in – as indeed has happened with respect to Florida's 13th Congressional District representative in 2006. Every state should have a procedure in place for resolving election disputes fairly and promptly. To be sure, these values will sometimes be in conflict. But finality, along with access and integrity, is an essential value in our democracy. Thus, state procedures must provide a means by which to conclusively resolve elections within a reasonable, prescribed time after Election Day.

12. Congress should revisit the federal law governing the resolution of presidential election disputes to allow states more time to complete their recount and contest processes.

We have been wary of making new recommendations for federal election reform in this report. That is partly because we believe Congress should remain cautious about imposing new requirements on the states without considering particular elements of state ecosystems that may make a one-size-fits-all solution inappropriate. Relatedly, we believe that the results of HAVA must be comprehensively evaluated before a new set of systemic reforms is mandated.

Notwithstanding this caution, the timetable for resolving presidential elections is an issue to which Congress should attend. Under the present system, there is relatively little time for states to resolve post-election disputes before the "safe harbor" date (thirty-five days after the election), or even by the date on which the presidential electors are to meet (forty-one days after the election). States that fail to reach a conclusive resolution of post-election disputes by the safe harbor date risk having the allocation of their electors decided by the House of Representatives. Accordingly, as one of us has previously suggested, Congress should move back the Electoral College timetable by several weeks, making the safe harbor date December 31 and having presidential electors cast their votes on January 3.[14] This reform would add from seventeen to twenty-three days (depending on the year) to the time available for resolving an election contest and could be accomplished without affecting the constitutionally established date for presidential transitions of January 20.

REFERENCES

1. *See* Craig Leonard Brians & Bernard Grofman, *Election Day Registration's Effect on U.S. Voter Turnout*, 82 SOC. SCI. Q. 170 (2001)(finding that Election Day Registration increased turnout); Mark J. Fenster, *The Impact of Allowing Day of Registration Voting on Turnout in U.S. Elections from 1960 to 1992*, 22 AM. POL. Q. 74 (1994)(same).

2. *See* electionline.org, *Statewide Voter Registration Database Status*, http://electionline.org/Default.aspx?tabid=288 (showing fifty states' compliance with HAVA).

3. *See* Brian Kavanagh, *et al.*, *Ten Years Later, A Promise Unfulfilled: The National Voter Registration Act in Public Assistance Agencies*, 1995-2005 (2005).

4. *See* U.S. Election Assistance Commission, *The Impact of the National Voter Registration Act of 1993 on the Administration of Elections for Federal Office*, 2005-2006, at 8 (2007).

5. *See* Lorraine Minnite, *Election Day Registration: A Study of Voter Fraud Allegations and Findings on Voter Roll Security* 6-9 (2007), *available at* http://www.demos.org/pubs/edr_fraud_v2.pdf (finding no evidence of widespread fraud in EDR states).

6. John B. Anderson & Ray Martinez III, *Voters' Ed*, N.Y TIMES, Apr. 6, 2006; *Letter from Mark Ritchie to Tim Pawlenty* (May 8, 2007), *available at* http://www.sos.state.mn.us/docs/replytogovsvetomsg.pdf.

7. *See* Lorraine Minnite, *The Politics of Voter Fraud*, 33-34.

8. *See* Daniel P. Tokaji, *Early Returns on Election Reform: Discretion, Disenfranchisement, and the Help America Vote Act*, 73 GEO. WASH. L. REV. 1206, 1234-36 (2005).

9. *See* U.S. Government Accountability Office, *The Nation's Evolving Election System as Reflected in the November 2004 General Election 119* (2006) (reporting on problems with the return of absentee ballot applications); R. Michael Alvarez, *et al.*, *Whose Absentee Votes Are Counted: The Variety and Use of Absentee Ballots in California*, Caltech/MIT Voting Technology Project, Working Paper #34 (July 2005), *available at* http://vote.caltech.edu/media/documents/wps/vtp_wp34.pdf 18-20, 26-27 (reporting on absentee ballots not returned or not counted).

10. *See* Adam J. Berinsky, *The Perverse Consequences of Electoral Reform in the United States*, 33 AM. POL. RES. 471 (2005)(reforms like early voting and liberalized absentee voting are likely to increase the socioeconomic bias of the electorate); Jeffrey A. Karp & Susan A. Banducci, *Absentee Voting, Mobilization, and Participation*, 29 AM. POL. RES. 183 (2001) (liberal absentee voting laws do not appear to increase voter turnout).

11. *See* Charles Stewart, III, *Residual Vote in the 2004 Election*, 5 ELECTION L.J. 158, 165 (2006).

12. *See* Mark Rollenhagen, *Bipartisan Panel to Test Voting Machines*, (CLEVELAND) PLAIN DEALER, Sept. 24, 2007, *available at* http://blog.cleveland.com/metro/2007/09/bipartisan_panel_to_test_votin.html.

13. *See* Edward B. Foley, *The Analysis and Mitigation of Electoral Errors*, 18 STAN. L. & POLY REV. 350, 378-79 (2007).

14. *See* Steven F. Huefner, *Reforming the Timetable for the Electoral College Process*, Election Law @ Moritz Weekly Comment, Nov. 30, 2004, http://moritzlaw.osu.edu/electionlaw/comments/2004/041130.php.

CHAPTER 10
SPECIFIC REFORMS FOR THE FIVE STATES

AS PART II DEMONSTRATES, the election ecosystems of Illinois, Michigan, Minnesota, Ohio, and Wisconsin vary widely in certain features, while having substantial similarities in others. Some of their similarities may reflect common historical roots, while others are the result of more recent innovations and approaches. The Help America Vote Act ("HAVA") obviously also has forced a certain similarity on these and other states. Yet important variations exist even with respect to how each state is meeting key HAVA requirements, such as the statewide voter database requirement and the demand for new voting technology. In some instances, these and other state-by-state variations reflect deliberate choices. In other cases, they are largely the result of historical circumstance.

In all five states, certain aspects of their election ecosystems seem quite stable, and other aspects remain quite fluid. Some matters of election administration are fluid today in part because they remain under intense pressure and scrutiny, even to the point that some reformers might be accused of promoting change merely for its own sake. As previously suggested, however, we believe that continuity also is critical to sound election administration. At the same time, some changes in election administration are inevitable, and often warranted.

Recognizing both the unique characteristics of each state, as well as the importance of maintaining continuity wherever appropriate, this final chapter recommends reforms tailored to the existing election ecosystems of each of the five states in this study. We have favored reforms that are practical and, we believe, politically feasible. We have also kept our list of recommendations short, presenting for each state only what we view as the three most important priorities, both to maximize the ability of policymakers to focus on a few critical goals and to reduce the prospects of destabilizing change.

We discuss the states in the same order that we presented our description of their election ecosystems in Chapters 3 through 7, starting with Ohio and then proceeding through Illinois, Michigan, Wisconsin, and Minnesota. Our specification of three priority reforms for each state should not be understood as a suggestion that policymakers ignore the other issues identified in the preceding chapter. Rather, the recommendations in Chapter 9 and the ones that follow in this chapter should be seen as complementary.

OHIO REFORMS

Our priority reforms for Ohio all involve steps to take partisan politics out of election administration. This is not to denigrate the efforts of current Ohio Secretary of State Jennifer Brunner, which if successful are likely to bring improvements to Ohio's statewide registration database, poll worker recruitment and training, voting technology, and other areas. Accordingly, our three proposed reforms – improving bipartisan cooperation, changing the method by which the state's chief elections official is selected, and creating a specialized neutral tribunal for the resolution of election contests – are far from the only possible improvements the state could make to its election ecosystem. They are, however, major systemic reforms with the potential to influence a number of more particular needs.

1. Develop bipartisan leadership over election administration.

What Ohio's election ecosystem needs more than anything else is a sense of shared stewardship. Consider Cuyahoga County, a thorn in Secretary Blackwell's side in 2004 and 2006, which Secretary Brunner addressed by removing the prior board of elections. When something next goes wrong in an election there, Secretary Brunner now owns the problem. This may have been a necessary step, but it would be better if there were bipartisan, joint ownership of Cuyahoga County's challenges, so that the Republicans no longer have the same incentive to claim there is a problem that the Democrats did in 2004 and 2006, and instead all are genuinely concerned about minimizing the risks and promoting sound election administration.

A useful model is the bipartisan advisory committee composed of county elections officials that Ohio recently created to verify the reliability of its voting machines.[1] Ohio should develop a similar bipartisan approach to prepare to handle the variety of election administration issues that can be expected to arise in the 2008 election and beyond. An election reform summit between Secretary Brunner, other key Democrats, and key Republicans, would be one method of doing so. Such an approach could establish bipartisan buy-in concerning both

Cuyahoga County and the rest of the state and promote a joint commitment to identifying and solving the key issues. This type of bipartisan planning and leadership ought to be within easy reach of Ohio's many thoughtful and genuinely concerned political leaders. Absent such shared stewardship, election administration problems all too often will continue to serve as fodder for partisan attacks, rather than promoting real improvements.

2. Replace the elected chief election officer with a nonpartisan appointee.

A related reform would be to take election administration entirely out of the hands of a partisan elected official and instead place it in the hands of an appointed professional. Without detracting from either Secretary Brunner's or Secretary Blackwell's knowledge and understanding of election administration matters, the fact that they became the state's chief election officer only by winning a partisan election inevitably compromises their effectiveness. A promising alternative would be to transfer responsibility for state election administration to a nonpartisan official with significant election administration experience.

In reflecting on the value of having a nonpartisan professional serve as a state's chief election officer, we have considered as an analogy the role of the chairman of the Federal Reserve in guiding and influencing the national economy. Although Alan Greenspan, recently retired, perhaps best exemplifies the substantial contributions that nonpartisan professionals can make in this position, his successor and his numerous predecessors also make the case that in certain matters of public administration appointed experts can provide highly effective leadership. We see no reason, other than political inertia and partisan interests, that matters of election administration should not be overseen by officials selected through a mechanism that will promote nonpartisanship and professionalism.

One possible model is that which Wisconsin has recently adopted (discussed in Chapter 6), in which a board nominated by former judges and appointed with bipartisan consensus is responsible for selecting a chief elections administrator. Another is that which Professor Rick Hasen has proposed, in which the state's chief election official would be nominated by the governor and confirmed by a supermajority of the state legislature.[2] Still another possibility is to have the governor appoint a chief election officer from three nominees submitted jointly by the majority and minority leaders in the state legislature. In any event, the chief election officer should be given substantial stature, akin to that of the secretary of state or the attorney general, and a term of at least four years.

3. Create nonpartisan tribunals to resolve election disputes.

When matters of election administration become the subject of a legal dispute, candidates and the public need a tribunal, whether within the state's regular judiciary or elsewhere, that all sides are prepared to trust. This is especially true in post-election proceedings, which traditional courts are not well-suited to handle, both in terms of how rapidly these proceedings should be resolved and in terms of the awkwardness of having the judicial branch of government determining the membership of another branch of government. Indeed, historically courts lacked jurisdiction over election contests, until state legislatures charged the courts with resolving them.[3]

As discussed in Chapter 9, one option would be to structure in advance an impartial administrative tribunal to handle election administration disputes, with members selected through bipartisan consensus. Having such a tribunal ready obviously would provide some advantages, in terms of both the speed with which it could resolve a contest and the preparation and insight it could bring to the task. But to the extent that empaneling such a tribunal as a form of contingency planning is too costly, another alternative would be to place responsibility for adjudicating certain election disputes in a special tribunal to be constituted only in response to the commencement of an election contest. The panel might be constituted like some arbitration panels, with both sides to the contest picking one member of the tribunal, and those members in turn agreeing upon a third person to serve with them in hearing the contest.[4]

Yet another alternative would be to leave election contests to the state's judiciary, but change the manner in which judges are chosen from election to merit selection. Such a reform obviously has ramifications well beyond election disputes, and may not be politically feasible. But an elected judiciary inevitably has the problem of an appearance of bias in its resolution of the elections of other officials. Letting judges who have been appointed on merit adjudicate election contests would reduce, but not necessarily eliminate, this problem.

ILLINOIS REFORMS

For somewhat different reasons, our top priority reforms for the election ecosystem of Illinois also involve steps that would reduce partisan influences on the system. More than in Ohio, however, these reforms also can be thought of as efforts to enhance the professionalism with which Illinois elections are administered. They are: replace the relatively toothless State Board of Elections with a single state elections director, make local election administrators more accountable for following proper procedures, and resolve election disputes before special tribunals, instead of leaving such matters to elected judges.

1. Replace the state board of elections with a statewide elections director.

Of the five states in this study, Illinois stands in the greatest need of sweeping change to the administrative structure of its election ecosystem. Compared to its counterparts in other states, the current state board of elections provides far less value to Illinois' local election jurisdictions, both as a result of its general disengagement from the practical difficulties facing local election officials, and in terms of its almost complete failure to promulgate administrative regulations and guidelines to help enhance statewide consistency. The state board of elections should be scrapped in favor of a single nonpartisan statewide chief election officer.

We recognize that this is a dramatic reform, one that will be politically difficult to implement. Still, it is desperately needed, and it will be unfortunate if its realization must come in response to a critical election failure that might otherwise have been prevented. Accordingly, with a hope that some Illinois reformers will pursue it seriously, we offer a few brief thoughts about the structure and function of this new position.

As with Ohio, we think the Federal Reserve model is instructive. In Illinois, a professional state elections director should be given authority to prescribe and enforce statewide uniformity with respect to certain election administration procedures, including the rules applicable to provisional voting. Without developing such uniformity, Illinois runs the risk of (and might even benefit from) a type of lawsuit akin to the Ohio case of *League of Women Voters v. Blackwell,* discussed in the Ohio chapter. Indeed, one federal district court in Illinois has already held that disparities in residual vote rates across jurisdictions sufficed to state an Equal Protection violation,[5] and barring a change in the state board of elections, similar litigation might be the only mechanism for prodding the state to produce appropriate statewide consistency. The state director also should have the ability to equalize funding for electoral resources throughout the state, as well as the authority to enforce state rules, and thus consistency among local jurisdictions, in the manner described in Chapter 9's recommendations on institutional reform.

2. Increase trust in the integrity of state elections by making local election officials more accountable.

In a number of respects, Illinois' local election officials could better fulfill their duties in a manner that would both enhance public understanding and trust while also reducing the likelihood of election problems. One specific improvement would be to require that all local boards of election be evenly bipartisan, in the Ohio model. Local boards that are effectively controlled by one party breed public cynicism and increase the chances of both mistakes and deliberate wrongdoing.

On a related note, Illinois must ensure that all steps of the vote counting and canvassing process remain both publicly transparent and auditable. Illinois also should redouble its efforts to ensure that local jurisdictions comply with the mandatory audit requirement, described in more detail in Chapter 4, which apparently is sometimes ignored. The state board of elections must take steps to ensure all localities satisfy this requirement, and serious penalties should result from noncompliance.

Local jurisdictions also should be required to comply strictly with the statutory requirement of ensuring partisan balance among precinct workers.[6] This will require more creative efforts to recruit poll workers in some locations, perhaps especially among youth. We discuss some possible approaches to recruiting election volunteers as a Minnesota reform below. But we note here that aggressive reliance on student poll workers might also have an additional value, to the extent that youth may be less likely to be tied to existing avenues of political corruption.

3. Create nonpartisan tribunals to resolve election disputes.

Our third recommended reform is that Illinois, like Ohio, create a special tribunal for adjudicating post-election contests. This would complete the creation of an impartial, nonpartisan, and trustworthy institutional architecture to handle the vote-counting process, including in the disputed elections where it comes under the most pressure. Short of creating a special elections tribunal, the state could move its judiciary as a whole to a merit selection basis, although as a political matter this seems much less likely to happen than creating a special elections court.

MICHIGAN REFORMS

Michigan faces the same need as Ohio and Illinois to develop an alternative tribunal to handle election litigation, other than its highly politicized supreme court. In other respects, however, Michigan's election ecosystem is in better health and does not cry out for systemwide reform like Ohio and Illinois. Nonetheless, some of its more particular problems still manage to affect many aspects of its ecosystem. Accordingly, our first recommendation is that the state redouble its efforts to update and correct its Qualified Voter File, particularly in Detroit and other urban centers. Second, we suggest that the state legislature consider granting the secretary of state greater authority over local election officials. Third, we encourage the state to do all that it can to ease the burden of finding and training local poll workers.

1. Update the Qualified Voter File.

Because of its importance in several areas of election administration – including the registration process, polling place operations, provisional voting, and absentee voting – Michigan's Qualified Voter File ("QVF") continues to warrant significant attention. Perhaps because the QVF has been in existence for a decade (much longer than most of the statewide databases developed in response to HAVA), it may be increasingly burdened by its outdated entries, most of which may have lingered in the database since its creation. These outdated entries, which have been declining sharply after each election but still may number close to one million, both increase administrative costs and burdens and provide opportunities for absentee ballot fraud of the kind that allegedly has occurred in Detroit in recent years. If done properly, purging these entries from the QVF would result in a meaningful improvement to the state ecosystem, particularly to the extent that it reduced absentee ballot issues.

Maintaining the QVF is primarily a local function, however. It is the larger urban areas of the state that have the greatest need to update their files, but also may face greatest difficulty finding sufficient resources to do so quickly. Michigan therefore should work to assist these areas to improve the accuracy of their QVF files, including providing them with funding and other forms of support for a short-term campaign to bolster existing efforts to eliminate the deadwood. Once these outdated entries are eliminated, it should be much easier for local jurisdictions to keep their lists updated using periodic references to change of address notices, master death files, and the like.

2. Ensure that the state's chief election authority has sufficient tools to enforce consistency among municipalities.

Michigan's chief election officer, its secretary of state, is a partisan elected official like Ohio's. Yet the Michigan office has not been affected by the same level of allegations of partisan behavior as has its Ohio counterpart. Instead, the Michigan Bureau of Elections has long been widely respected for its professionalism. Meanwhile, however, Michigan's state administrative structure does partake of a weakness not shared by Ohio, in that the Michigan Secretary of State has less authority to ensure consistency in the administration of elections among municipalities.

Consider, for instance, the absentee ballot problems that came to light in Detroit in 2005. As described in Chapter 5, a state court eventually stripped the Detroit clerk of all authority over absentee balloting in the city and brought in the secretary of state and the county clerk's office to take it over from the city. Yet without the court's involvement, the secretary of state appears to have been relatively powerless to take any direct action against the city clerk. It would benefit the state's election system if the state's chief election officer had some direct authority to enforce compliance with state policies or withhold funds from local jurisdictions that fail to do so, perhaps supplemented by additional ability to audit the conduct and performance of local jurisdictions on a regular basis. We discussed these possible enforcement mechanisms in more detail in Chapter 9, as among the institutional reforms that all states should consider. This reform may have particular salience for Michigan, given the state's recent history and the diffusion of authority among so many municipal officials.

3. Improve poll worker recruitment and training.

In hindsight, it seems likely that at least some substantial portion of the difficulties that Detroit has experienced in recent years resulted from inadequate training of "election judges" or poll workers. When poll workers do not perform their duties properly, all kinds of election problems can and usually will occur. Accordingly, as described in Chapter 9, this is a weak link in all state election ecosystems today. Indeed, we feature it as our top reform in our discussion of Minnesota below, where we present a few thoughts about experimental approaches to recruiting more youth as poll workers.

We believe that Michigan also would be well-served by focusing attention on this reform in two fairly different respects. First, a number of the state's smaller municipalities report having to work harder each election to find an adequate number of election judges. Before this recruiting difficulty becomes a true crisis, state officials should work with local officials to create and implement a strategy for ensuring that all polling places are adequately staffed. Second, in the state's larger jurisdictions, such as Detroit, the problem just as often may be that the poll workers are not sufficiently trained and prepared to handle the array of issues that arise under the pressures and stresses of Election Day. Some form of enhanced training, as Detroit has begun to use, and perhaps an audit of the training programs, therefore may be in order to ensure that these programs in fact accomplish what they need to accomplish.

WISCONSIN REFORMS

Because of the creation earlier this year of its new Government Accountability Board ("GAB"), Wisconsin is in the middle of a major realignment of its statewide election administration system. Its first priority therefore should be to ensure continuity and effectiveness in the manner in which state officials oversee state elections. At the same time, Wisconsin must continue working to resolve the problems that have plagued its statewide registered voter database. Finally, the state legislature should consider how to improve its post-election processes.

1. Create a strong election division of the new Government Accountability Board.

In contrast to other states, Wisconsin has a state institutional structure that seems well-de-signed to promote evenhanded decision making. Rather than vesting power in a partisan elected official or a board controlled by one of the parties, Wisconsin has just created a Government Accountability Board ("GAB") consisting of retired judges who must be confirmed by a supermajority of the state senate, as described more fully in Chapter 6. This structure provides a basis for optimism that the new GAB will operate by consensus, rather than serving the narrow interest of one party or the other. But the GAB must work expeditiously to establish its election division and to give that division the authority and resources needed to ensure consistency in the state's administration of elections.

Indeed, while this institutional structure is promising, it is much too early to say whether it will actually work, and a number of institutional issues remain to be worked out. Foremost among them is the precise relationship among the components of the GAB. What is quite clear is that, with the 2008 election season already upon us, it is essential for any necessary institutional changes to be made promptly – including the board's selection and appointment of its legal counsel and its elections division administrator, as well as the delineation of the responsibilities of these two offices.

As discussed next, Wisconsin also faces a pressing need to improve its statewide voter registration system ("SVRS"), if it is to serve the needs of local election officials (and voters) and the purposes contemplated by Congress. A well-functioning elections division is critical to accomplishing these improvements. In this respect, Wisconsin might learn from the difficult experience of the U.S. Election Assistance Commission, which was hampered both by the late appointment of its commissioners, and by Congress' failure to fund it adequately in the initial stages of its work.[7] Analogously, the GAB's elections division must be given adequate enforcement authority, to ensure consistency among the state's 1,851 municipalities. The large number of electoral jurisdictions in Wisconsin creates an enormous challenge in promoting uniformity and avoiding differential practices among municipalities that could give rise to Equal Protection concerns. The GAB's elections division must have the power not only to clarify the procedures that localities are supposed to follow, but also to enforce those uniform procedures.

2. Improve the statewide voter registration system.

Wisconsin's statewide registration database is currently the most problematic aspect of its election ecosystem. The registration system, whose software was developed by Accenture under contract with the state, has failed to meet the needs and expectations of the municipal election officials who rely upon it. These problems have serious consequences for voters as well. To the extent that election officials find the system difficult to operate, it will consume time and energy that otherwise could be spent on pre-election preparations. If registration lists are inaccurate, they will occupy poll workers' time – an undervalued though essential resource – on Election Day. While Wisconsin's Election Day registration system reduces the risk of voters being disenfranchised through registration glitches, delays caused by registration list problems can undoubtedly cause inconvenience for voters.

It is therefore important that Wisconsin election authorities act expeditiously to correct the components of the SVRS that still fall short of expectations. As described in Chapter 6, complaints include the slow speed of the system, the failure of the absentee voter module to function properly, inability to cross-check against felon and death records, and difficulty in generating lists of voters for those who need them, including candidates and their campaigns. Because there is no easy solution to these problems, state and local officials will need to devote substantial time and resources to improving the functioning of the database. Given the centrality of voter registration to all aspects of election administration, the failure to do so would surely have a major negative impact on Wisconsin's entire election ecosystem in 2008 and beyond.

3. Reform the post-election dispute resolution processes.

Although Wisconsin's system for resolving post-election disputes generally has functioned well, there is good cause to worry about what might happen in the event of a disputed statewide election, particularly a presidential election. That is true for two reasons. The first is that the canvass and recount process is conducted by boards of canvassers, which will have two members of one party and one member of the other. With many Wisconsin municipalities using optical-scan ballots, inevitably some ballots will be ambiguously marked, making this process all the more important. The second reason has to do with timing. Under state law, the state and federal canvass need not be completed until December 1,[8] and a recount petition may not even be filed until after the time for completing the canvass.[9] As a practical matter, it would be difficult if not impossible to conduct a meaningful recount – much less to obtain judicial review of the recount – prior to the "safe harbor" date for presidential elections.[10] Even for non-presidential elections, in a bitterly contested election this process could drag out the result for weeks.

Wisconsin is certainly not the only state to have this problem, but its likely centrality in presidential electoral politics makes this reform especially urgent for the state. Accordingly, Wisconsin should re-examine its system for resolving post-election disputes, both to minimize the possibility of partisanship in the vote-counting (and recounting) process, and to ensure an adequate opportunity for judicial review, particularly in presidential elections. With respect to the recount process, one possibility would be to develop a new procedure, perhaps overseen by the GAB, for statewide elections. Rather than entrusting the canvass and recount process to partisan officials, this process might be placed under the control of nonpartisan officials selected by the GAB. If authority remains with county boards of canvassers, then there must be a procedure by which to secure prompt judicial review of their decisions. As explained in Chapters 8 and 9, the court with authority to review these matters must be one that is above the partisan fray.

Prompt resolution of post-election disputes is particularly essential for presidential elections, given the early December "safe harbor" and Electoral College meeting dates under federal law. In Chapter 9 we have suggested changes to these federal laws to facilitate the timely resolution of state recounts and contests. But until that happens, states like Wisconsin will be faced with the difficult task of expediting their post-election processes to conform to the presidential timetable. This means that states must find a way to complete the canvass, recount, contest, and any judicial review before the "safe harbor" date. As a practical matter, this will probably require: 1) moving up the date for completing the canvass in presidential elections; 2) allowing recounts and contests to proceed simultaneously on parallel tracks; and 3) providing a procedure for expedited judicial review of recount and contest decisions. This is undoubtedly a formidable task, but we believe it is essential to minimize the risk of a post-election meltdown similar to the one that the country faced in 2000, and came close to facing in 2004.

MINNESOTA REFORMS

Minnesota's system for administering elections has much to commend it – indeed, it may be among the strongest in the nation – but it is not perfect. The state would do well to develop a master plan for the recruitment, training, and retention of poll workers for the next decade or so, at least through the presidential election of 2020. Such a plan could then serve as a model for the many other states also struggling with this issue. The state also should address the risks of absentee ballot improprieties. Finally, Minnesota would benefit from some of the structural reforms recommended for Ohio and Illinois, designed to promote neutral and nonpartisan decisionmaking, including on the part of the state's judiciary. While the need for structural reform may be less urgent in Minnesota, given its history and political culture, nevertheless the increasing polarization of American elections makes this an issue to which even the most high-functioning states should attend.

1. Improve poll worker recruitment and training.

Minnesota's track record of experimentalism means that it is well-positioned to try to create a youth "Election Corps" for staffing its polling places. Modeled loosely on the Peace Corps, or City Year, or Teach for America, or other similar youth-based initiatives, such a program would seek to capitalize on the idealism and public spiritedness of many American young people. Of course, an Election Corps would be dramatically different in that its participants would be volunteering to serve for only one or two days, rather than for an entire year or two. But participants might move around the state, serving in counties (or even states) other than where they live. To facilitate such a program, it might be linked with a high school civics curriculum, or perhaps Election Day could become a school holiday.

Of course, many states already encourage youth, sometimes as young as 16 who therefore cannot themselves vote, to serve as poll workers. But the successes of these programs have to date been sporadic and highly contingent on the efforts of individual local elections directors. Minnesota, like the rest of the country, would benefit from an aggressive statewide effort to reach out widely to this still largely untapped pool of potential election volunteers.

2. Experiment with in-person early voting instead of expanding mail-in absentee voting.

Minnesota should systematically assess the extent to which it can minimize the risks of absentee ballot improprieties, consistent with the countervailing policy goal of promoting convenient access. As discussed in Chapter 9, in-person early voting provides the benefits of absentee voting, without the risks of fraud and

error associated with mailed-in ballots. Thus, Minnesota could explore the alternative of promoting in-person early voting in locations like public schools, public libraries, and other places of easy access. Early voting can provide many of the advantages of no-excuse absentee voting, without introducing nearly the same risks of voting improprieties. Minnesota could be on the forefront of this reform, particularly if it addressed the challenges of developing and implementing transparent and non-partisan chain-of-custody procedures for all early voting materials, so that there is no doubt about the accuracy and integrity of the vote count.

3. Develop nonpartisan institutions for administering elections and resolving disputes.

Minnesota would benefit from having its political leaders endeavor to reinvigorate the culture of fair-minded bipartisanship that enabled the remarkable agreement for resolving the 1962 governor's race. Of course, as part of this effort, Minnesota also could consider transferring the election administration duties of its elected secretary of state to an appointed nonpartisan official, along the lines described above in the reforms we view as priorities for Ohio and Illinois. But well short of that step, Minnesota should consider transferring the election administration duties of its elected local authorities to appointed nonpartisan election boards in each jurisdiction. Perhaps most feasibly, Minnesota should create a nonpartisan judicial tribunal for the resolution of election disputes. Because we have already discussed the need for a nonpartisan tribunal in Chapter 9, as well as in our recommendations for Ohio and Illinois in this chapter, we do not repeat that discussion here. At the same time, Minnesota also should conform its presidential recount timetable to meet the federal "safe harbor" date, a reform discussed in more detail above as one of our Wisconsin recommendations.

∗   ∗   ∗

We close with one final, overarching theme that has repeatedly arisen throughout our study and again in our priority recommendations for each state in this chapter: Improvement of each state's election ecosystem depends upon non-partisan and professional administration at every level. This echoes Chapter 8's observation that all states should strive for statesmanship in these matters, but it carries it one step further by calling for structural changes, not just for attitudinal changes. We are optimistic about the prospects for reaching this goal, but recognize that it will take dedicated and concerted efforts on the part of elected officials, administrators, and citizens to get us there.

REFERENCES

1. *See* Mark Rollenhagen, *Bipartisan Panel to Test Voting Machines*, (CLEVELAND) PLAIN DEALER, Sept. 24, 2007, *available at* http://blog.cleveland.com/metro/2007/09/bipartisan_panel_to_test_votin.html.

2. Richard L. Hasen, *Beyond the Margin of Litigation: Reforming U.S. Election Administration to Avoid Electoral Meltdown*, 62 WASH. & LEE L. REV. 937, 983-84 (2005).

3. *See* Steven F. Huefner, *Remedying Election Wrongs*, 44 HARV. J. ON LEGISLATION 265, 270 (2007).

4. *See id.* at 322.

5. *Black v. McGuffage*, 209 F.Supp.2d 889, 899 (N.D.Ill., 2002).

6. ILL. COMP. STAT. 5/13-1; 5/13-2; 5/14-1.

7. *See* Daniel J. Tokaji, *Early Returns on Election Reform: Discretion, Disenfranchisement, and the Help America Vote Act*, 73 Geo. Wash. L. Rev. 1206, 1218-20 (2005).

8. WIS. STAT. ANN. §7.70(3)(a).

9. WIS. STAT. ANN. § 9.01(1).

10. For a description of this problem, see recommendations 11 and 12 in Chapter 9.

APPENDIX A
INDIVIDUALS CONSULTED

A number of individuals graciously shared with us their knowledge of matters of election administration in their respective states, either during in-person meetings or through telephone or email communications. In addition to the individuals specifically named below, we also benefitted greatly from the contributions and feedback we received from participants in the meetings of the *Midwest Democracy Network* that occurred during the period of our study, and we appreciate the opportunity to attend these meetings.

ILLINOIS

James P. Allen, *Communications Director, Chicago Board of Election Commissioners*

Cindi Canary, *Director, Illinois Campaign for Political Reform*

Bruce Clark, *Kankakee County Clerk*

Christina Cray, *Legislative Liaison, State Board of Elections*

Diane Felts, *Director of Voting Systems & Standards, State Board of Elections*

Esther Fox, *Chief Deputy, Kankakee County Clerk*

Lance Gough, *Executive Director, Chicago Board of Election Commissioners*

James Lewis, *Executive Director, East St. Louis Board of Election Commissioners*

Stephen Liehr, *County Board, Kankakee County*

Geetha Lingham, *Director of Information Technology, Cook County Clerk's Office*

Daniel Madden, *Legal Advisor to the Cook County Clerk*

Peter McLennon, *Policy Analyst, Cook County Clerk's Office*

Ronald Michaelson, *former Director, State Board of Elections*

Stephanie Miller, *Elections Staffer, Kankakee County Clerk*

Mark Mossman, *Director/Election Information, State Board of Elections*

David Orr, *Cook County Clerk*

Matt Ostrom, *Elections Staffer, Kankakee County Clerk*

Robert Saar, *Executive Director, DuPage County Election Commission*

Gail Siegel, *Communications Director, Cook County Clerk's Office*

Kyle Thomas, *Database Coordinator, State Board of Elections*

Daniel W. White, *Director, State Board of Elections*

MICHIGAN

Terry G. Bennett, *Clerk, Canton Township*

Todd Blake, *City Clerk/Finance Director, City of Fremont*

Patricia Donath, *Special Projects Director, League of Women Voters of Michigan*

Terri Kowal, *Clerk, Shelby Charter Township*

Anne Magoun, *President, League of Women Voters of Michigan*

Dana L. Muscott, *City Clerk, City of Bay City, and President, Michigan Association of Municipal Clerks*

Rich Robinson, *Executive Director, Michigan Campaign Finance Network*

Janet Santos, *Clerk, Bangor Charter Township, and Past President, Michigan Association of Municipal Clerks*

Christopher M. Thomas, *Director of Elections, Office of the Secretary of State*

Shirley Wazny, *Clerk, Saginaw Charter Township*

Bradley S. Wittman, *Director, Elections Liaison Division, Office of the Secretary of State*

MINNESOTA

Dean Alger, *Project Consultant to the Secretary of State*

C. Scott Cooper, *Education Fund Director, TakeAction Minnesota*

Thomas P. Ferber, *City Clerk, City of Bloomington*

Debra Mangen, *City Clerk, City of Edina*

Joseph Mansky, *Elections Manager, Ramsey County, and former Director of Elections Office of the Secretary of State*

Patty O'Connor, *Director of Taxpayer Services, Blue Earth County*

Gary Poser, *Director of Elections, Office of the Secretary of State*

Mark Ritchie, *Secretary of State*

Rachel Smith, *Elections Supervisor, Anoka County*

OHIO

Jerolyn Barbee, *Executive Director, League of Women Voters of Ohio*

Jennifer Brunner, *Secretary of State*

Keith Cunningham, *Director, Allen County Board of Elections, and former President, Ohio Association of Election Officials*

Matthew Damschroder, *Director, Franklin County Board of Elections, and President, Ohio Association of Election Officials*

David M. Farrell, *Deputy Assistant Secretary of State and Director of Elections*

Brian Green, *Elections Counsel, Office of the Secretary of State*

Steve Harsman, *Director, Montgomery County Board of Elections, and former President, Ohio Association of Election Officials*

Tom Hayes, *former Director, Cuyahoga County Board of Elections*

Ann Henkener, *Legislative Director, League of Women Voters of Ohio*

Christopher B. Nance, *Assistant Secretary of State*

Anne Nelson, *Project Manager, Ohio Democracy Project, League of Women Voters of Ohio*

Mark Niquette, THE COLUMBUS DISPATCH

Peg Rosenfield, *Election Specialist, League of Women Voters of Ohio*

Catherine Turcer, *Campaign Finance Reform Director, Ohio Citizen Action Education Fund*

John Williams, *Director, Hamilton County Board of Elections*

Patricia Wolfe, *Elections Administrator, Office of the Secretary of State*

WISCONSIN

Neil V. Albrecht, *Assistant Director, City of Milwaukee Election Commission*

Jay Heck, *Executive Director, Common Cause Wisconsin*

Andrea Kaminski, *Executive Director, League of Women Voters of Wisconsin*

Marcia Kelly, *Town Clerk, Town of Dale*

Kevin J. Kennedy, *Executive Director, Wisconsin State Elections Board*

Bruce Landgraf, *Assistant District Attorney, City of Milwaukee*

E. Michael McCann, *former District Attorney, City of Milwaukee*

Robert Ohlsen, *County Clerk, Dane County*

James R. Villiesse, *City Clerk/Treasurer, City of New London*

Sandra L. Wesolowski, *City Clerk, City of Franklin*

APPENDIX B
BIBLIOGRAPHY OF WORKS CONSULTED

ACCURATE, *Public Comment on the Manual for Voting System Testing & Certification Program* (Oct. 2006).

Michael Alvarez & Thad E. Hall, *How Hard Can it Be: Do Citizens Think it is Difficult to Register to Vote?* (Caltech/MIT Voting Technology Project, Working Paper No. 48, July 2006), *available at* http://www.vote.caltech.edu/electmgmt.htm.

Michael Alvarez, *et al.*, *Election Day Voter Registration in the United States: How One-Step Voting Can Change the Composition of the American Electorate*, Caltech / MIT Voting Technology Project (2002).

Michael Alvarez, *et al.*, *Whose Absentee Votes Are Counted: The Variety and Use of Absentee Ballots in California*, Caltech/MIT Voting Technology Project, Working Paper #34 (July 2005).

Stephen Ansolabehere, *Voting Machines, Race, and Equal Protection*, 1 ELECTION L. J. 61 (2002).

Adam J. Berinsky, *The Perverse Consequences of Electoral Reform in the United States*, 33 AM. POL. RES. 471 (2005).

Adam J. Berinsky, Nancy Burns, & Michael W. Traugott, *Who Votes By Mail? A Dynamic Model of the Individual-Level Consequences of Voting-By-Mail Systems*, 65 PUBLIC OPINION Q. 178 (2001).

John Berry, *Comment, Take the Money and Run: Lame-Ducks "Quack" and Pass Voter Identification Provisions*, 74 U. DET. MERCY L. REV. 291 (1997).

Henry E. Brady, Matt Jarvis, & John McNulty, *Counting All the Votes: The Performance of Voting Technology in the United States (2001)*, *available at* http://ucdata.berkeley.edu:7101/new_web/countingallthevotes.pdf.

Kimball W. Brace & Michael P. McDonald, *Final Report of the 2004 Election Day Survey* (Sept. 2005).

Brennan Center for Justice, *Citizens Without Proof: A Survey of Americans' Possession of Documentary Proof of Citizenship and Photo Identification* (Nov. 2006), *available at* http://www.brennancenter.org/dynamic/subpages/download_file_39242.pdf.

Craig L. Brians & Bernard Grofman, *Election Day Registration's Effect on U.S. Voter Turnout*, 82 SOC. SCI. Q. 170 (2001).

----------, *When Registration Barriers Fall, Who Votes? An Empirical Test of a Rational Choice Model*, 99 PUB. CHOICE 161 (1999).

Robert D. Brown & Justin Wedeking, *People Who Have Their Tickets But Do Not Use Them: "Motor Voter," Registration, and Turnout Revisited*, 34 AM. POL. RES. 479 (2006).

William P. Browne & Kenneth VerBurg, MICHIGAN POLITICS AND GOVERNMENT (1995).

Caltech/MIT Voting Technology Project, *Voting: What Is, What Could Be* (July 2001), *available at* www.vote.caltech.edu.

Tracy Campbell, DELIVER THE VOTE (2005).

The Century Foundation, *Balancing Access and Integrity: The Report of The Century Foundation Working Group on State Implementation of Election Reform* (July 2005).

Michael F. Curtin, THE OHIO POLITICS ALMANAC (1996).

Commission on Federal Election Reform (Carter-Baker Commission), *Building Confidence in U.S. Elections* (Sept. 2005).

James K. Conant, WISCONSIN POLITICS AND GOVERNMENT: AMERICA'S LABORATORY OF DEMOCRACY (2006).

Congressional Research Service, *What Do Local Election Officials Think About Election Reform?: Results of a Survey* (June 2005).

CQ Researcher, *Voting Controversies: Can All Citizens Vote, and are All Votes Counted?* (Sept. 2006).

Richard N. Current, THE HISTORY OF WISCONSIN: THE CIVIL WAR ERA, 1848-1873 (1976).

Cuyahoga County Collaborative Audit Committee, *Collaborative Public Audit of the November 2006 General Election, Final Report* (April 2007).

Cuyahoga County Election Review Panel, *Final Report* (July 2006).

Jonathan E. Davis, *Comment, The National Voter Registration Act of 1993: Debunking States' Rights Resistance and the Pretense of Voter Fraud*, 6 TEMP. POL. & CIV. RTS. L. REV. 117 (1996/1997).

Tina Ebenger & Darren Henderson, *Do Voter Registration Drives Increase Voter Turnout?*, Prepared For Presentation at the 2007 Annual Meeting of the Midwest Political Science Association (Apr. 12, 2007), *available at* http://convention2.allacademic.com/one/mpsa/mpsa07/index.php?click_key=1.

Daniel J. Elazar, *American Federalism: A View From the States* (3d ed. 1984).

Daniel J. Elazar, Virginia Gray & Wyman Spano, MINNESOTA POLITICS & GOVERNMENT (1999).

electionline.org, *Briefing: The 2006 Election*, Nov. 2006, *available at* http://www.electionline.org/Portals/1/Publications/EB15.briefing.pdf.

----------, *Election Preview 2004: What's Changed, What Hasn't, and Why*, *available at* http://www.electionline.org/Portals/1/Publications/Election.preview.2004.report.final.update.pdf.

----------, *Election Preview 2006: What's Changed, What Hasn't, and Why*, *available at* http://www.electionline.org/Portals/1/Publications/Annual.Report.Preview.2006.Final.pdf.

Alec Ewald, *A "Crazy-Quilt" of Tiny Pieces: State and Local Administration of American Criminal Disenfranchisement Law*, 2005 THE SENTENCING PROJECT 1.

----------, *Punishing At The Polls: The Case Against Disenfranchising Citizens With Felony Convictions* (2003), *available at* http://www.demos.org/pubs/FD__Punishing_at_the_Polls.pdf.

Brandon Fail, *Comment, HAVA's Unintended Consequences: A Lesson for Next Time*, 116 YALE L.J. 493 (2006).

Gerald M. Feige, *Comment, Refining the Vote: Suggested Amendments to the Help America Vote Act's Provisional Balloting Standards*, 110 PENN. ST. L. REV. 449 (2005).

Felony Disenfranchisement Laws in the United States, 2007 THE SENTENCING PROJECT 1, *available at* http://www.sentencingproject.org/Admin/Documents/publications/fd_bs_fdlawsinus.pdf.

Mark J. Fenster, *The Impact of Allowing Day of Registration Voting on Turnout in U.S. Elections from 1960 to 1992*, 22 AM. POL. Q. 74 (1994).

Edward B. Foley, *The Analysis and Mitigation of Electoral Errors: Theory, Practice, Policy*, 18 STAN. L. & POL'Y REV. 350 (2007).

----------, *The Future of* Bush v. Gore?, 68 OHIO ST. L. J. (forthcoming 2007).

----------,*The Promise and Problems of Provisional Voting*, 73 GEO. WASH. L. REV. 1193 (2005).

----------,*Uncertain Insurance: Provisional Ballots Confuse and Complicate Voting, in* 4 VOTING IN AMERICA: AMERICAN VOTING SYSTEMS IN FLUX: DEBACLES, DANGERS AND BRAVE NEW DESIGNS (Morgan E. Felchner ed., forthcoming 2008).

John C. Fortier, ABSENTEE AND EARLY VOTING: TRENDS, PROMISES, AND PERILS (2006).

Anne K. Friedman, *Voter Disenfranchisement and Policy Toward Election Reforms*, 22 REV. OF POL'Y RES. 787 (2005).

John Fund, STEALING ELECTIONS (2004).

Samuel K. Gove & James Nowlan, ILLINOIS POLITICS & GOVERNMENT (1996).

Government Accountability Office, *The Nation's Evolving Election System as Reflected in the November 2004 General Election* (June 2006).

R. Bradley Griffin, *Note, Gambling with Democracy: The Help America Vote Act and the Failure of the States to Administer Federal Elections*, 82 WASH. U. L.Q. 509 (2004).

Paul Gronke, *Ballot Integrity and Voting By Mail: The Oregon Experience*, 2005 THE EARLY VOTING INFORMATION CENTER 1.

----------, *Early Voting Reforms and American Elections,* Paper Presented at the Annual Meeting of the American Political Science Association, Chicago, IL (Sept. 2-5, 2004).

Thad Hall, J. Quin Monson, & Kelly Patterson, *The Human Dimension of Elections: How Poll Workers Shape Confidence in Elections* (unpublished manuscript, Feb. 2006)

Michael J. Hanmer & Michael W. Traugott, *The Impact of Voting by Mail on Voter Behavior*, 32 AM. POL. RES. 375 (2004).

Richard L. Hasen, *Beyond the Margin of Litigation: Reforming U.S. Election Administration to Avoid Electoral Meltdown*, 62 WASH. & LEE L. REV 937 (2005).

Ronald E. Hero & Caroline J. Tolbert, *A Racial/Ethnic Diversity Interpretation of Politics and Policy in the States of the U.S.*, 40 AM. J. POL. SCI. 851 (1996).

Benjamin Highton, *Easy Registration and Voter Turnout*, 59 THE J. OF POL. 565 (1997).

M.V. Hood III & Charles S. Bullock, III, *Worth a Thousand Words?: An Analysis of Georgia's Voter Identification Statute*, 2007 ELECTION REFORM PROJECT 1, *available at* http://electionlawblog.org/archives/GA%20Voter%20ID%20%28Bullock%20%26%20Hood%29.pdf.

Steven F. Huefner, *Remedying Election Wrongs*, 44 HARV. J. LEGISLATION 265 (2007).

Deborah S. James, *Voter Registration: A Restriction on the Fundamental Right to Vote*, 96 YALE L. J. 1615 (1987).

Eric G. Juenke & Julie M. Shepherd, *Not the If But the How: Vote Procedure Changes and Voter Turnout, An Elite or Mass-Based Process?*, Prepared For Presentation at the 2007 Annual Meeting of the Midwest Political Science Association (April 12-15, 2007), *available at* http://64.112.226.77/one/mpsa/mpsa07/index.php?click_key=1&PHPSESSID=5f785b685486038f6cf6fff3c683e9a8.

Jeffrey A. Karp & Susan A. Banducci, *Absentee Voting, Mobilization, and Participation*, 29 AM. POL. RES. 183 (2001).

----------, *Going Postal: How All-Mail Elections Influence Turnout*, 22 POL. BEHAV. 223 (2000).

Brian Kavanagh, *et al., Ten Years Later, A Promise Unfulfilled: The National Voter Registration Act in Public Assistance Agencies, 1995-2005* (2005).

John Kincaid, *Political Cultures of the American Compound Republic*, 10 PUBLIUS 1 (1980).

Ryan S. King, *A Decade of Reform: Felon Disenfranchisement Policy in the United States*, 2006 THE SENTENCING PROJECT 1, *available at* http://www.sentencingproject.org/Admin/Documents/publications/fd_decade_reform.pdf.

Stephen Knack, *The Voter Participation Effects of Selecting Jurors from Registration Lists*, 36 J. OF L. AND ECON. 99 (1993).

Stephen Knack & James White, *Election-Day Registration and Turnout Inequality*, 22 POL. BEHAV. 29 (2000).

Justin Levitt, Wendy R. Weiser, & Ana Munoz, *Making The List: Database Matching And Verification Processes For Voter Registration* (Brennan Center for Justice, Mar. 24, 2006), *available at* http://www.brennancenter.org/dynamic/subpages/download_file_49479.pdf.

William W. Liles, *Challenges to Felony Disenfranchisement Laws: Past, Present, and Future*, 58 ALA. L. REV. 615 (2007).

David B. Magleby, *Participation in Mail Ballot Elections*, 40 W. POL. Q. 79 (1987).

Jeff Manza & Christopher Uggen, *Punishment and Democracy: Disenfranchisement of Nonincarcerated Felons in the United States*, 2 PERSP. ON POL. 491 (2004).

Michael P. McDonald, *May I See Your ID, Please? Measuring the Number of Eligible Voters with Photo Identification*, Prepared for Presentation at the 2006 California Institute of Technology and Massachusetts Institute of Technology Voter Identification Registration Conference (Oct. 4-5, 2006).

Michael P. McDonald & Samuel L. Popkin, *The Myth of the Vanishing Voter*, 95 AM. POL. SCI. REV. 963 (2001).

Lorraine C. Minnite, *Election Day Registration: A Study of Voter Fraud Allegations and Findings on Voter Roll Security* (Sept. 6, 2007), *available at* http://www.demos.org/pubs/edr_fraud_v2.pdf.

----------, *The Politics of Voter Fraud*, *available at* http://projectvote.org/fileadmin/ProjectVote/Publications/Politics_of_Voter_Fraud_Final.pdf.

Glenn E. Mitchell & Christopher Wlezien, *The Impact of Legal Constraints on Voter Registration, Turnout, and the Composition of the American Electorate*, 17 POL. BEHAV. 179 (1995).

Daniel S. Murphy & Adam J. Newmark, *Felon Disenfranchisement Policies in the States*, Prepared for Presentation at the 2005 Annual State Politics and Policy Conference (May 13-14, 2005), *available at* http://polisci.msu.edu/sppc2005/papers/satam/Murphy,%20Newmark,%20Ardoin.doc.

The National Commission on Federal Election Reform (Carter-Ford Commission), *To Assure Pride and Confidence in the Electoral Process* (Aug. 2001).

The National Research Commission on Elections and Voting, *Challenges Facing the American Electoral System: Research Priorities for the Social Sciences* (Mar. 2005).

Grant W. Neeley & Lilliard E. Richardson, Jr. *Who Is Early Voting? An Individual Level Examination*, 38 THE SOC. SCI. J. 381 (2001).

Robert C. Nesbit, WISCONSIN: A HISTORY (2d ed. 1989).

Albert Nicosia, THE ELECTION PROCESS IN THE UNITED STATES (2003).

Note, Toward a Greater State Role in Election Administration, 118 HARV. L. REV. 2314 (2005).

J. Eric Oliver, *The Effects of Eligibility Restrictions and Party Activity on Absentee Voting and Overall Turnout*, 40 AM. J. OF POL. SCI. 498 (1996).

Spencer Overton, *Voter Identification*, 105 MICH. L. REV. 631 (2007).

Samuel C. Patterson & Gregory A. Caldeira, *Mailing In the Vote: Correlates and Consequences of Absentee Voting*, 29 AM. J. OF POL. SCI. 766 (1985).

John Pawasarat, *The Driver License Status of the Voting Age Population in Wisconsin*, Emp. and Training Inst., University of Wisconsin-Milwaukee 2005, *available at* http://www.uwm.edu/Dept/ETI/.

Gillian Peele, *The Legacy of Bush v. Gore*, 1 ELECTION L.J. 263 (2002).

PERSPECTIVES ON MINNESOTA GOVERNMENT AND POLITICS (Steven M. Hoffman, *et al.*, eds. 2003).

Brian Pinaire, Milton Heumann, & Laura Bilotta, *Barred from the Vote: Public Attitudes Toward the Disenfranchisement of Felons*, 30 FORDHAM URB. L.J. 1519 (2003).

Richard A. Posner, BREAKING THE DEADLOCK: THE 2000 ELECTION, THE CONSTITUTION, AND THE COURTS (2001).

Project Vote, *Survey of State and Local Voter Registration & List Maintenance Practices in Michigan* (June 2006), *available at* http://projectvote.org/fileadmin/ProjectVote/ pdfs/Michigan_Voter_Registration___List_Maintenance_Sur vey_2006.pdf

Project Vote, *Your Ballot's in the Mail: Vote By Mail and Absentee Voting* (July 9, 2007), *available at* http://projectvote.org/fileadmin/ProjectVote/Policy_Briefs/PB 13-Vote_by_Mail.pdf.

Miles Rapoport, *Restoring the Vote*, 12 AM. PROSPECT 1314 (2001), *available at* http://www.prospect.org/cs/ articles?article=restoring_the_vote.

P. Orman Ray, *Absent-Voting Legislation, 1924-1925*, 20 THE AM. POL. SCI. REV. 347 (1926).

Recounting Election 2000 (symposium),13 STAN. L. & POL'Y REV. 1 (2002).

Gabrielle B. Ruda, *Comment, Picture Perfect: A Critical Analysis of the Debate on the 2002 Help America Vote Act*, 31 FORDHAM URB. L.J. 235 (2003).

Paul M. Schwartz, *Voting Technology and Democracy*, 77 N.Y.U. L. REV. 625 (2002).

Leonard Shambon & Keith Abouchar, *Trapped by Precincts? The Help America Vote Act's Provisional Ballots and the Problem of Precincts*, N.Y.U. J. LEGIS. & PUB. POL'Y 133 (2006/2007).

Andrew L. Shapiro, *Challenging Criminal Disenfranchisement under the Voting Rights Act: A New Strategy*, 103 YALE L. J. 537 (1993).

Sixth Circuit Employs Clear Statement Rule in Holding that the Help America Vote Act Does Not Require States to Count Provisional Ballots Cast Outside Voters' Home Precincts: Sandusky County Democratic Party v. Blackwell, 387 F. 3D 565 (6th Cir. 2004) (Per Curiam), 118 HARV. L. REV. 2461 (2005).

Peter A. Shocket, Neil R. Heighberger, & Clyde Brown, *The Effect of Voting Technology on Voting Behavior in a Simulated Multi-Candidate City Council Election: A Political Experiment of Ballot Transparency*, 45 THE W. POL. Q. 521 (1992).

Priscilla L. Southwell, *Five Years Later: A Re-Assessment of Oregon's Vote by Mail Electoral Process*, 83 PS: POL. SCI. AND POL. 89 (2004).

Priscilla L. Southwell & Justin I. Burchett, *The Effect of All-Mail Elections on Voter Turnout*, 28 AM. POL. Q. 72 (2000).

----------, *Vote-By Mail in the State of Oregon*, 34 WILLIAMETTE L. REV. 345 (1998).

Robert M. Stein & Patricia A. Garcia-Monet, *Voting Early But Not Often*, 78 SOC. SCI. Q. 657 (1997).

Robert M. Stein & Greg Vonnahme, *Election Day Vote Centers and Voter Turnout,* Prepared For Presentation at the 2006 Annual Meeting of the Midwest Political Science Association (April 20-23, 2006), *available at* http://www3.brookings.edu/gs/ projects/electionreform/20060418Stein.pdf.

Charles Stewart, III, *Residual Vote in the 2004 Election*, 5 ELECTION L.J. 158 (2006).

Ronald F. Stinnett & Charles H. Backstrom, RECOUNT (1964).

Daniel P. Tokaji, *The Birth and Re-Birth of Election Administration*, 6 ELECTION L.J. 118, 126-31 (2007).

----------, *Early Returns on Election Reform: Discretion, Disenfranchisement, and the Help America Vote Act*, 73 THE GEO. WASH. L. REV. 1206 (2005).

----------, *The New Vote Denial: Where Election Reform Meets the Voting Rights Act*, 57 S.C. L. REV. 689 (2006).

----------, *The Paperless Chase: Electronic Voting and Democratic Values*, 73 FORDHAM L. REV. 1711.

Michael Tomz & Robert P. Van Houweling, *How Does Voting Equipment Affect the Racial Gap in Voided Ballots*, 47 Am. J. of Pol. Sci. 46 (2003).

Christopher Uggen & Jeff Manza, *Voting and Subsequent Crime and Arrest: Evidence From a Community Sample*, 36 COLUM. HUM. RTS. L. REV. 193 (2004-2005).

----------, *2003 Summary of Changes to State Felon Disenfranchisement Law 1865-2003, available at* http://www.demos.org/page29.cfm.

U.S. Election Assistance Commission, *Election Crimes: An Initial Review and Recommendations for Further Study* (Dec. 2006).

U.S. Election Assistance Commission, *The Impact of the National Voter Registration Act of 1993 on the Administration of Elections for Federal Office, 2005-2006* (2007).

Timothy Vercellotti & David Anderson, *Protecting the Franchise, or Restricting It? The Effects of Voter Identification Requirements on Turnout*, Prepared for Presentation at the 2006 Annual Meeting of the American Political Science Association (Aug. 31-Sept. 3, 2006), *available at* http://www.electionreformproject.org/Topic/ 7/rl/Default.aspx?FGuid=5a5a7e76-6790-4732-917d-24f86aab95ef.

THE VOTE: BUSH, GORE, AND THE SUPREME COURT (Cass R. Sunstein & Richard A. Epstein, eds. 2001).

Voting: What Is What Could Be, 2001 Caltech/MIT Voting Technology Project 1, *available at* http://www.vote.caltech.edu/media/documents/july01/July01_ VTP_Voting_Report_Entire.pdf.

Tova A. Wang, *Competing Values or False Choices: Coming to Consensus on the Election Reform Debate in Washington State and the Country*, 29 SEATTLE U. L. REV. 353 (2006).

Audra L. Wassom, *Comment, The Help America Vote Act of 2002 and Selected Issues in Election Law Reform*, 28 T. MARSHALL L. REV. 345 (2003).

Wendy R. Weiser, *Are HAVA's Provisional Ballots Working?* (Brennan Center for Justice, Mar. 29, 2006), *available at* http://www.brennancenter.org/dynamic/subpages/download_file_39043.pdf.

Mitchell K. Wunsh, *Note, No Photo Necessary: Georgia's Short-Lived Voter-Photo Statute*, 17 GEO. MASON U. CIV. RTS. L.J. 267 (2006).

ABOUT THE AUTHORS

Steven F. Huefner, *Election Law @ Moritz ("EL@M") Senior Fellow, Associate Professor of Law at The Ohio State University Moritz College of Law ("Moritz"), and Director of the Moritz Legislation Clinic,* has wide-ranging election law experience and interests, including the specific areas of contested elections, term limits in state legislative elections, legislative redistricting, and poll worker responsibility and training. Prior to joining the faculty at Moritz, Professor Huefner spent five years in the U.S. Senate Office of Legal Counsel, where his responsibilities included advising the U.S. Senate in contested Senate elections, as well as assisting in the 1999 presidential impeachment trial. Since arriving at Moritz, Professor Huefner has put his experience to use in teaching Legislation and directing the Legislation Clinic. As director of the Legislation Clinic, Professor Huefner has studied many aspects of Ohio's electoral processes, including campaign finance law, lobbying regulation, other campaign practices, legislative term limits, and the initiative and referendum processes of direct democracy. Professor Huefner's previous election law scholarship includes: "Term Limits in State Legislative Elections: Less Value For More Money?" (*Indiana Law Journal*), and "Remedying Election Wrongs" (*Harvard Journal on Legislation*).

Daniel P. Tokaji, *Associate Professor of Law at Moritz, and the Associate Director of EL@M,* is an authority on election law and voting rights. He specializes in election reform, including voting technology, voter ID, provisional voting, and other subjects addressed by the Help America Vote Act of 2002. He also specializes in issues of fair representation, including redistricting and the Voting Rights Act of 1965. Professor Tokaji's published work addresses questions of election administration, political equality, and racial justice. Among the publications in which his scholarship has appeared are the *Michigan Law Review, Stanford Law & Policy Review*, and *Yale Law Journal*. Professor Tokaji's publications in the past two years include "The New Vote Denial: Where Election Reform Meets the Voting Rights Act" (*South Carolina Law Review*), "Early Returns on Election Reform: Discretion, Disenfranchisement, and the Help America Vote Act" (*George Washington Law Review*), and "The Paperless Chase: Electronic Voting and Democratic Values" (*Fordham Law Review*). Professor Tokaji authors the *Equal Vote* blog (www.moritzlaw.osu.edu/blogs/tokaji/index.html), which provides analysis and commentary on developments in the area of election reform and voting rights. Prior to arriving at Moritz, he was a staff attorney with the ACLU Foundation of Southern California. Among the cases he has litigated are challenges to voting equipment in California and Ohio.

Edward B. Foley, *Robert M. Duncan/Jones Day Designated Professor of Law at Moritz, and Director of EL@M,* is one of the nation's preeminent experts on election law. Professor Foley teaches and writes in all areas of this field, including substantial writings on campaign finance regulation. His current work focuses on the less-developed law of voting administration: provisional voting, registration rules and procedures, HAVA, and recounts and judicially disputed elections. His contributions to this study are part of the effort to bring more attention to this area. In addition, he has written a major article on "The Future of *Bush v. Gore*?," as well as a follow-up, "Refining the *Bush v. Gore* Taxonomy," both part of a symposium sponsored by *EL@M* and the *Ohio State Law Journal*. His re-examination of the future significance of that major precedent has led him to complete for the *Election Law Journal* an analysis of the Indiana voter identification case before the U.S. Supreme Court in its 2007-2008 term. His earlier article, "The Analysis and Mitigation of Electoral Errors: Theory, Practice, Policy," published in the *Stanford Law & Policy Review*, formed a basis for some of the recommendations of this study. His commentary on election law can be found at Free & Fair (www.electionlaw.osu.edu/freefair).

Nathan A. Cemenska is an election law consultant and web editor of *EL@M (www.electionlaw.osu.edu)*, an online legal publication dedicated to covering the law of election administration. He is a 2004 graduate of Moritz and a 2001 graduate of Northwestern University. Before coming to *EL@M*, he practiced general civil litigation at a small law firm in Cleveland.